I0793193

IMAGES
*of America*

# EARLY COLUMBIA COUNTY

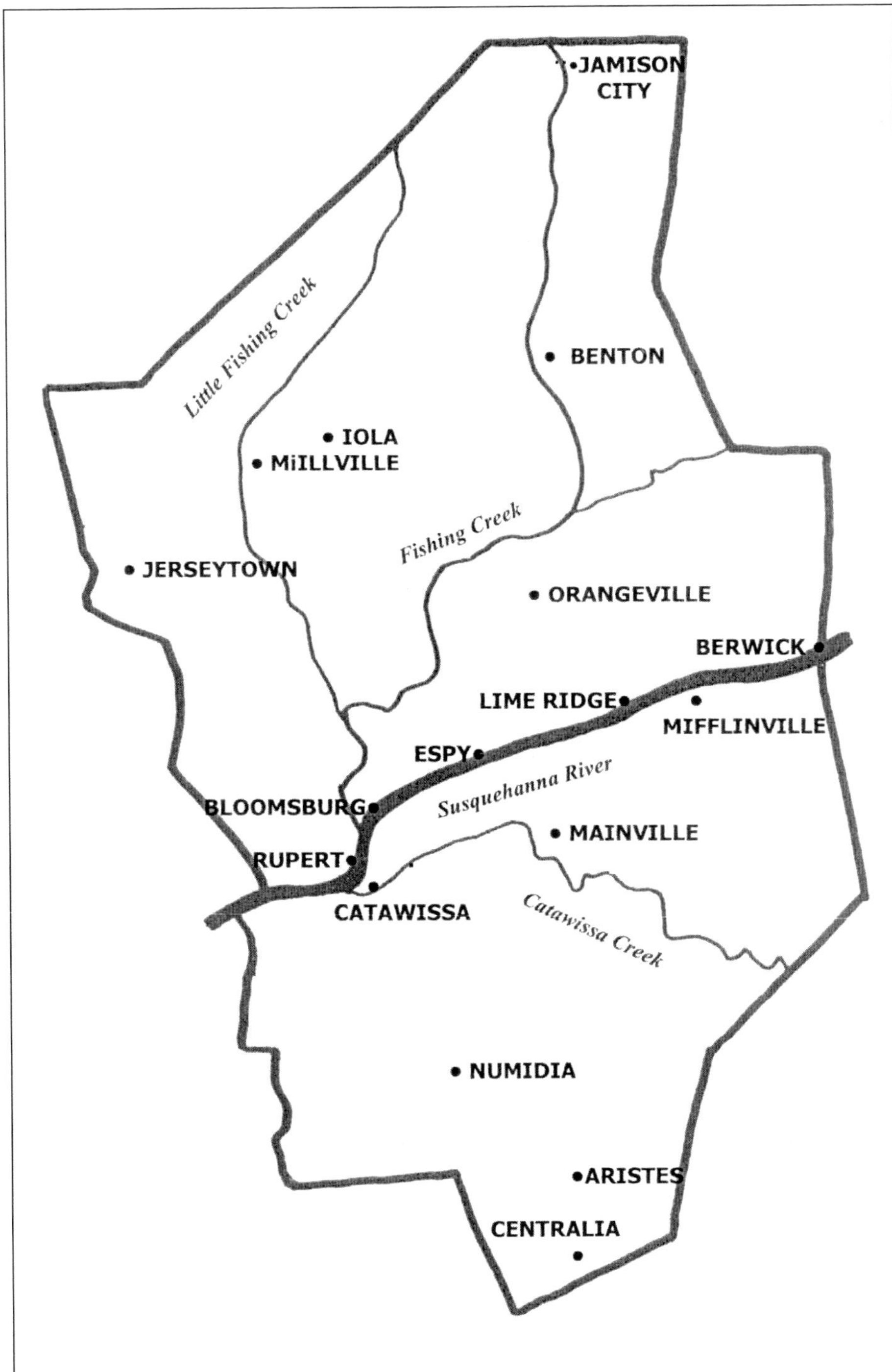


**COLUMBIA COUNTY MAP.** This map shows the principal waterways and towns of Columbia County. (Courtesy of Columbia County Historical and Genealogical Society.)

*On the cover*: **MIFFLINVILLE BRIDGE.** This image offers a view of the Mifflinville Bridge upon completion in 1908 and the work crew. (Courtesy of Bill Hartzell.)

IMAGES
*of America*

# EARLY COLUMBIA COUNTY

Columbia County Historical and
Genealogical Society

ARCADIA
PUBLISHING

ISBN 978-0-7385-7201-7

Published by Arcadia Publishing
Charleston, South Carolina

Printed in the United States of America

Library of Congress Control Number: 2009926124

For all general information contact Arcadia Publishing at:
Telephone 843-853-2070
Fax 843-853-0044
E-mail sales@arcadiapublishing.com
For customer service and orders:
Toll-Free 1-888-313-2665

Visit us on the Internet at www.arcadiapublishing.com

*To all the dedicated volunteers at
the Columbia County Historical and Genealogical Society.*

# Contents

# ACKNOWLEDGMENTS

We have many people to thank for bringing this project to completion. Archiving the photograph collection of the Columbia County Historical and Genealogical Society over these past 10 years has truly been a collaborative effort on the part of the members of the photograph committee. It has been educational, productive, and, above all, lots of fun. The committee includes Nina Feldser, Jean Groner (past chairman), Bill Hartzell, Donna Laubach, Bob Mosteller, Malinda Price (chairman), Cary Rhodomoyer, and Glenn Rupert.

Those who helped with compiling, researching, or scanning the photographs for this book are William Baillie, Dani Crossley, André Dominguez, Alex Dubil, Robert Dunkelberger, Nina Feldser, Dennis Hartzell, David Kline, Sue Koch, Donna Laubach, Bob Mosteller, Pat Parker, Burt Price, Malinda Price, Cary Rhodomoyer, and Sue Seiple. The editing team consisted of William Baillie, Ann Diseroad, Robert Dunkelberger, and Malinda Price.

Special thanks go to André Dominguez, Bonnie Farver, and George Holdren, who were ready, willing, and able to help no matter what the request. A special thank-you goes to George Turner for allowing use of many of his "photos of the month." Much gratitude goes to William Baillie, our president, for unsurpassed dedication to getting the job done. And to everyone who offered a word of encouragement along the way, I thank you.

Unless otherwise noted, all images appearing in this book are from the photograph collection of the Columbia County Historical and Genealogical Society.

Malinda Price
Project Chairman

# INTRODUCTION

An interesting history is revealed in the more than 8,000 archived photographs on file at the Columbia County Historical and Genealogical Society in Bloomsburg, Pennsylvania. For 10 years, volunteers have been archiving the photographs that were in boxes, drawers, and scrapbooks and many more that are still being donated. It indeed has been a labor of love.

Drawing upon this collection, *Early Columbia County* attempts to provide a glimpse of life here through some 210 photographs dating from 1870 to 1920. The reader will find a representative sample of various aspects of life as it was during this early time period. Six chapters, arranged from north to south in the county, look at historic landmarks and buildings, events and celebrations, schools, houses of worship, industries and businesses, transportation, and some of the organizations of the day. Scenes of everyday life are also offered. What is not attempted with this book is to present a comprehensive history of Columbia County. It is impossible to cover the entire span of the county history in one photograph book.

Columbia County was formed from Northumberland County on March 22, 1813. The major population centers are the borough of Berwick and the town of Bloomsburg, which is also the county seat. Unique industries characterized each of these and lent a particular personality to them.

The earliest settlers were English Quakers who came into the Catawissa Valley from Berks County between 1774 and 1778. The Friends meetinghouse in Catawissa, still standing today, was built in 1775. By 1840, Catawissa had a population of 800, surpassing Bloomsburg's by 150. The building of the Catawissa Railroad precipitated a boom period for the village, which brought with it an increase in the number of residents. Catawissa enjoyed the status of "railroad center" through the late 1800s.

Evan Owen laid out the town of Owensville, as named by the settlers, in 1786. However, Owen was a modest Quaker and gave the town the name Berwick after Berwick-on-Tweed, his hometown in England. The Pennsylvania canal system in this part of the commonwealth had its beginning in Berwick on July 4, 1828, when a ceremony was held and ground broken for the construction of the canal. Its building brought Irish workers into the community, and they settled in next to the earlier settlers, many of whom were of German descent. Berwick became best known for the production of steel railroad cars, beginning in 1904 at the American Car and Foundry Company, which were sold around the world.

Ludwig Eyer laid out the town of Bloomsburg in 1802. At the time, the only buildings standing were the Episcopal church, a tavern, and a log house. The early name for Bloomsburg was Oyertown. The discovery of iron ore nearby and the building of the iron furnaces in the

1850s provided a growth spurt for the community. The advent of the railroad only increased the attractiveness of the area for newcomers. Eventually numerous small-to-medium-sized industries were developed and flourished for a long period of time. These included textile mills and manufacturing plants for such products as furniture, ore, cars, and bricks. Some are still in operation, although employment is lower than in earlier days. The growth and development over the years of the Bloomsburg State Normal School, now Bloomsburg University of Pennsylvania, has certainly helped to put Bloomsburg on the map. The Bloomsburg Fair draws more than a quarter million visitors for a traditional-style agricultural fair each year.

Other areas were unique for different reasons. There is the Quaker community of Millville, the former lumbering boomtown of Jamison City, and the rich, natural resources of coal around Centralia at the southern tip of the county. The riverside villages of Espy, Almedia, and Lime Ridge were home to the North Branch Canal and a few small businesses. Not to be forgotten is the rich history of agriculture in the county, with there being many small-to-medium-size farms still operating today.

Common to all communities were the gristmill, the blacksmith, the general store, the schools, and the churches. Patriotism was very evident in photographs of holiday celebrations. Music played an important role in the lives of folks, as evidenced by the many bands—it seems every village had one.

Today Columbia County's population exceeds 65,000. Many of the residents trace their roots to the early settlers. A surprising number of surnames encountered today also show up in the earliest records of the county. Come along, step back in time, and visit early Columbia County from 1870 to 1920. Enjoy the ride!

# *One*

# Benton, Jamison City, and the Northern County

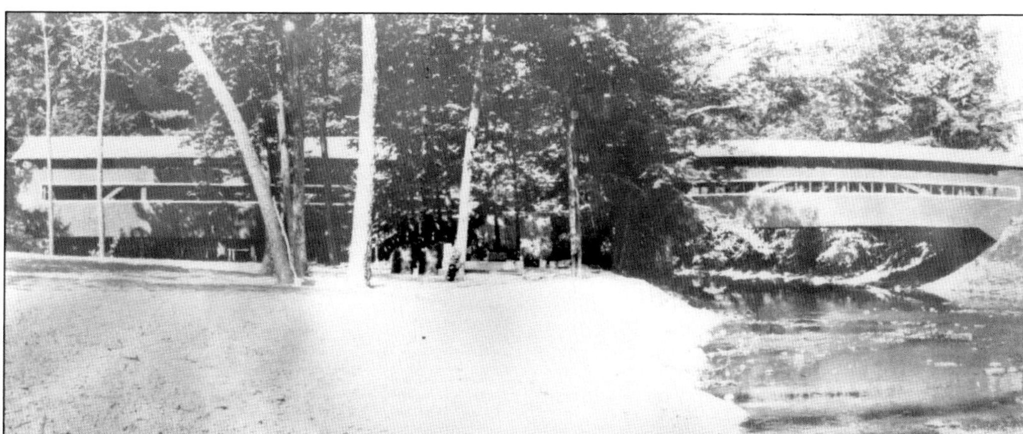

**Twin Covered Bridges.** The twin bridges over Huntington Creek, known as the East Paden and West Paden, are located off Route 487 near Forks. They were built in 1850 and named for John Paden, operator of a nearby sawmill. Over the years, both bridges have been damaged by flooding but have been reconstructed, most recently after the flood of June 2006 washed the West Paden Bridge away.

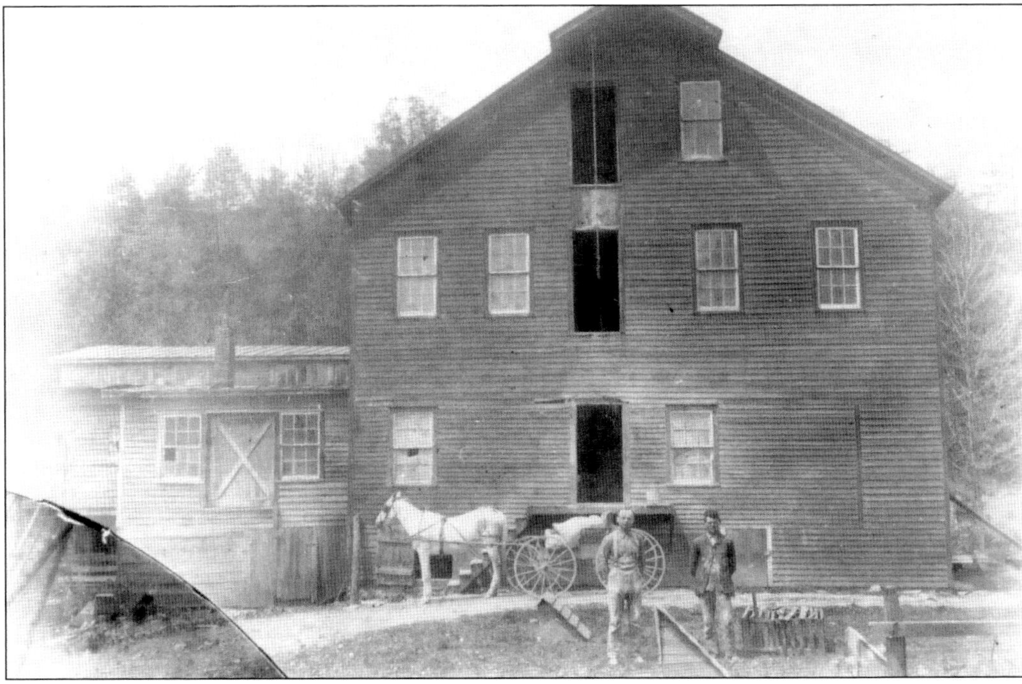

**IKLERTOWN MILL.** This 1910 photograph shows Iklertown gristmill owner T. Millard (Mill) Golder and his son Bertie Golder. Iklertown (or Eichleretown) is within the borough of Stillwater. Mill Golder owned a gristmill and a lumber-planing mill in Iklertown. Rock lime was shipped in by freight on the Bloomsburg and Sullivan Railroad and ground at this mill. (Courtesy of David Kline.)

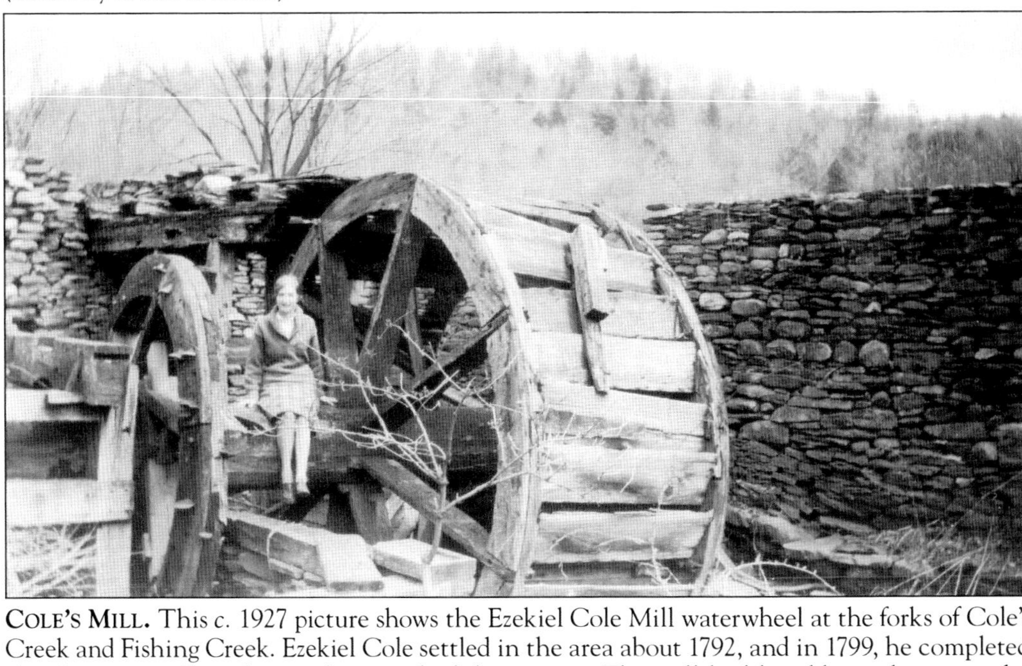

**COLE'S MILL.** This *c.* 1927 picture shows the Ezekiel Cole Mill waterwheel at the forks of Cole's Creek and Fishing Creek. Ezekiel Cole settled in the area about 1792, and in 1799, he completed this first gristmill in the northern end of the county. The mill had hand-hewn beams and a handmade waterwheel. Four generations of the family successively owned Cole's mill.

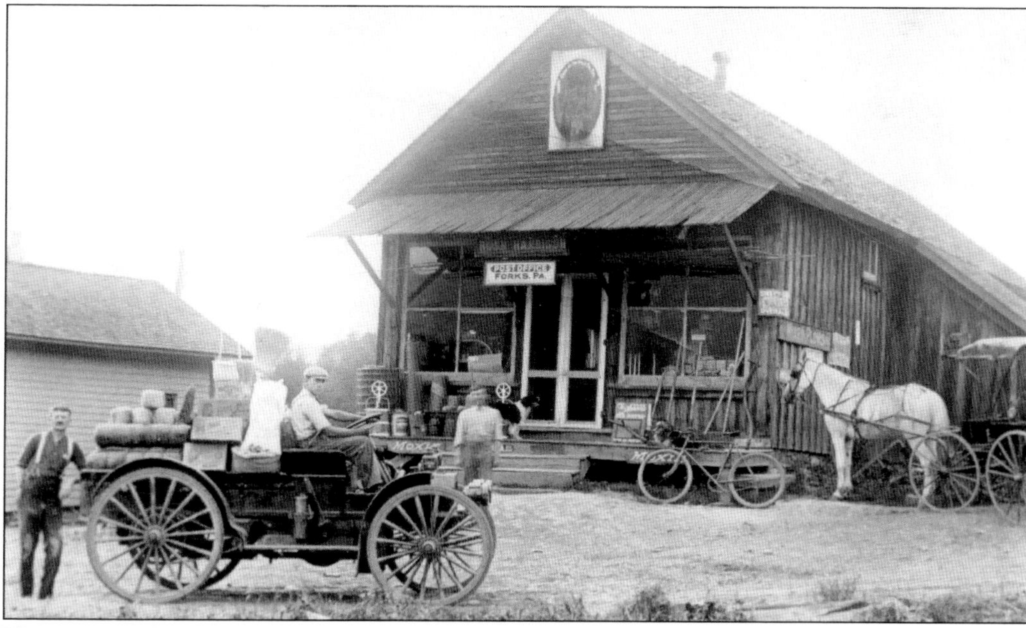


**HARRISON'S STORE AT FORKS, 1910.** Rush Harrison's general store at Forks was also the village post office. Here Harrison stands at the rear of his first International Harvester delivery truck; behind the wheel is his son Neil Harrison.

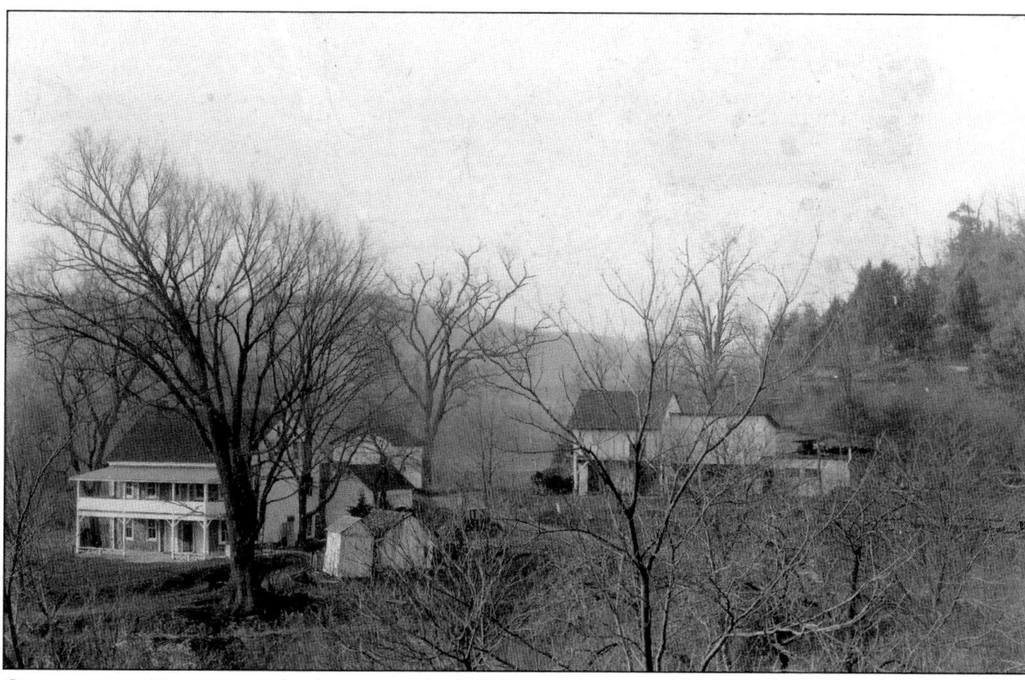

**GREYSTONE.** Greystone, the homestead of Cole, was built in 1806 at "Cole Town at the mouth of Cole's Creek." It was home to the Cole family until 1916. The Kettle Club purchased the home in the early 1920s after the cabin it owned near Jamison City burned. The building fell into disrepair, and in the late 1980s, it was torn down.

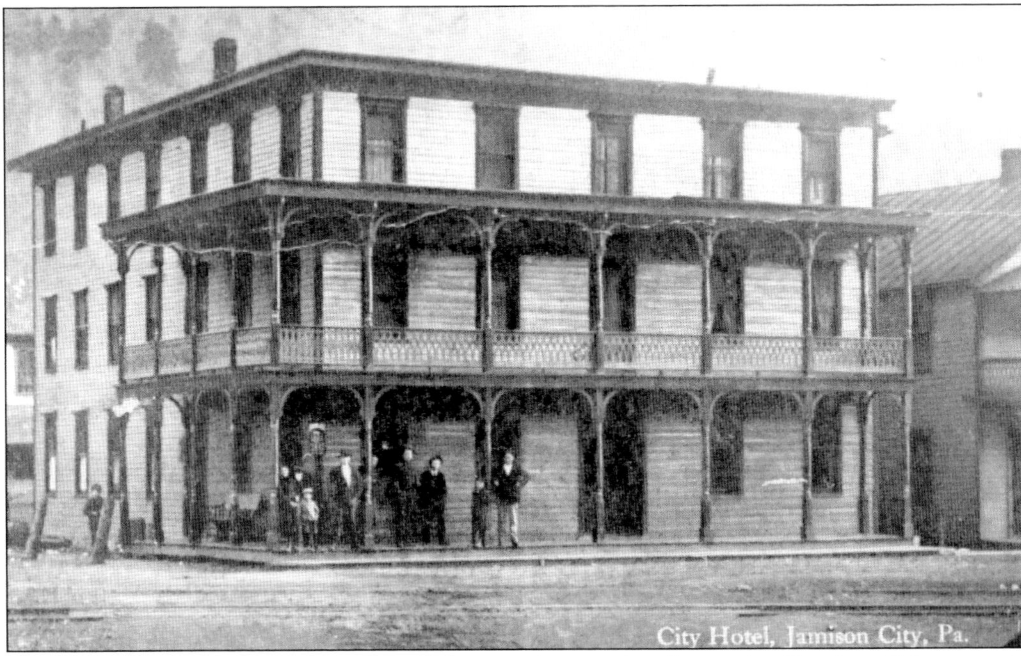


**CITY HOTEL, JAMISON CITY.** This edifice was known locally as the "big hotel" because its three-story front dominated the structures around it. The City Hotel, by design, strove to attract a respectable business and tourist clientele. The room rate of $1 a day attracted drummers (commercial travelers and salesmen) but discouraged the "rougher sort" from the lumbering and bark-peeling camps.

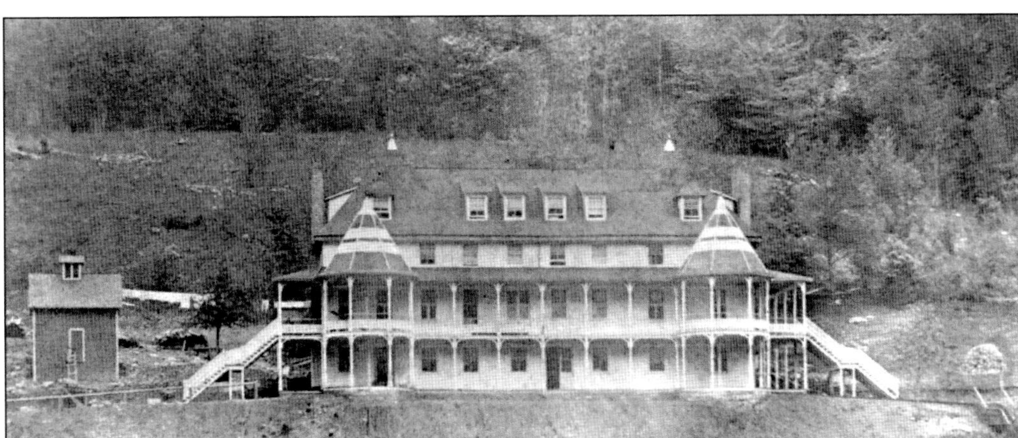

**PROCTOR INN, JAMISON CITY.** This vacation hotel was constructed on a hillside 75 feet above the valley. It was also known locally as the "big onion," perhaps from the conical roofs at each end of the extensive verandas on the first two floors. At first, the hotel catered to wealthy guests who arrived by train, but the odors from the nearby tannery limited its appeal. The building was demolished in 1908.

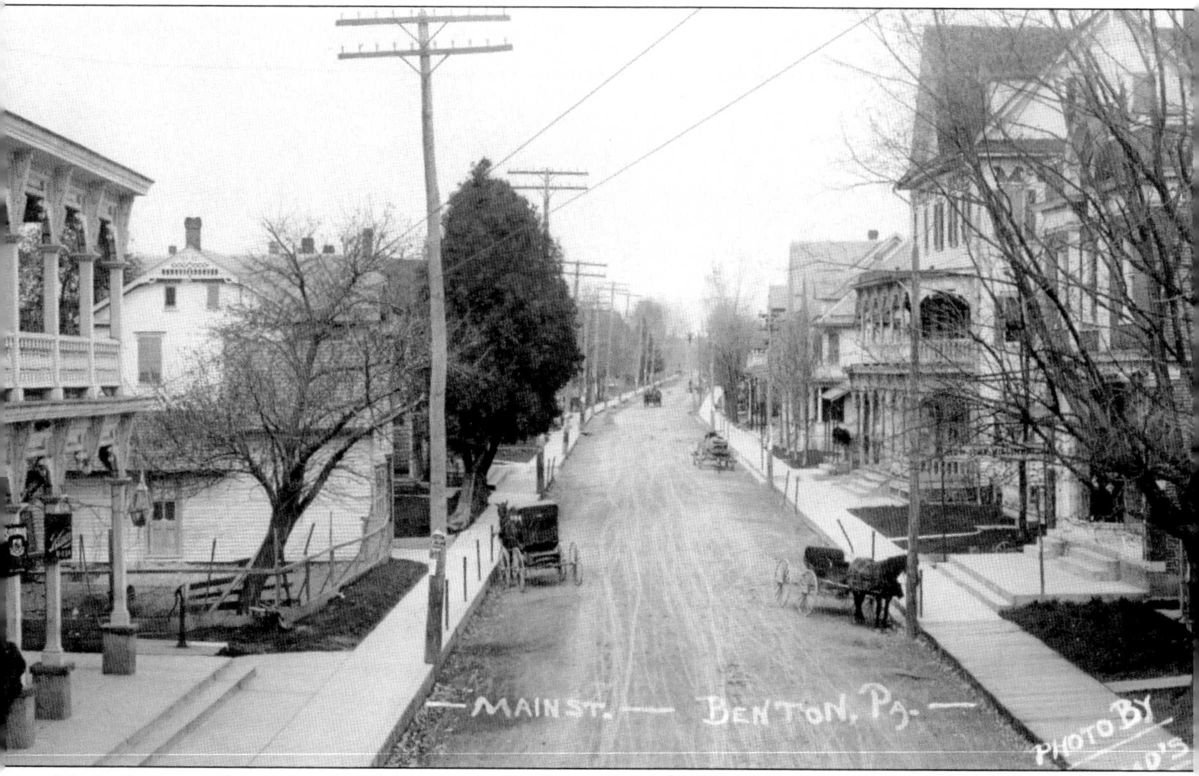


**MAIN STREET, BENTON, 1908.** The view looks north on Main Street in Benton. The Exchange Hotel is on the left in the foreground. A sign reads "New York Millinery" on the lower right, where there is also a wooden sidewalk. Notice the unpaved streets and the electric utility poles. (Courtesy of Helen Yoder.)

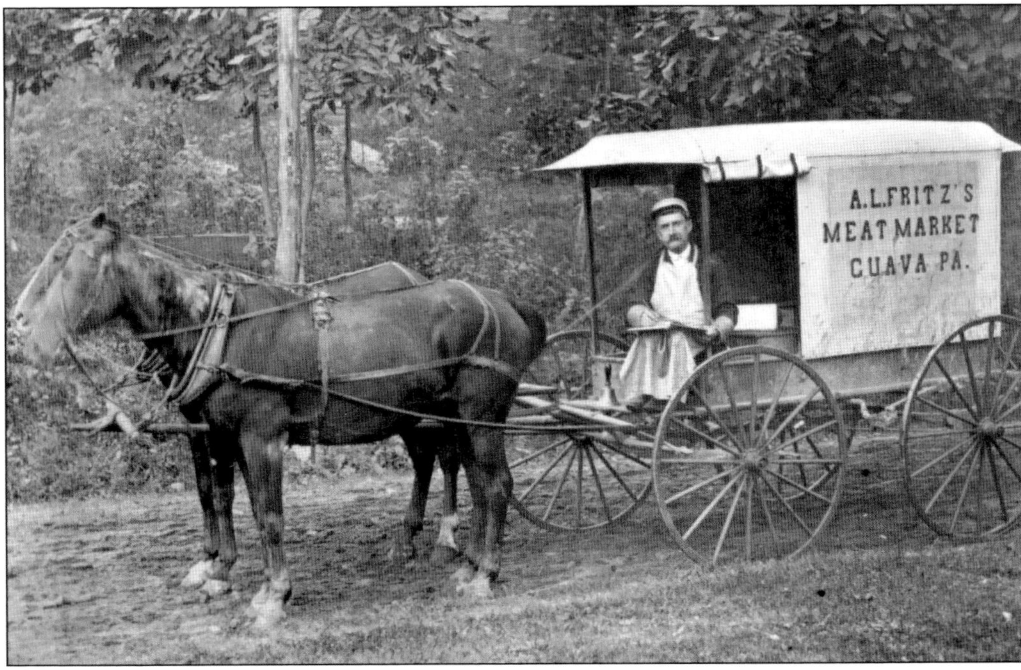


**FRITZ MEAT MARKET.** This view from about 1900 shows the butcher wagon of "A. L. Fritz's Meat Market, Guava, PA." The driver is Amandus L. Fritz. The village of Guava was located just south of Central and had its own post office. It eventually was renamed Laubach for its first postmaster, Andrew Laubach, grandfather of famed missionary Dr. Frank Laubach.

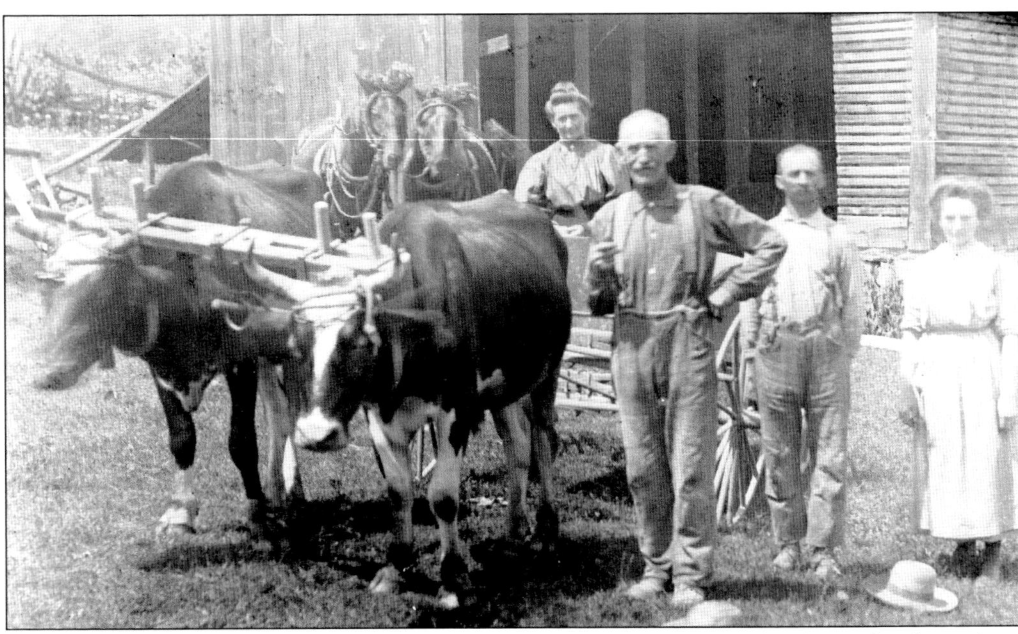

**OXEN TEAM, 1908.** John Hess, son of Barney Hess of Central, was the driver for this yoke of oxen. This was the last team of oxen used around the up-creek section of northern Columbia County. The photograph was taken on the George W. Smith farm in Central, with George and Alverda Smith also at right in the picture.

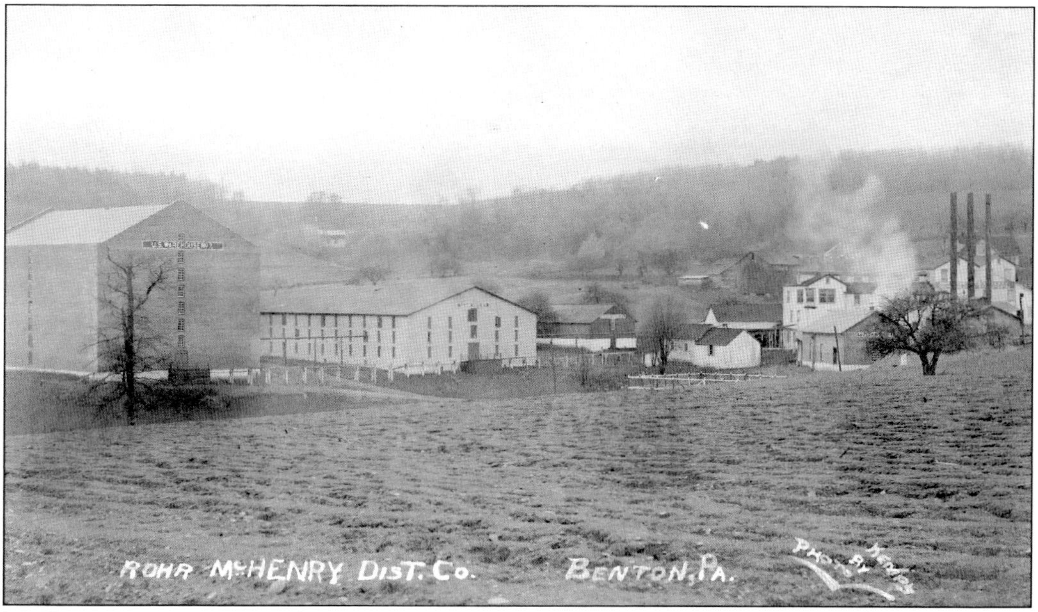


**McHENRY DISTILLERY.** The McHenry family began the manufacture and sale of whiskey at Benton in 1812. Under the ownership of Rohr McHenry and known by the trademark catchphrase "Born in 1812," the whiskey grew steadily in popularity through the 19th century. In 1911, a fire destroyed the distillery's warehouse, and production ceased after the death of John C. McHenry in 1912.

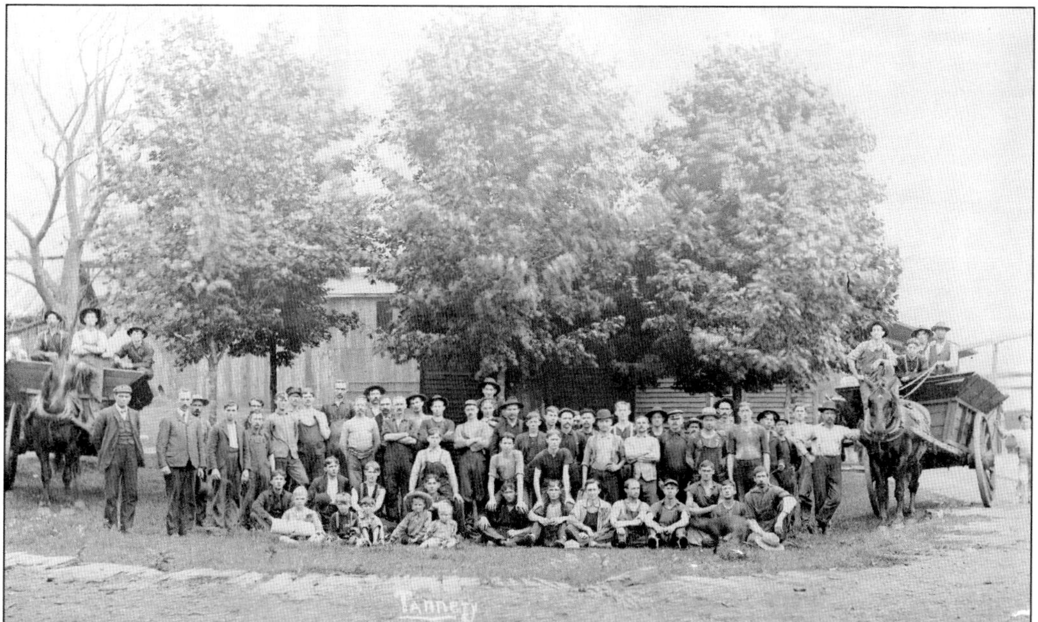


**ELK TANNING COMPANY WORKERS, 1905.** Besides the thriving lumbering business in northern Columbia County, the tanning industry emerged in the late 1880s. The Elk Tanning Company at Jamison City became the largest tanning operation in Pennsylvania. It operated until 1925 and outlived the lumber business in the North Mountain area.

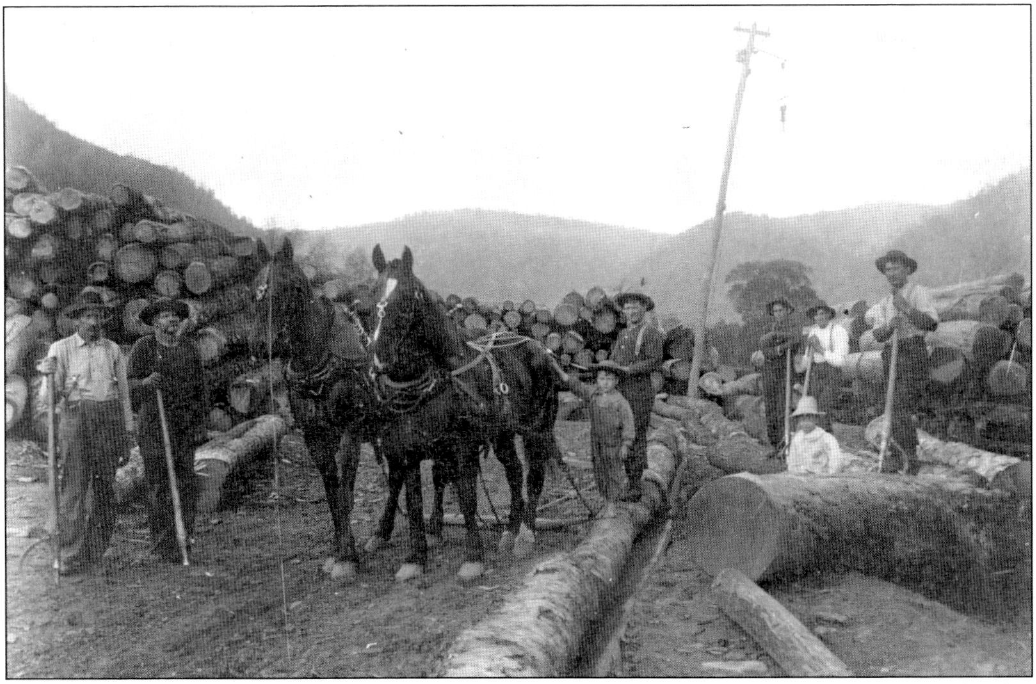

**LOGGING AND A LOGGERS' BUNKHOUSE.** Large-scale logging began in northern Columbia County in the 1880s and spurred the development of boomtowns such as Jamison City. Once the Bloomsburg and Sullivan Railroad reached the area in 1889, logging crews (above, about 1890) cleared the hills for many miles around in about 20 years. The loggers lived in the woods, as in the log bunkhouse below, with 32 men at a lumbering camp run by the Central Pennsylvania Lumber Company on North Mountain. The trees went to the company's large sawmill at Jamison City at the northern boundary of Columbia County in Sugarloaf Township. Also in Jamison City was the Elk Tannery, which used huge quantities of hemlock bark in its tanning process.

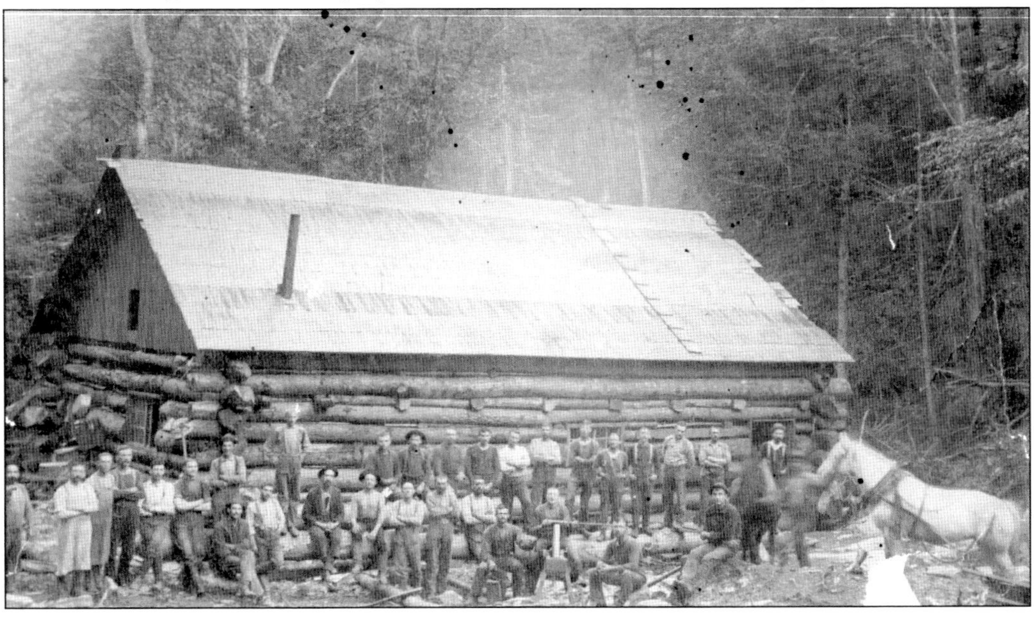

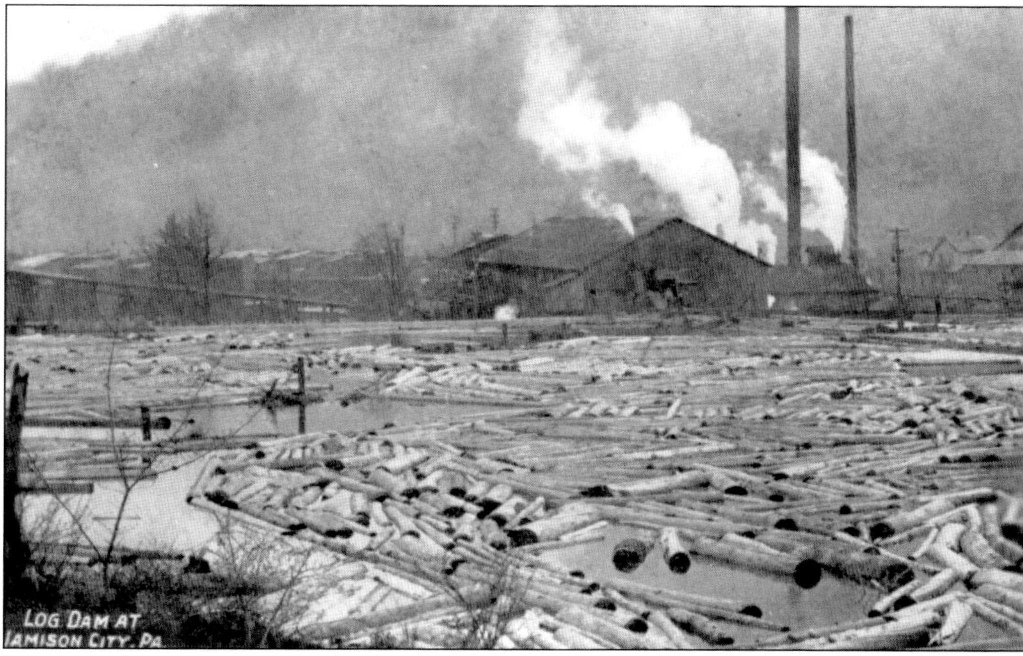


**LOGGING OPERATIONS.** The lumber company dammed a tributary of Fishing Creek (above) at Jamison City to create a millpond for storing 10 million feet of logs before they went to the saws. The log train (below) is shown on a mountain track, loaded and ready to return to the mill at Jamison City.

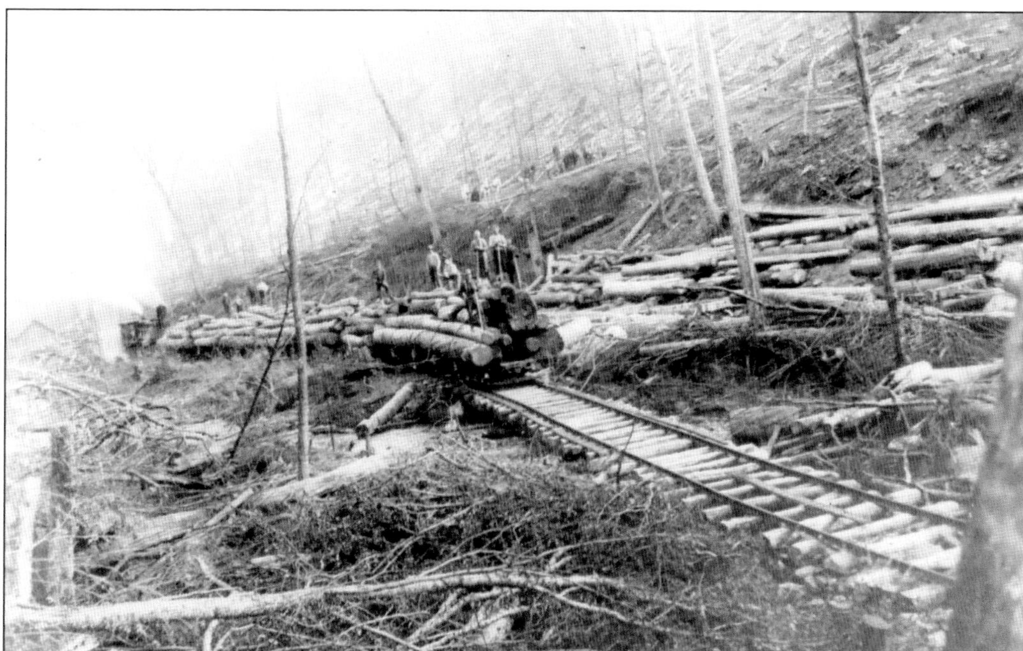

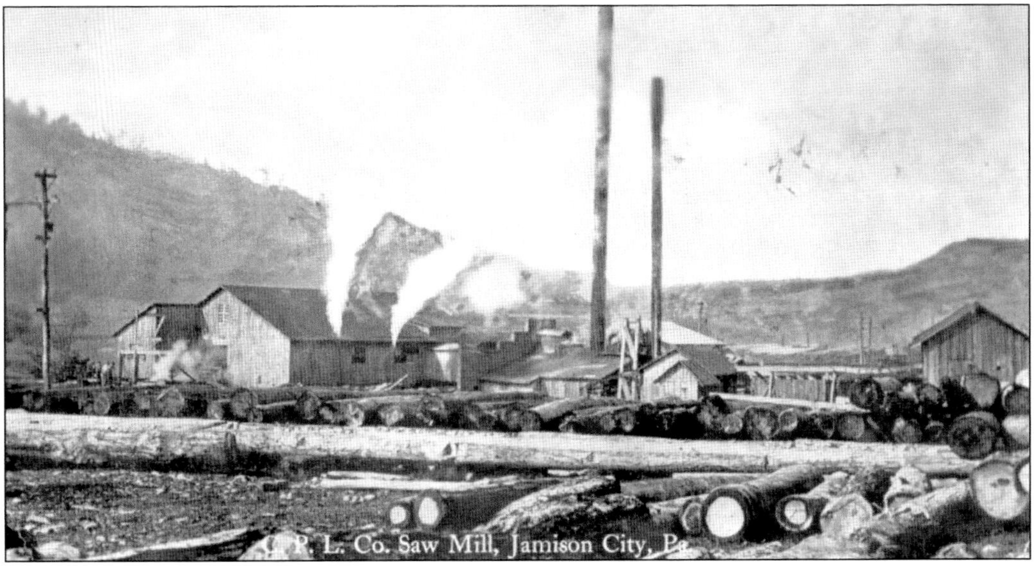


**SAWMILL AND LUMBERYARD, JAMISON CITY.** The Central Pennsylvania Lumber Company sawmill (above) processed hundreds of large logs every day; it had multiple saws powered by a steam engine. In its crowded yard (below), lumber was stacked for drying and to await loading onto flatcars for delivery to markets across the eastern United States. At the peak of production, the sawmill and tannery employed hundreds of workers and indirectly supported many others in commercial and professional venues in the village.

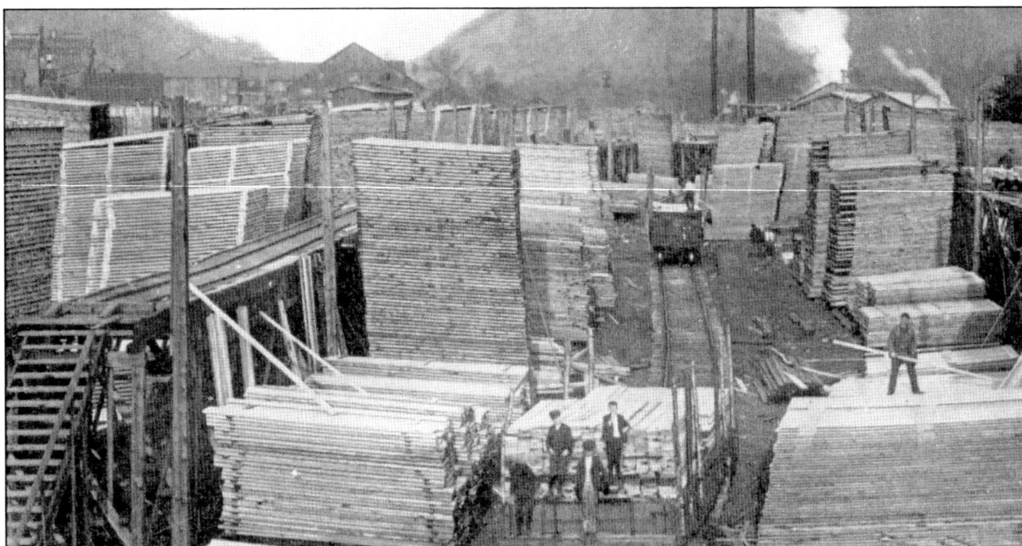

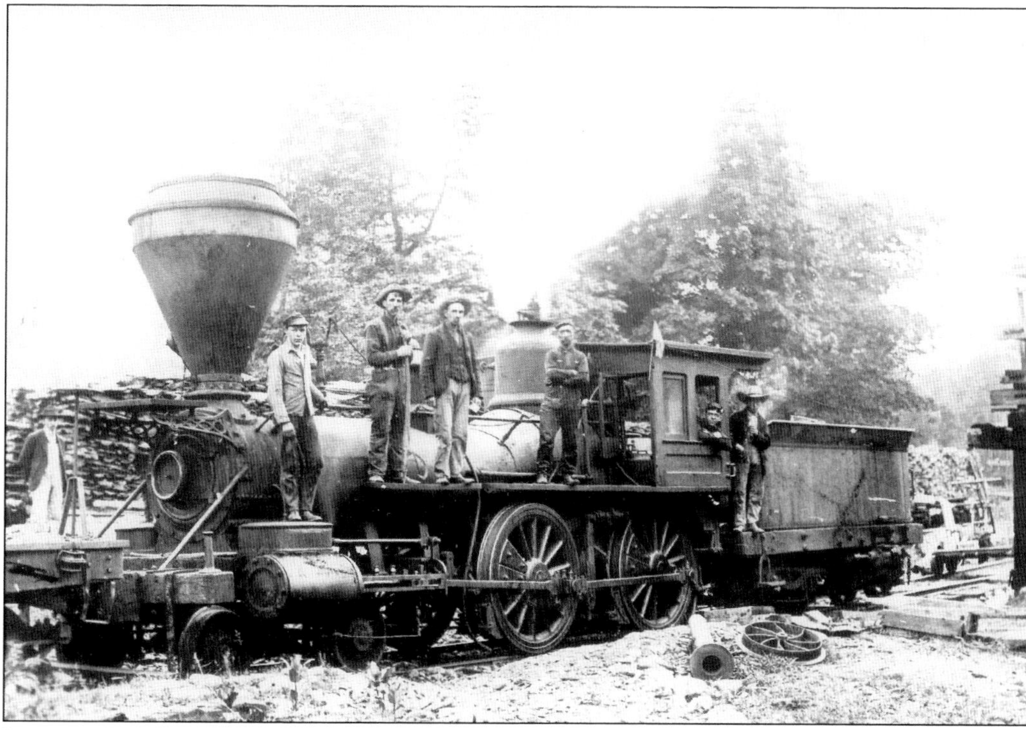

**LOGGING LOCOMOTIVE AT JAMISON CITY.** This first logging locomotive hauled logs until the Central Pennsylvania Lumber Company took over the operations of the Jamison City mill and introduced more modern equipment. The Central Pennsylvania Lumber Company laid many miles of track onto North Mountain so its trains could transport logs to the mill at Jamison City. Once the loggers had finished clear-cutting, the track was torn up to be used elsewhere.

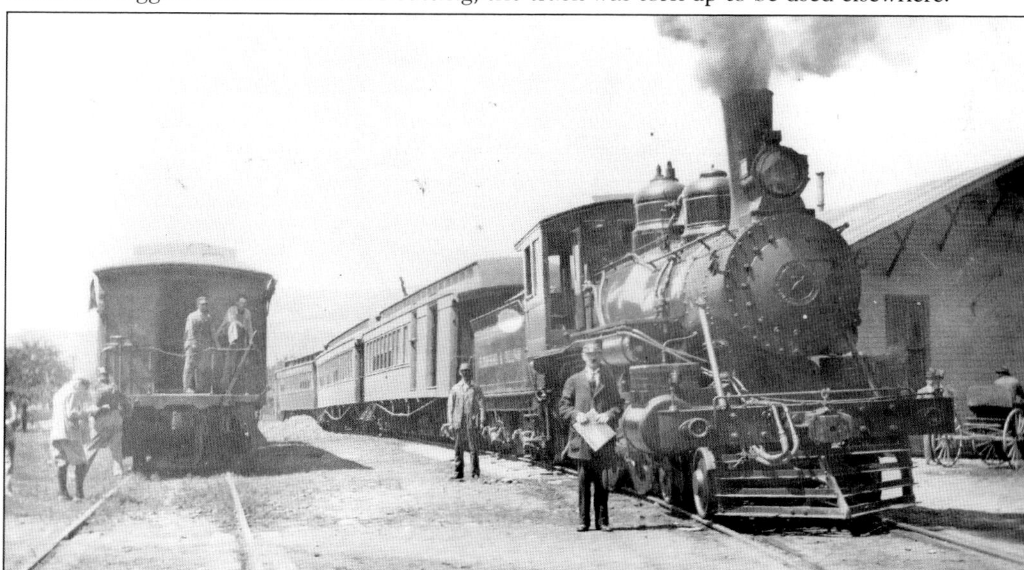

**BLOOMSBURG AND SULLIVAN RAILROAD TRAIN.** The No. 7 locomotive of the Bloomsburg and Sullivan Railroad pulls into the station at Jamison City (right), as a freight train (left) prepares to leave.

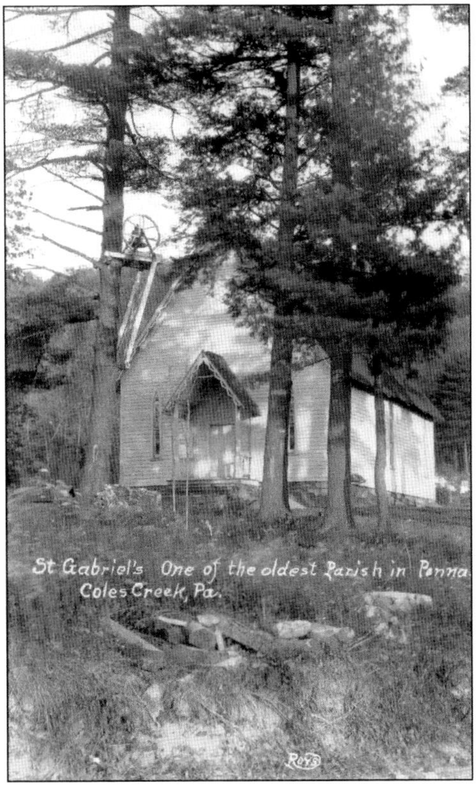


**ST. GABRIEL'S EPISCOPAL CHURCH, COLES CREEK.** Located three miles north of Benton, this church was known as "the Church in the Wildwoods," as well as "St. Gabriel's in the Pines," and is one of the oldest churches in the county. The original edifice of pine logs was completed in 1812 at a cost of slightly more than $200. The cemetery behind the church is still in use today.

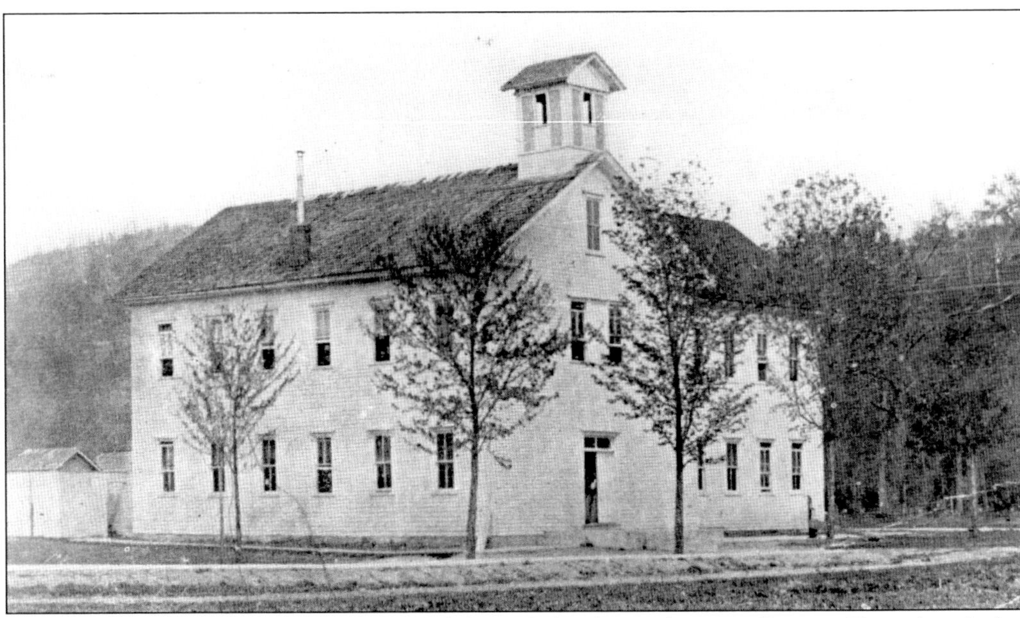

**BENTON PUBLIC SCHOOL.** Leveling off of the early lumber industry in Benton Township shifted development from township to borough. With the increase of small industries and homes in the borough, there arose a need for more schools. In 1913, a four-year high school was established and was housed in this building.

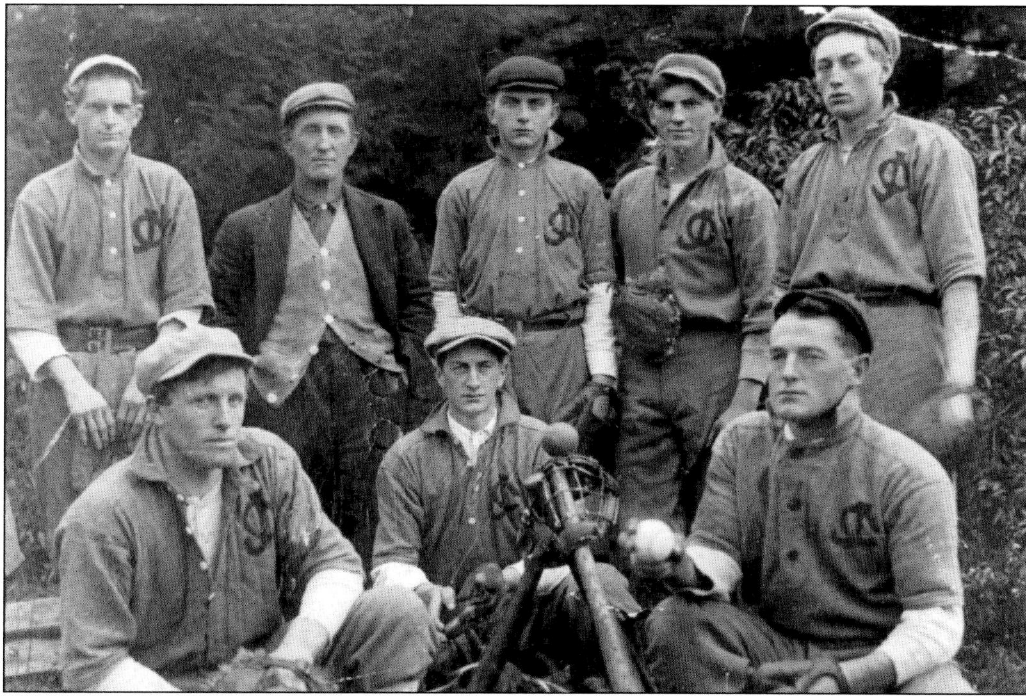

**JAMISON CITY BASEBALL TEAM, 1908.** In the early 20th century, baseball was truly America's pastime. Jamison City's team had storied success for several years, perhaps owing to the lumberjacks' well-developed arm muscles.

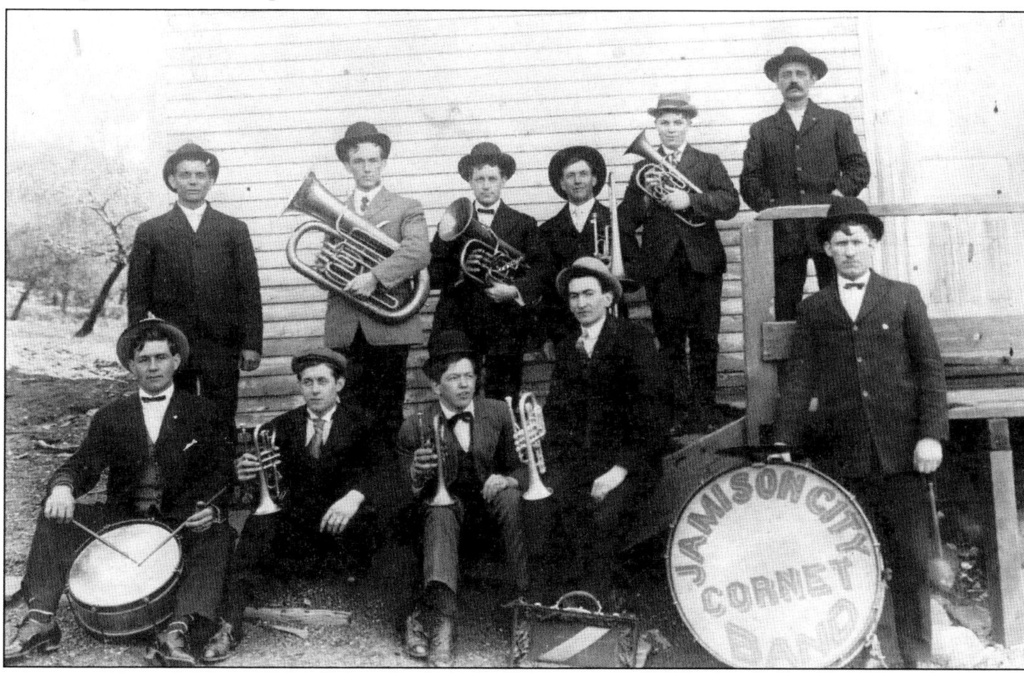


**JAMISON CITY CORNET BAND.** Around 1900, when this photograph was taken, even the smaller communities proudly sponsored bands and drum corps for local entertainment, parades, and competitions.

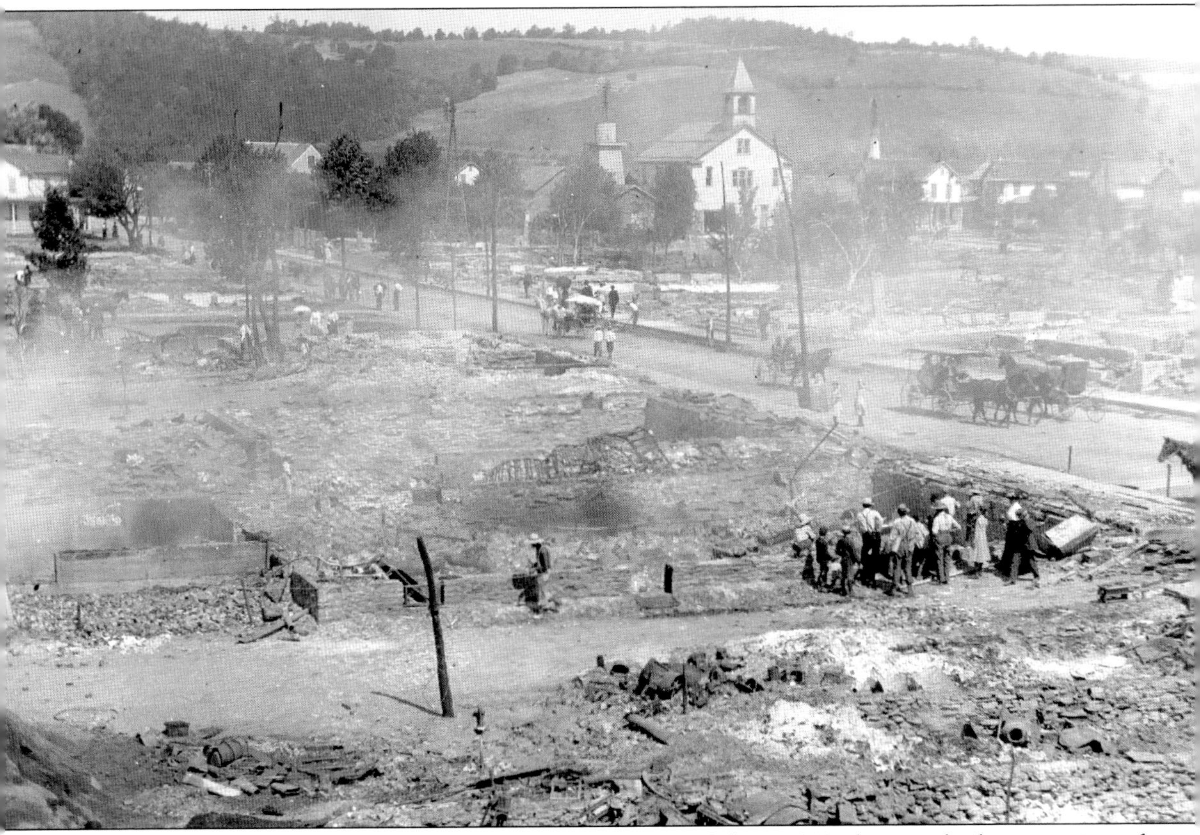

**BENTON FIRE, 1910.** A devastating fire at Benton on July 4, 1910, destroyed a large section of the town. Within two or three hours, the fired leveled 38 homes and stores and 48 barns and left 29 families homeless. The blaze started when boys playing with firecrackers sparked the flames. Five years later, a dam was built to provide ample water for fighting fires.

*Two*

# MILLVILLE, ORANGEVILLE, AND THE CENTRAL COUNTY

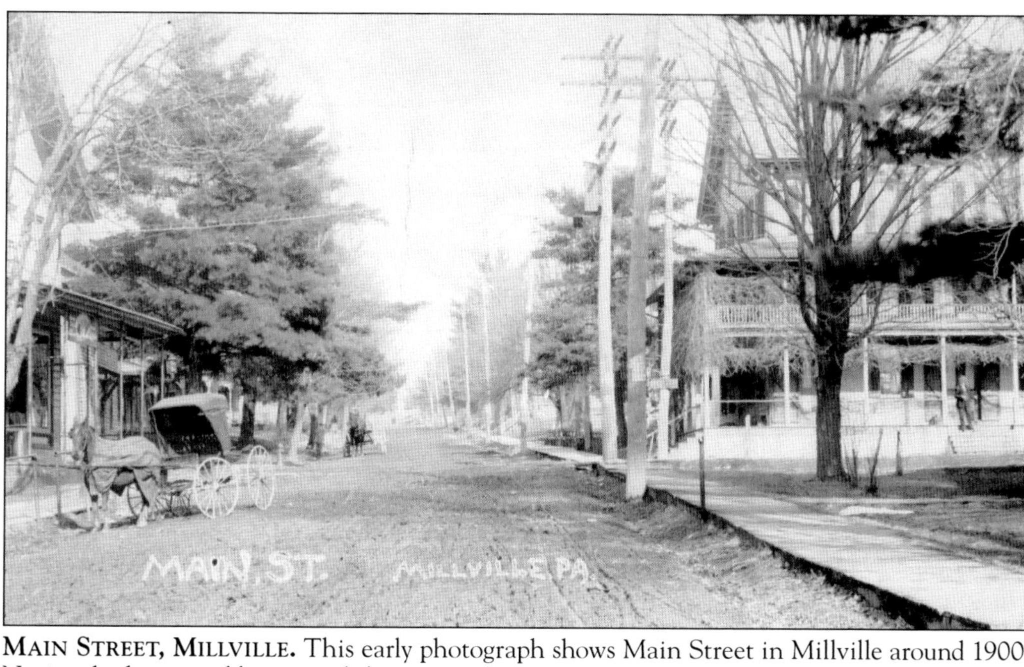


**MAIN STREET, MILLVILLE.** This early photograph shows Main Street in Millville around 1900. Notice the horse and buggy and the unpaved streets.

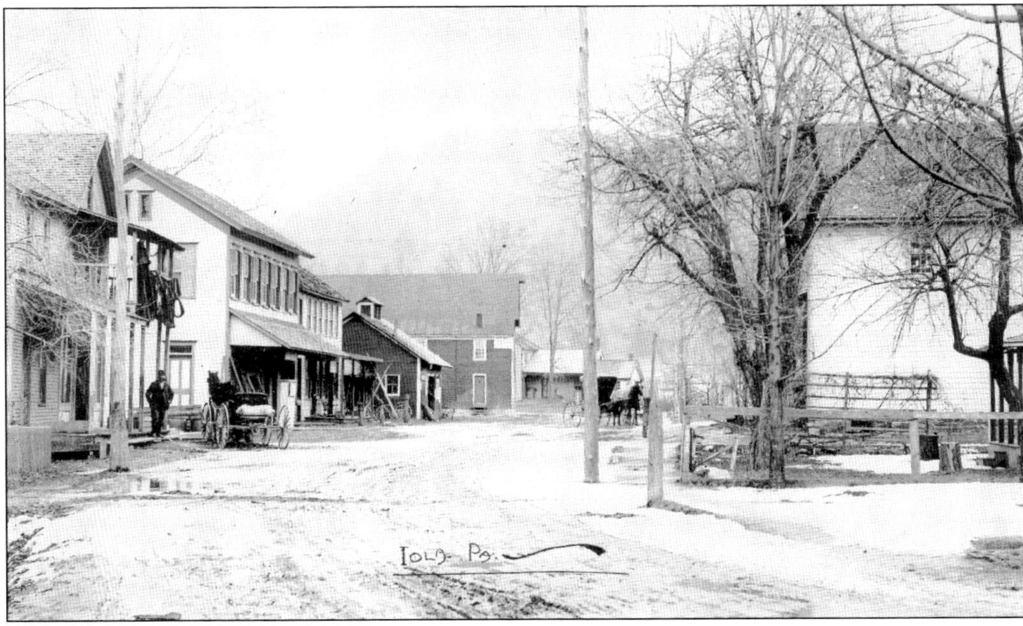


**EARLY SCENE, IOLA.** This early scene of Main Street in Iola around 1912 shows the Louis Brenner store, the blacksmith shop of Cappy Meyers, the Sam Fought gristmill, and the Quill Eves store.

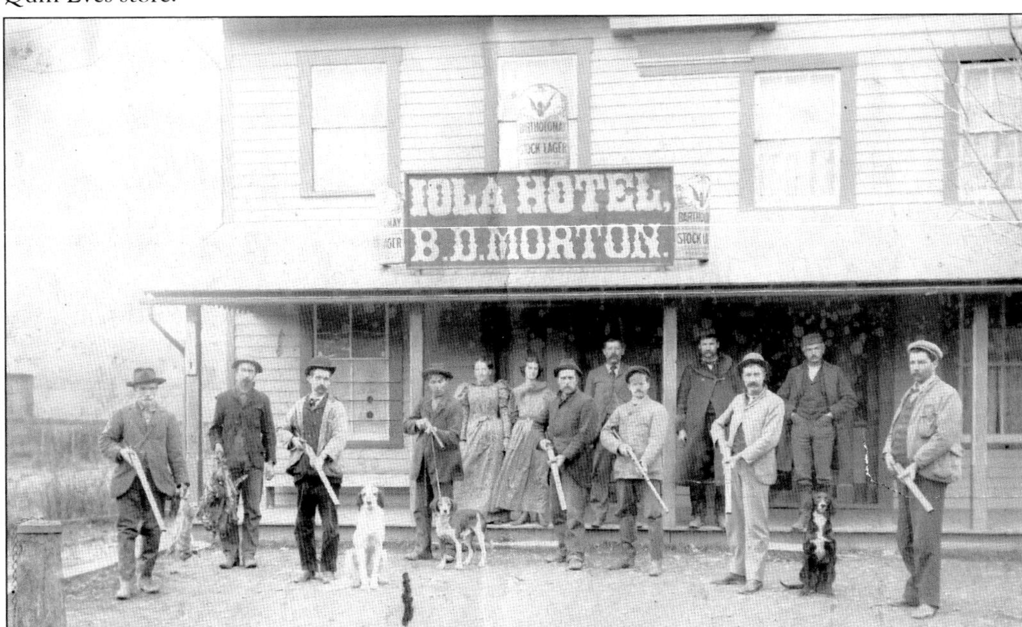


**HUNTING PARTY IN FRONT OF IOLA HOTEL.** Iola is just north of Millville on Little Fishing Creek. The village was founded in 1828 when John and Joseph Robbins built a gristmill and settled there. Elisha Hayman, who owned the mill from 1851 to 1880, named the town after his daughter. In the photograph the village men are dressed up for a hunting party.

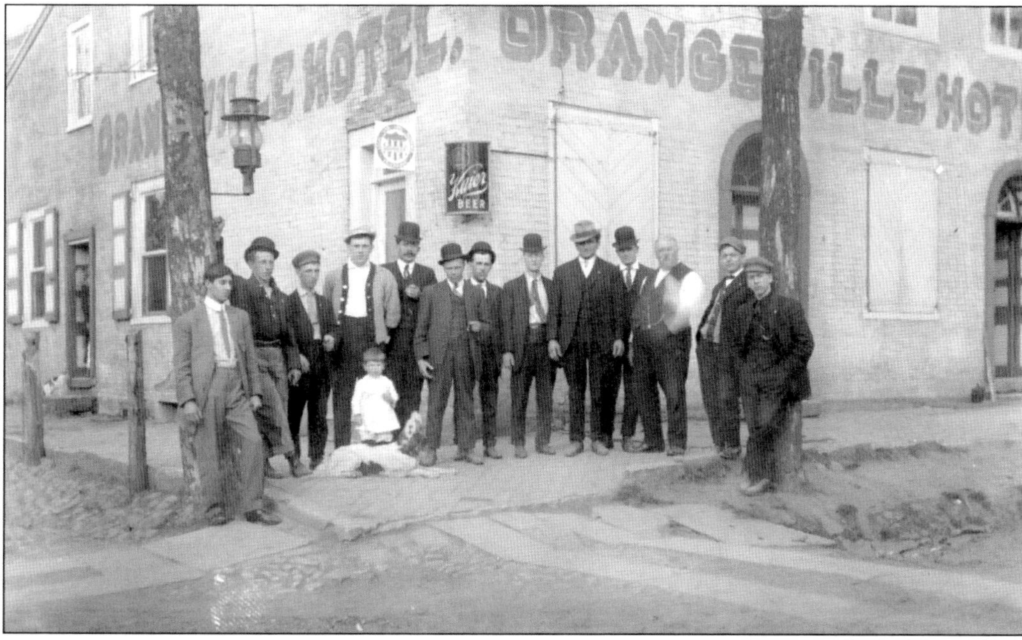


**ORANGEVILLE HOTEL, c. 1900.** A number of people are shown in front of the Orangeville Hotel at the corner of Main and Pine Streets. Clemuel Ricketts, who laid out the village of Orangeville, built the brick hotel about 1822. It was owned for many years by Samuel Hagenbuch. It was replaced by a modern building, and today the site is occupied by First Columbia Bank and Trust Company. (Courtesy of David Brewer.)

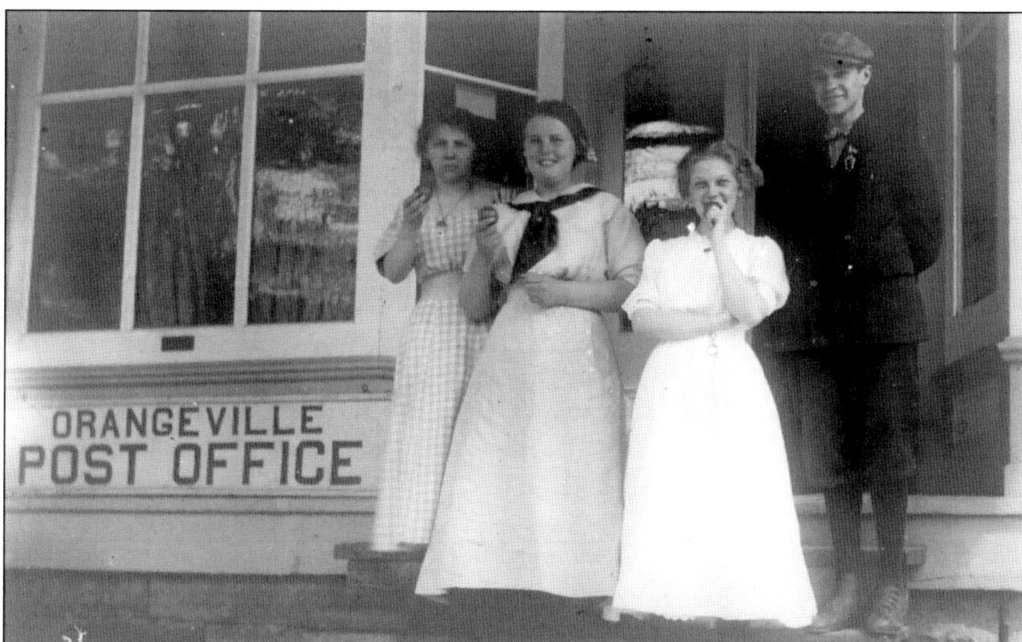


**ORANGEVILLE POST OFFICE.** This photograph shows a front view of the Orangeville Post Office in the early 1900s. This is now the location of the bank parking lot at Main and Pine Streets. The people in the photograph are not identified. (Courtesy of David Brewer.)

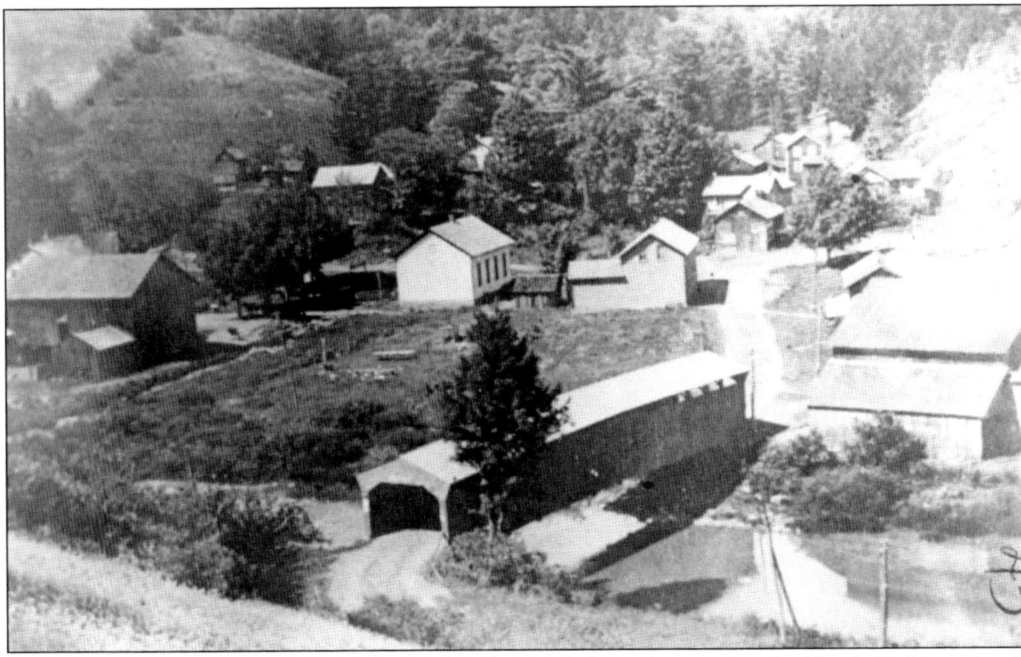

**VILLAGE OF MORDANSVILLE.** Mordansville is located along the east bank of Little Fishing Creek, five miles north of Bloomsburg in Mount Pleasant Township. It evolved from a sawmill established by John Mordan in the early 19th century. At one time, the Susquehanna, Bloomsburg and Berwick Railroad, running from Berwick to Watsontown, passed through the village.

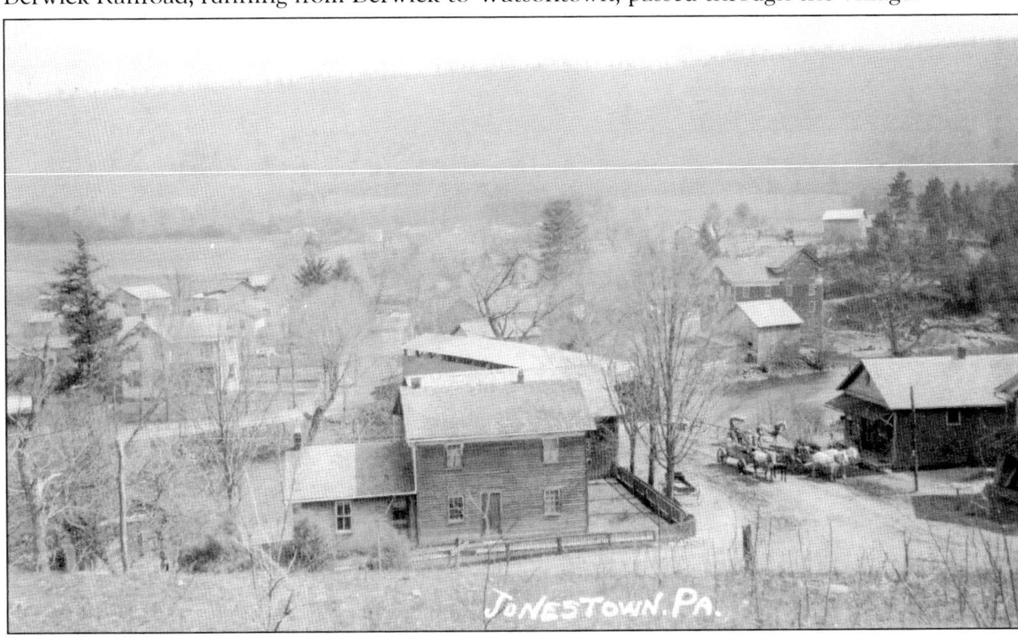


**JONESTOWN.** Jonestown is a small village south of Bendertown in the eastern part of Fishingcreek Township. This image was taken from a hill overlooking the community around 1909. In front of the store are wagons, horses, and a few people. There is a covered bridge over Huntington Creek, which flows past the village into Fishing Creek at Forks. The road across the bridge goes over Jonestown Mountain and on to Berwick.

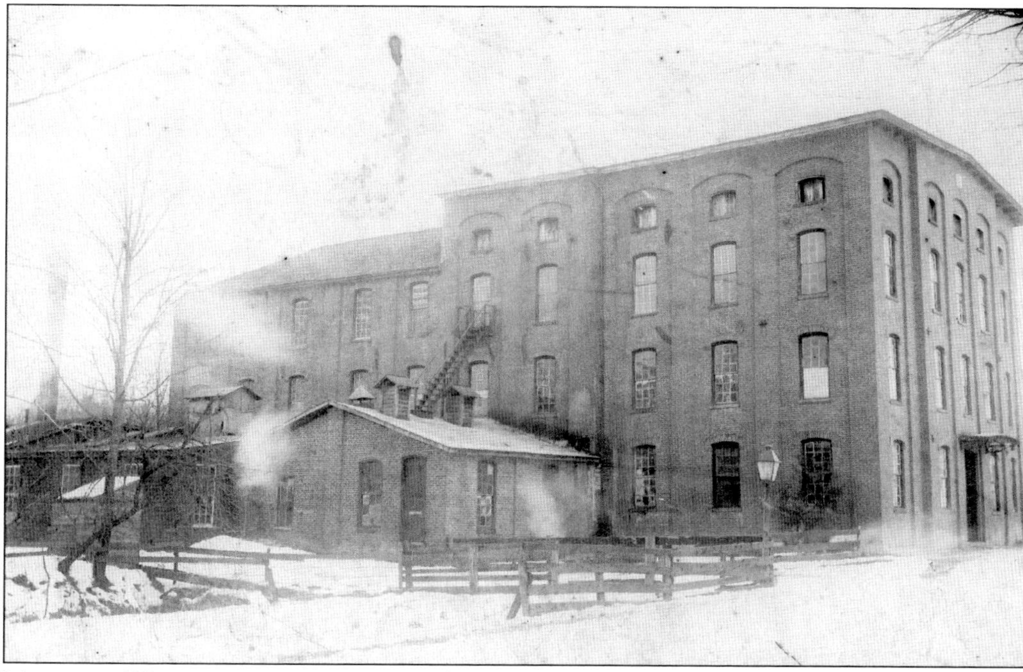

**MILLVILLE WOOLEN WORSTED MILL.** Charles Eves built this mill in 1866 on the east bank of Little Fishing Creek north of Millville. Having changed owners several times, at one time it made blankets for the U.S. Army. Later it shifted to manufacturing woolen yarns, with a weekly capacity of 5,000 pounds. Still later, it was converted to a hatchery. The building was destroyed by fire in 1940.

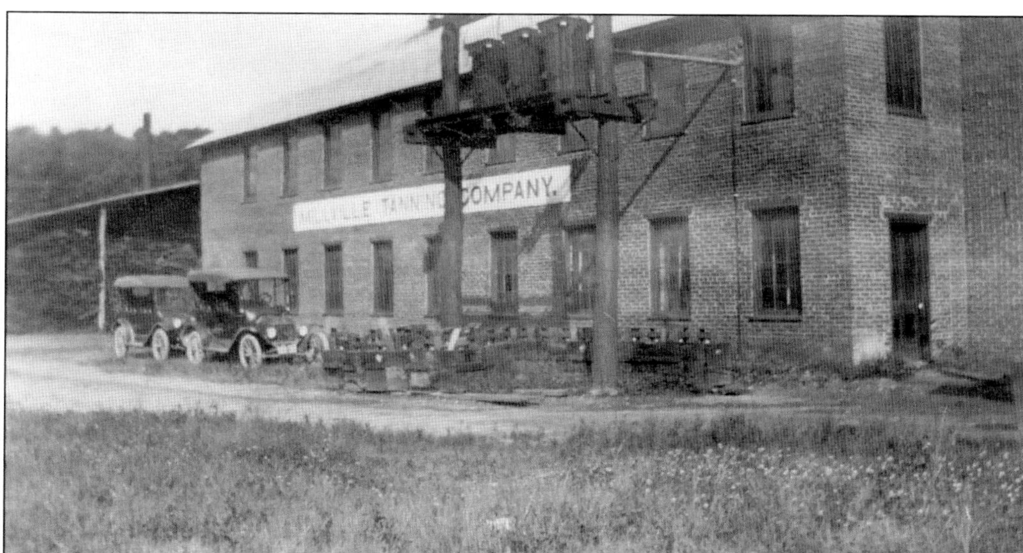


**MILLVILLE TANNERY.** The tannery received "green" hides from the slaughterhouses to be made into leather. Tannic acid, used in the finishing process, was made from tree bark of local timber harvests. As local timber supplies were depleted, the needed acid was purchased. The tanning process produced a characteristic foul odor, a disadvantage to the surrounding community. Fire destroyed the Millville Tannery on March 2, 1933. (Courtesy of Martha McMullen.)

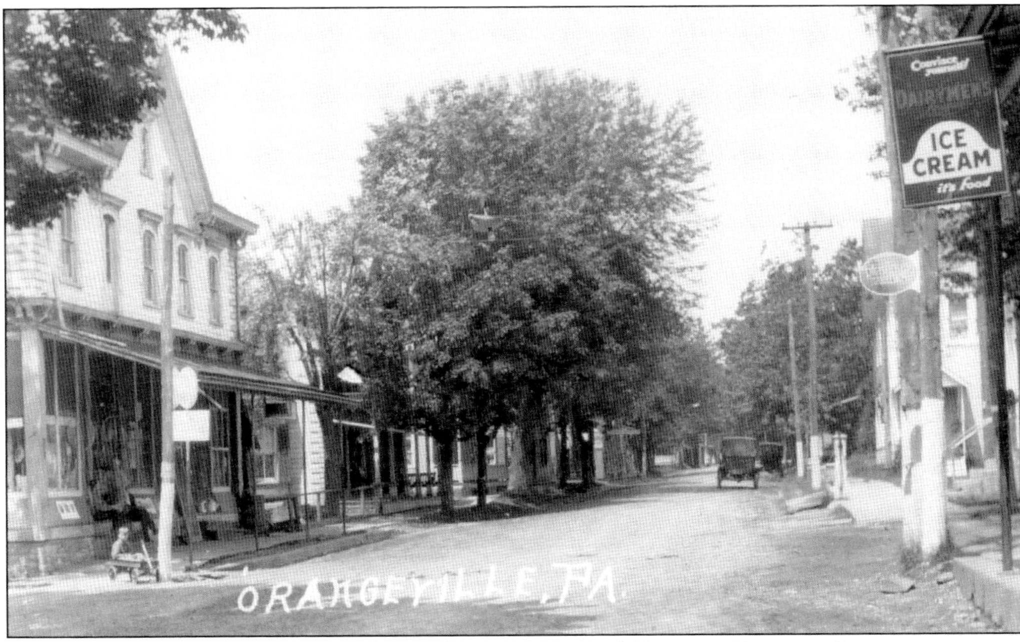


**MAIN STREET, ORANGEVILLE.** This early-1900s view of Orangeville is at the intersection of Main and Pine Streets. Leon Brewer's general store is the first building on the left. Orangeville received its name because many of the people in the Fishing Creek valley came from Orange, New Jersey, and Orange County, New York. (Courtesy of Donald Brewer.)

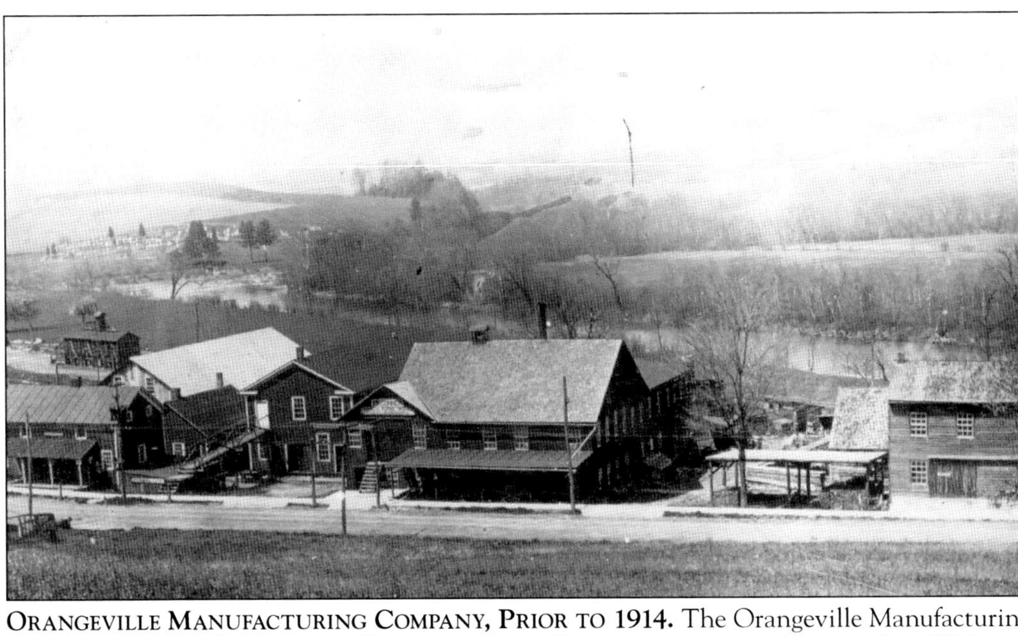

**ORANGEVILLE MANUFACTURING COMPANY, PRIOR TO 1914.** The Orangeville Manufacturing Company was founded by C. B. White in 1879. J. W. Conner later joined him and in 1896 took full control. The company produced threshers, wagons, wheelbarrows, wood saws, bobsleds, and more. The building was lost to fire in June 1914 but was soon rebuilt. In 1920, it was renamed the Orangeville Agricultural Works and began making truck bodies. The firm became the largest employer in the borough. (Courtesy of David Brewer.)

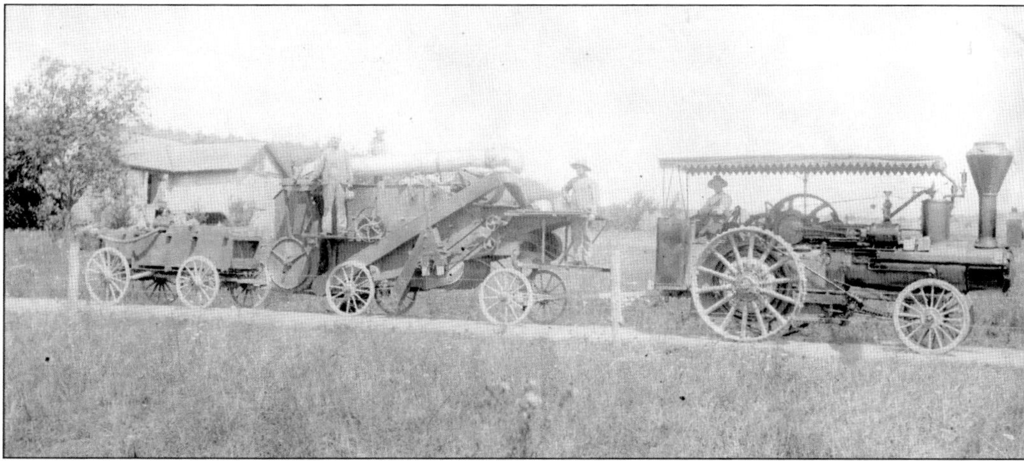

**THRESHING OPERATION, MOUNT PLEASANT TOWNSHIP.** Buckwheat was the main crop in the county in the early 1900s, and most of it was grown in and around Millville, Benton, Orangeville, and Washingtonville. Buckwheat flour was used in making the ever-popular buckwheat griddle cakes, still featured in local restaurants today. The photograph depicts a steam thresher in operation.

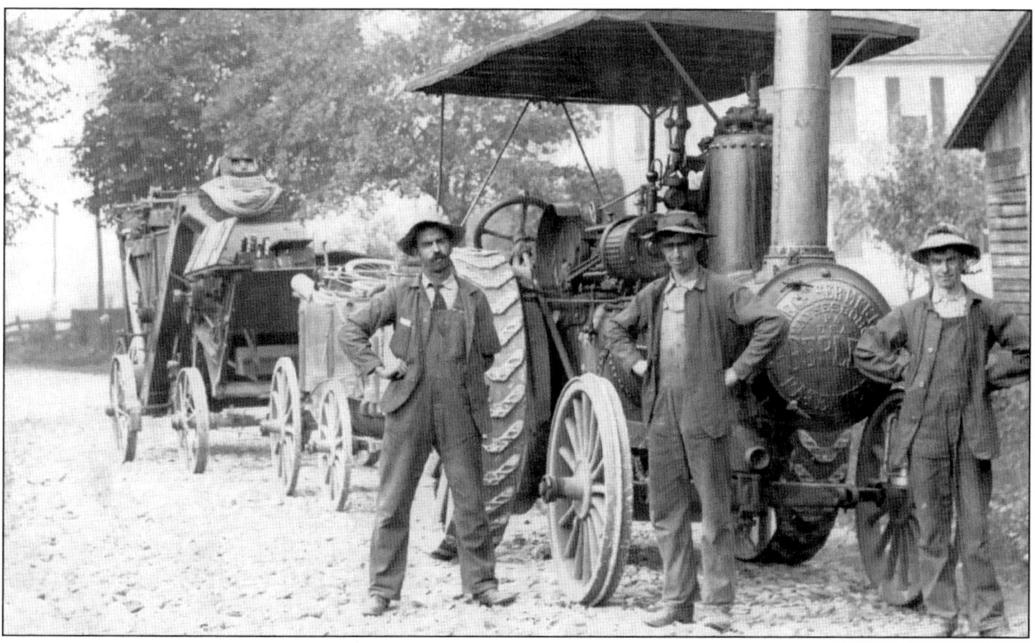

**STEAM-POWERED TRACTOR.** Orangeville workers Atwood and Elmer Keller and Ray Karns are shown here with a steam-driven tractor in the early 1900s. (Courtesy of David Brewer.)

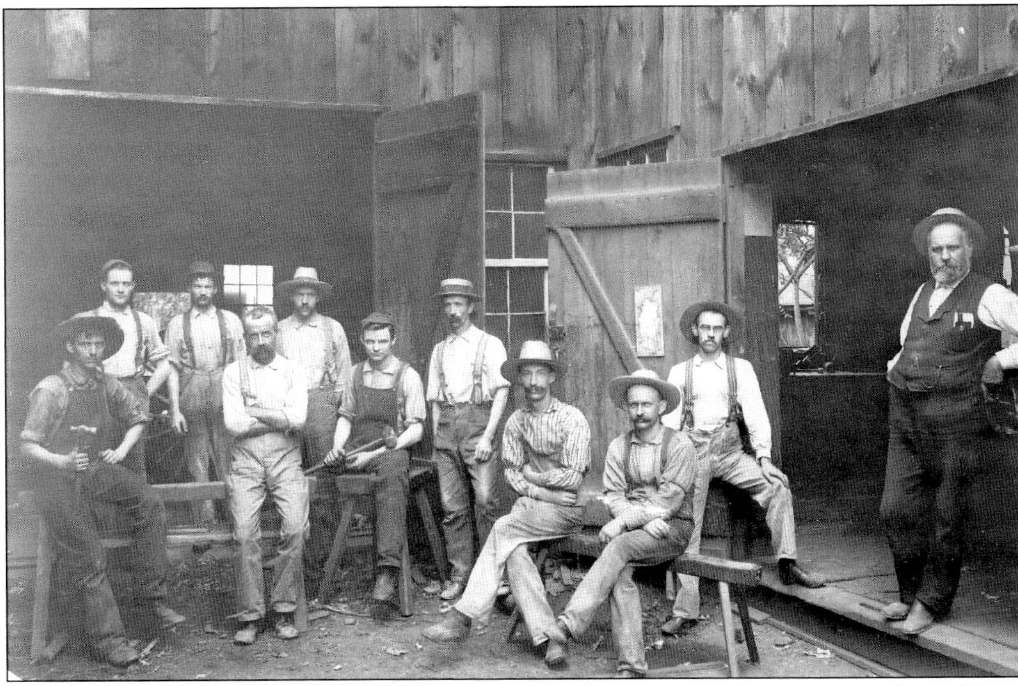

**JOHN EVES WAGON WORKS IN MILLVILLE.** Charles Eves founded the wagon works in 1837. It was continued by his four sons, John, Ellis, Webster, and Bart. It later became the John Eves Company. John is the man to the far right in the photograph, standing in the building. His son Charles, who also had a role in the operation, is the man with one leg in the building. The company made farm wagons, buggies, carriages, and bobsleds. The Eves wagons were noted for their excellent reputation and sold at auction for a much higher price than any other wagon. The company closed in the 1930s due to the advent of the automotive industry. The photograph below shows an example of a wagon made by John Eves.

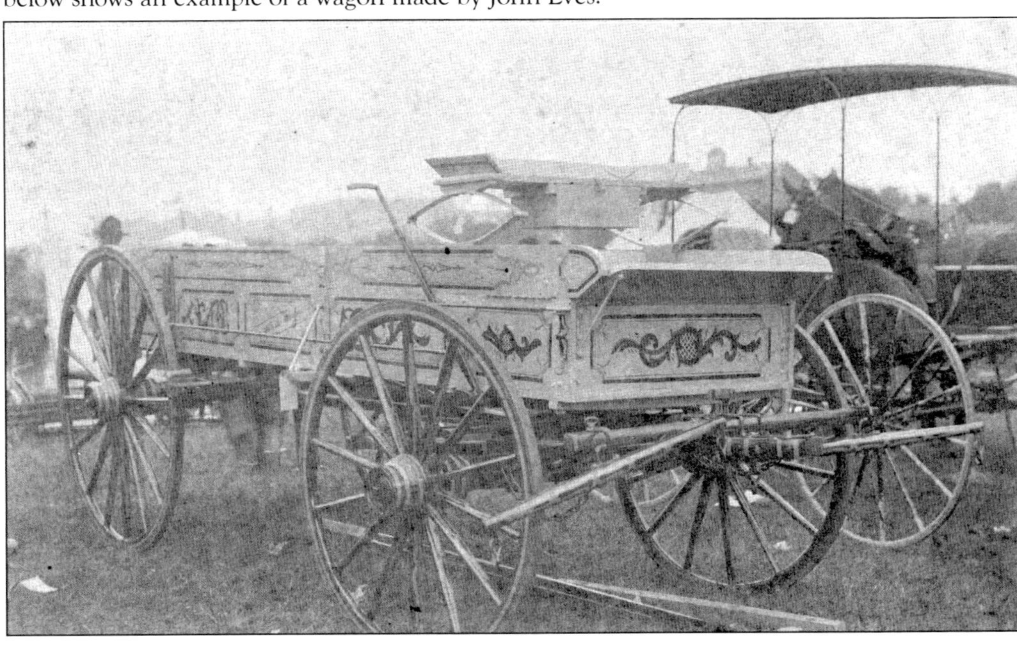

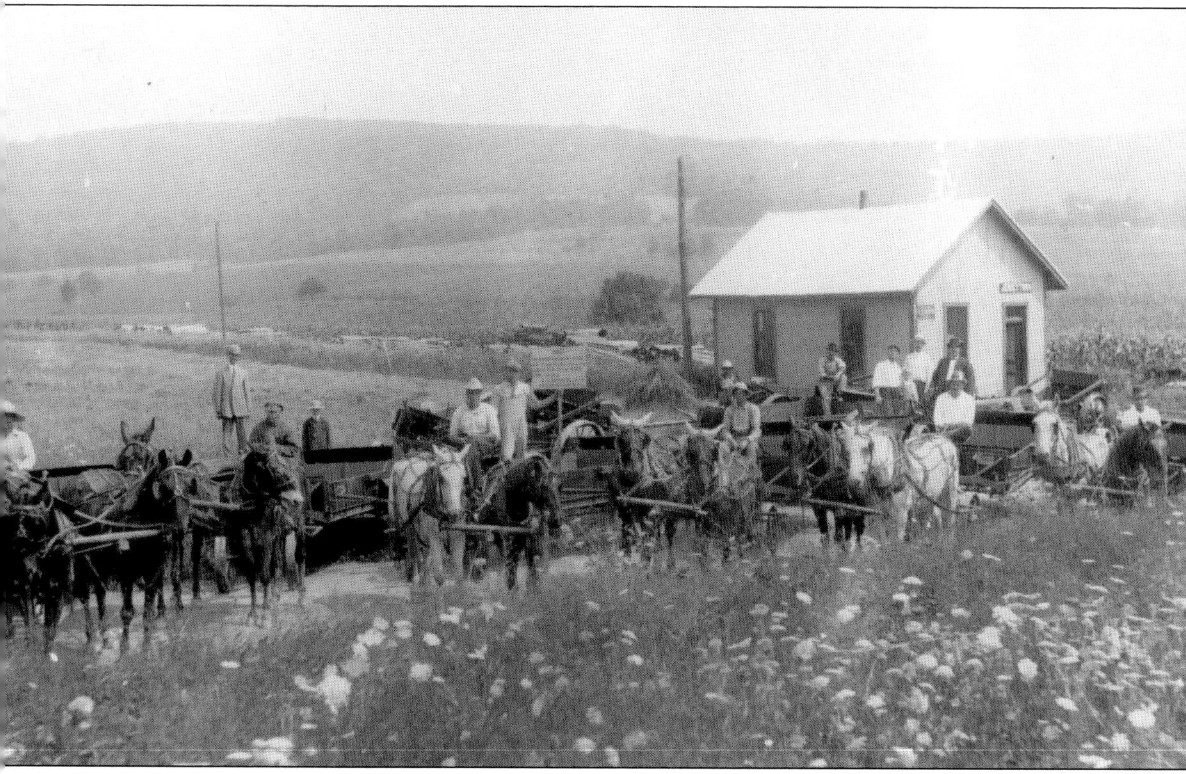

**RAILROAD STATION, JERSEYTOWN.** Numerous men on horse-drawn wagons are assembled at the railroad station in Jerseytown. The sign reads, "the Prosperous Way of Farming in and Around Madison Township, Columbia County Pennsylvania. J. G. Rishel, Agent, Jerseytown, Pennsylvania." The Sunbury, Bloomsburg and Berwick Railroad owned the line in 1891, which was part of the line that originally was supposed to go from Watsontown to Wilkes-Barre.

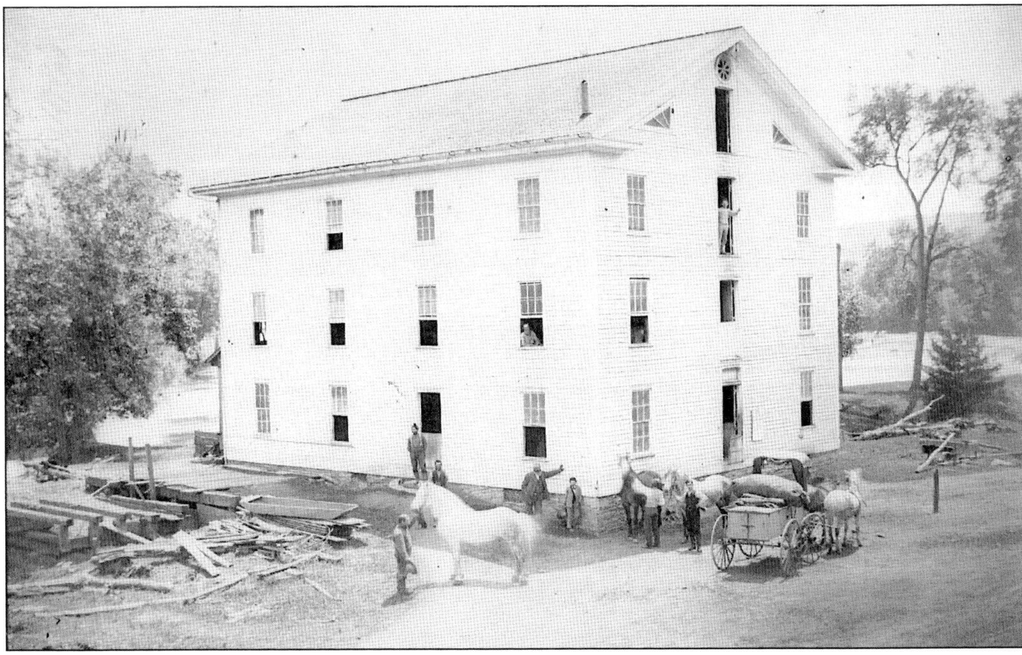

**BOWMAN'S MILL.** Bowman's Mill, along Fishing Creek west of Orangeville, was built by Henry Geiger. He sold it in 1822 to Jacob Seidle. In 1845, Wesley Bowman bought it and completely rebuilt it. In 1915, the mill was still running and was owned by Benjamin C. Bowman. The mill produced wheat flour and buckwheat flour that was sold throughout the county.

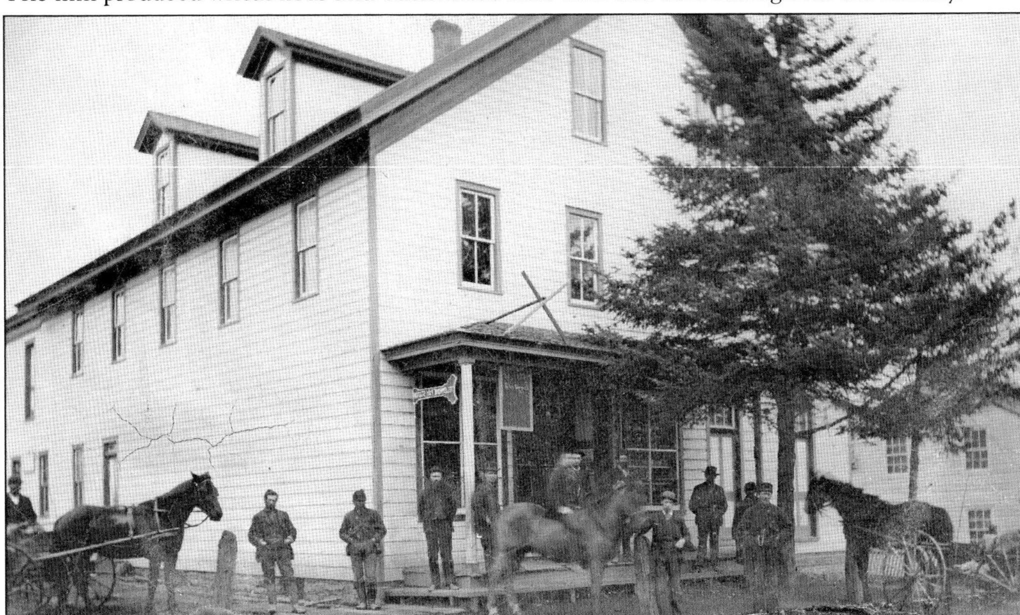

**EYERS GROVE GENERAL STORE.** Originally a private dwelling, this general store was owned and operated by the Eyer family in the late 1800s. General stores in those days were known as dry goods stores and sold very few groceries; they were actually small department stores. They sold everything from notions to clothing to hardware to medical items. An example of the latter was the popular Oil of Gladness.

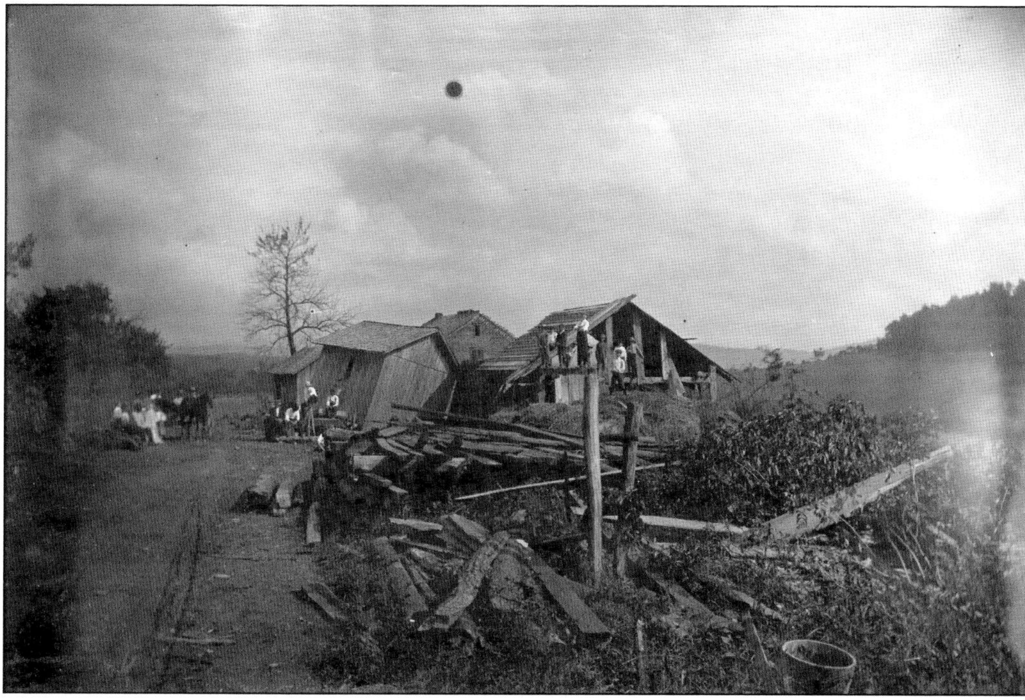

**IOLA CYCLONE.** This scene depicts the aftermath of a cyclone near Iola, which occurred in the summer of 1905.

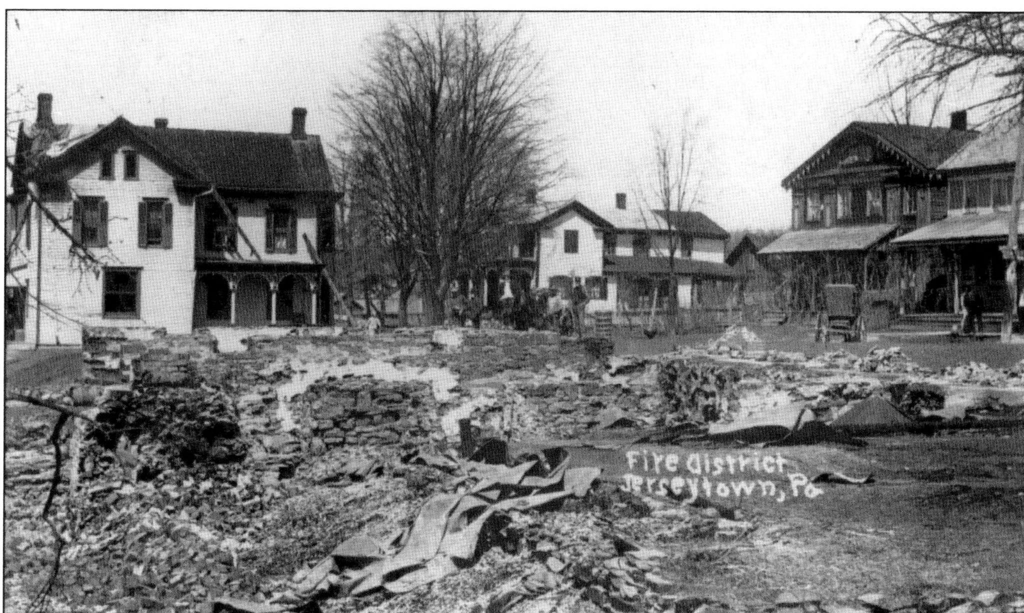


**FIRE SCENE AT JERSEYTOWN.** This 1911 photograph shows a fire scene of Hotel Harvey and the Gingles store. Looking northeast from left to right are the Gingles home, the Convers home, Dr. Jessie Gordner's office and home, and Ben Shultz's tavern. A night fire destroyed a dwelling, the hotel, and the Gingles store. The Gingles family rebuilt and continued in business. However, that building has since been razed.

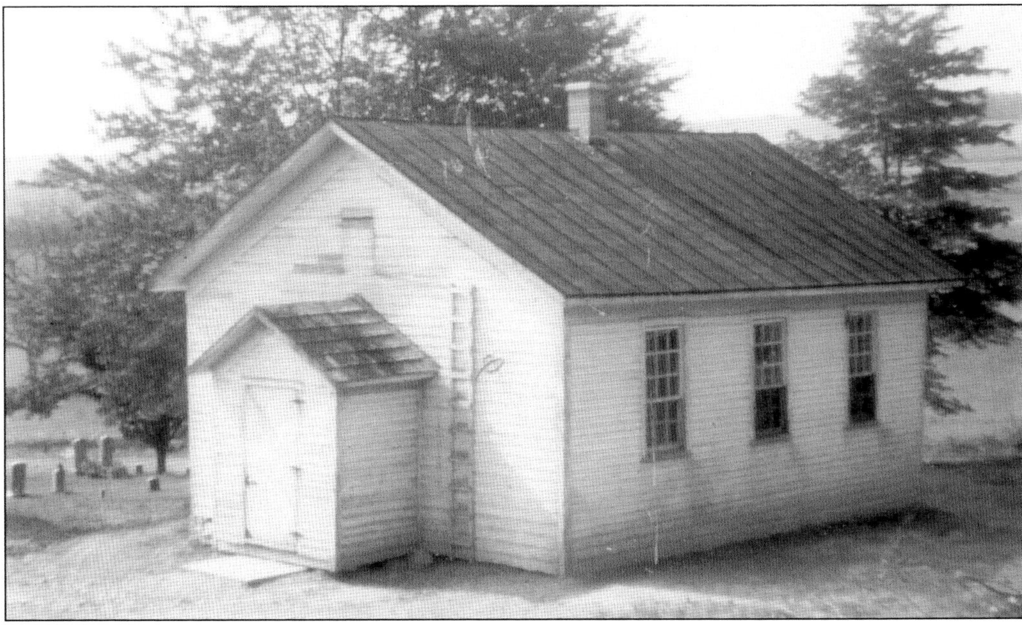

**McHenry School.** McHenry School, one of many one-room schoolhouses in Columbia County, was located on Bowman's Mill Road in Orange Township. It was named for the McHenry family, including Thomas McHenry, a Revolutionary War soldier who came to the county in 1791. The building was later moved to Elk Grove and used as a hunting cabin.

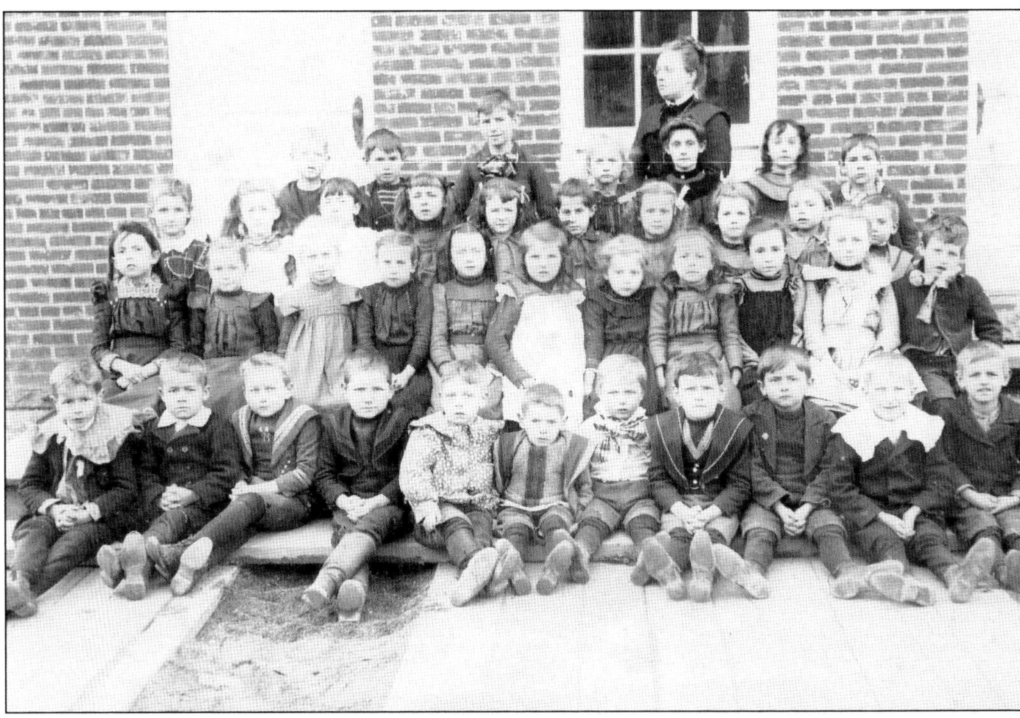

**Millville Grammar School Students.** This photograph shows a class of Millville Grammar School students in 1901. Fanny Hill was the teacher.

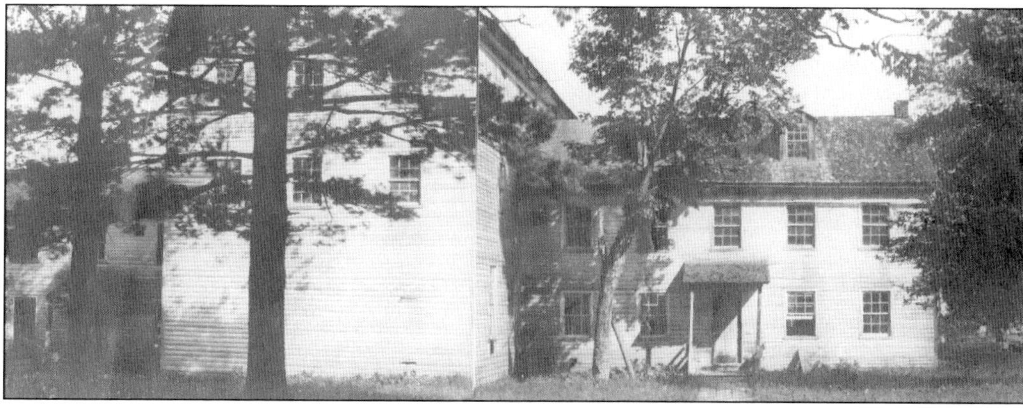

**GREENWOOD SEMINARY.** Greenwood Seminary, established in 1850 by the Quakers, was a three-story building on Main Street in Millville. Today this is the site of Millville Park. In the 1880s, it served as a public and private school. After it fell into disrepair during World War I, Millville citizens provided financial support to turn the building into a community hall. It served the community as such until it was demolished in 1966.

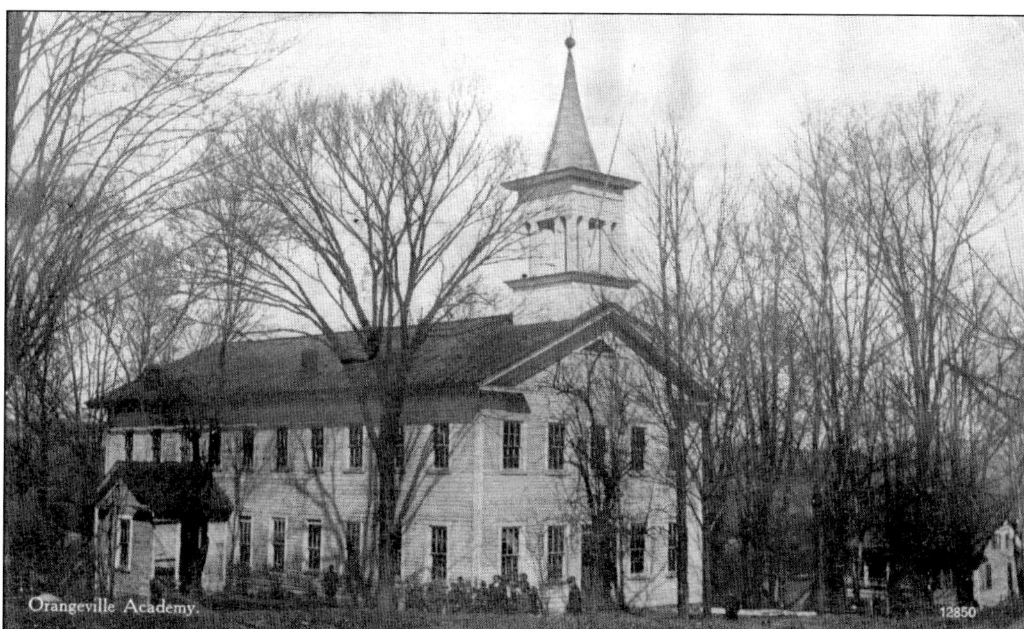


**ORANGEVILLE ACADEMY.** Orangeville Academy was chartered in 1860 and constructed in 1861. It served as a Civil War Soldiers' Orphan School from 1864 to 1868. The academy resumed operation in 1870 and continued until 1894 when it was purchased by Orange Township for use as a public school, housing all 12 grades. The building was razed in the 1960s.

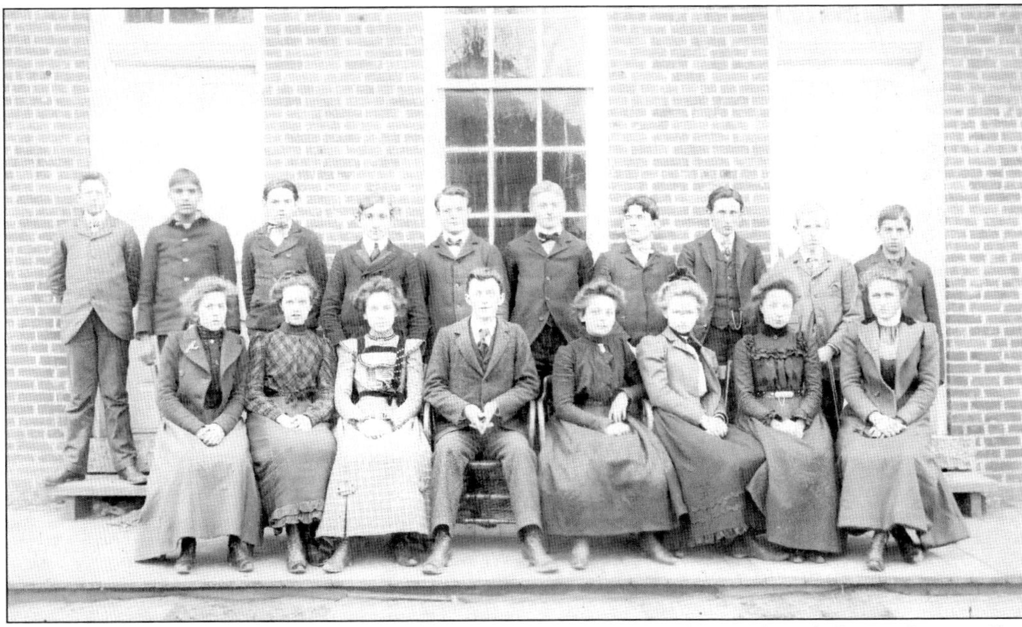

**MILLVILLE HIGH SCHOOL CLASS, 1901.** Members of the class of 1901, from left to right, are (first row) Elizabeth Strauser, Emma Wright, Lovina Kester, S. J. Johnston (principal), Pearl Eckman, Leona Kester, Irene Parks, and Elsie Vandine; (second row) Frank Fortner, William Brown, Barton Mendenhall, Jessie Gordner, Harry Pegg, Norman Smith, Wilson Mendenhall, Irvin Vandine, Earl Heacock, and Raymond Buck.

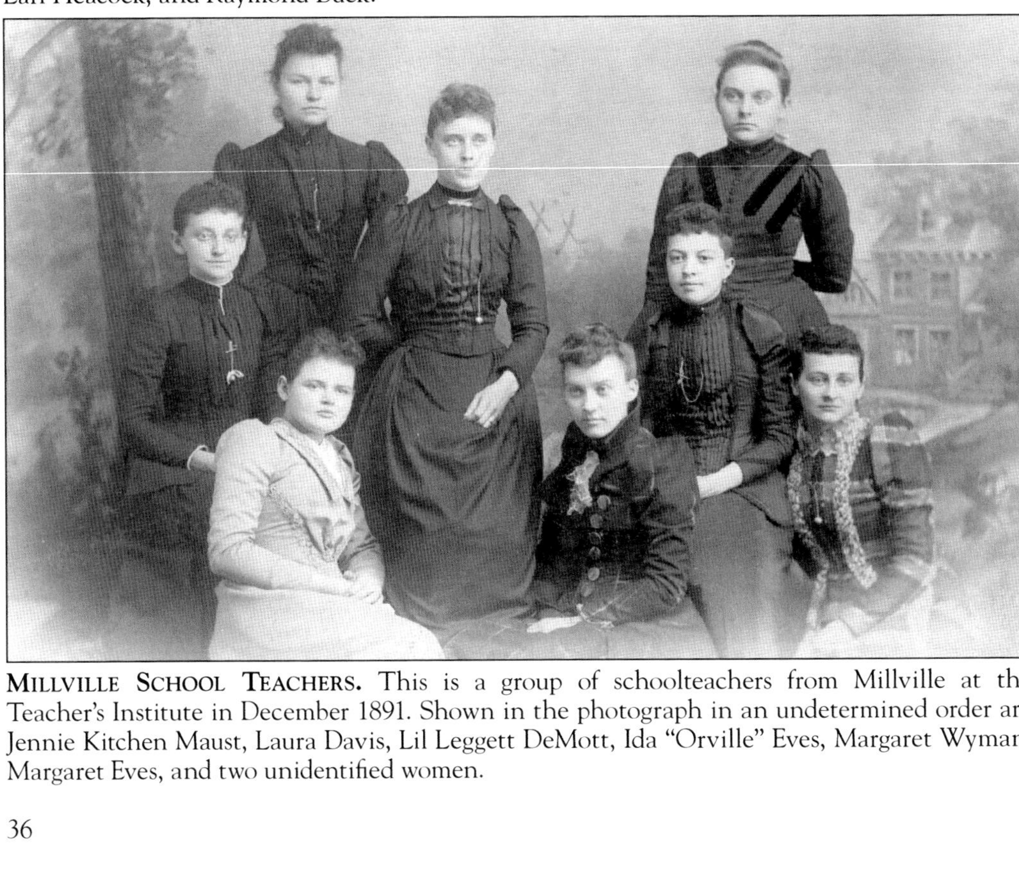

**MILLVILLE SCHOOL TEACHERS.** This is a group of schoolteachers from Millville at the Teacher's Institute in December 1891. Shown in the photograph in an undetermined order are Jennie Kitchen Maust, Laura Davis, Lil Leggett DeMott, Ida "Orville" Eves, Margaret Wyman, Margaret Eves, and two unidentified women.

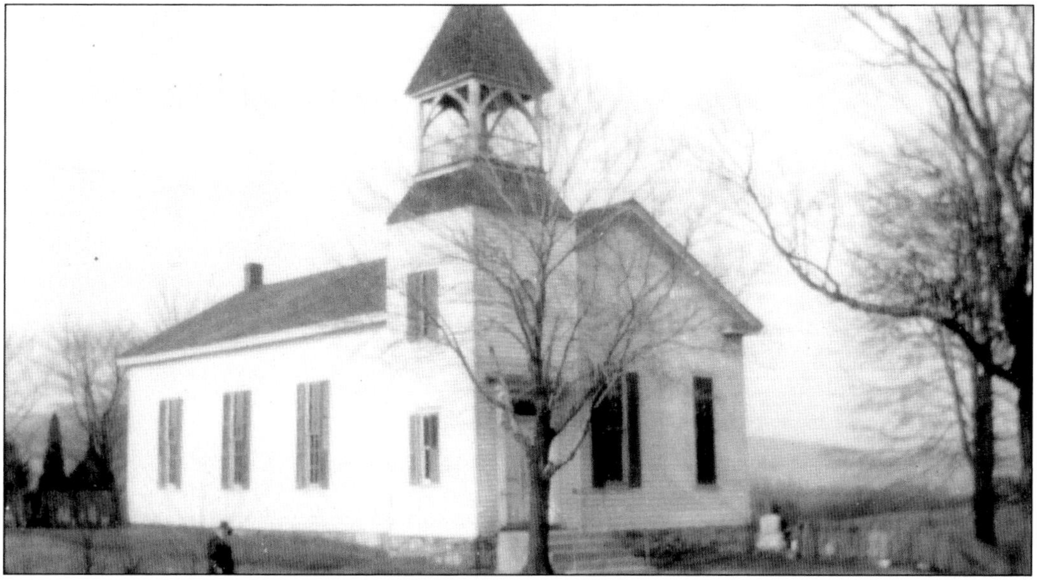

**Hidlay Church, North Centre Township.** The first building was a log structure erected in 1796 by Presbyterians. They joined forces with the Lutherans and Dutch Reformed, and in 1838, a large frame building replaced the former one. In 1872, the church was rebuilt and named Hidlay Union Church. Today it is Hidlay Lutheran Church. There are many gravestones from the 1820s in the adjacent cemetery.

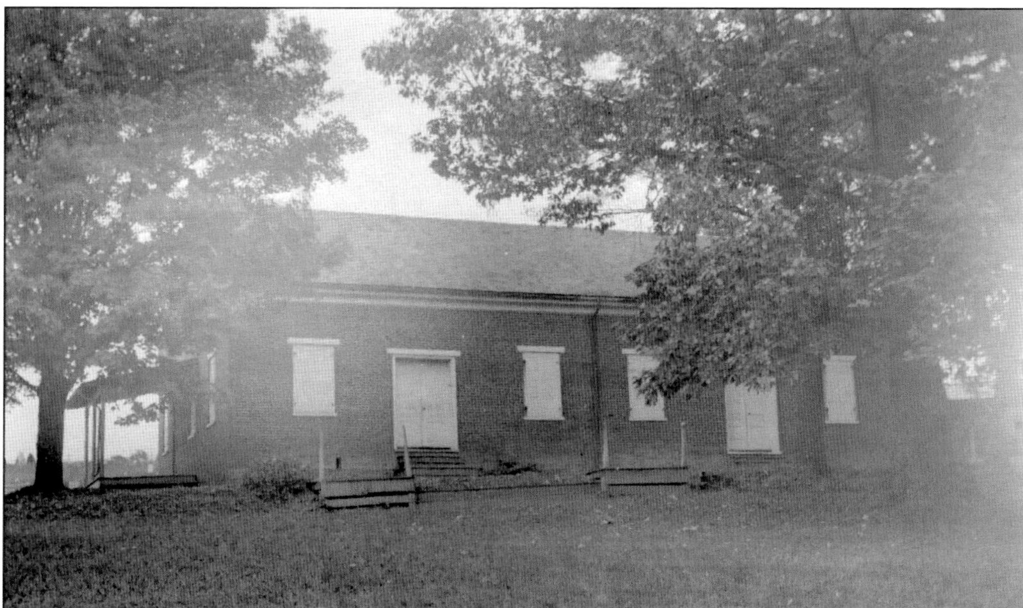

**Friends Meetinghouse, Millville.** A log building, erected in 1795, was replaced in 1846 with a brick structure at a cost of $500. Worship meetings have been continuous since 1785. Landowner John Eves gave the property indenture for 999 years at the cost of one peppercorn per year to be paid to his descendants.

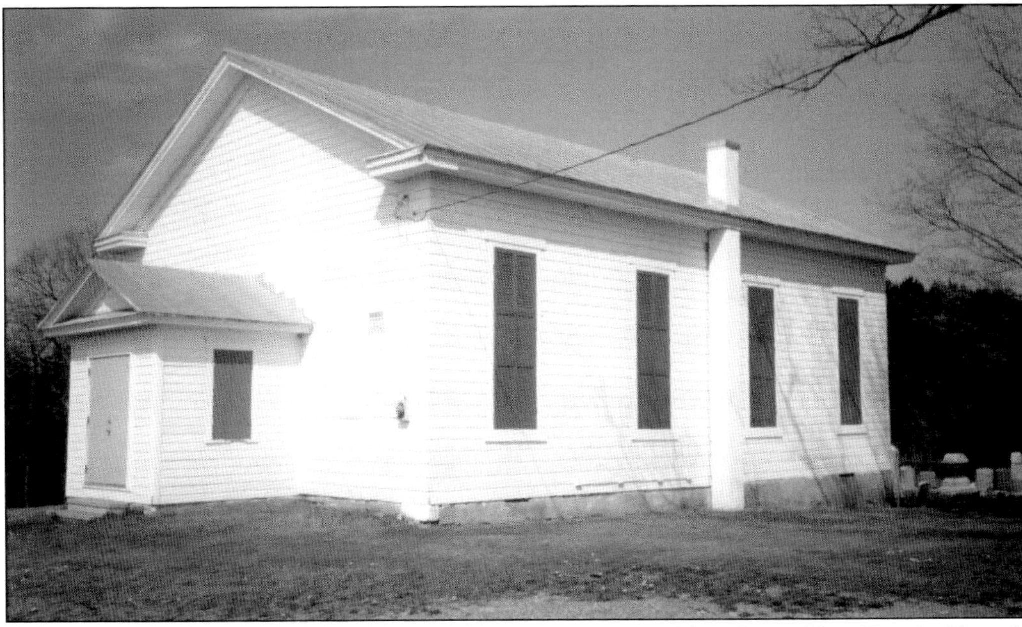

**IMMANUEL LUTHERAN CHURCH.** Also known as Katy's Church or Van Dine's Church, Immanuel Lutheran Church is located two miles north of White Hall in Madison Township. It was founded on August 31, 1869, as a "no frills" church—no cushioned pews, no carpeting, no stained glass. The church served the needs of the hardworking farm community of which it was a part.

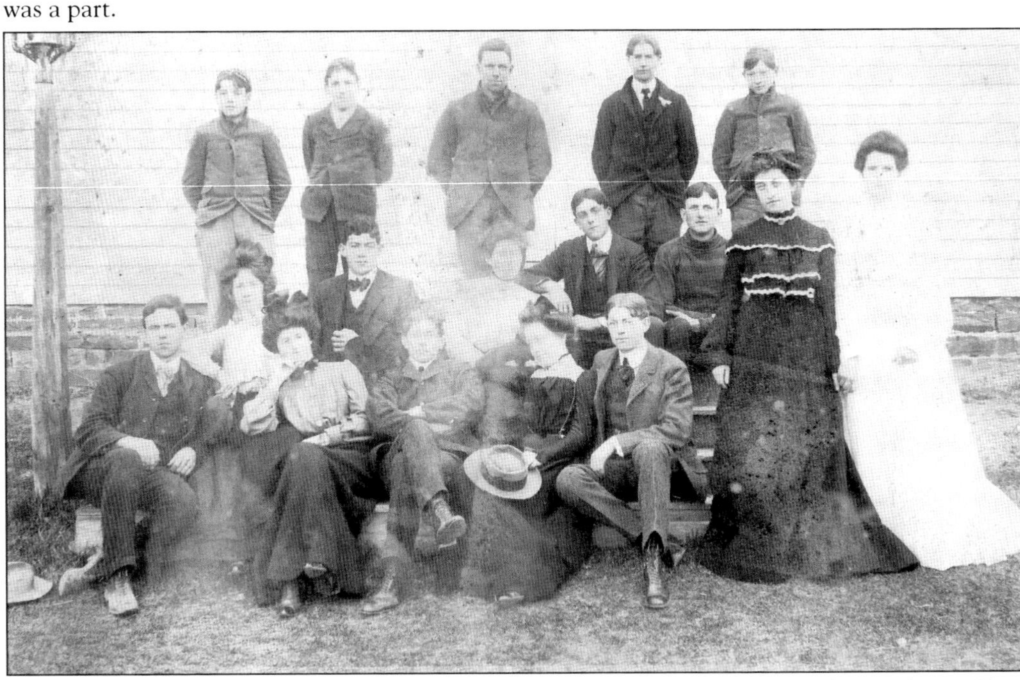

**GREENWOOD DRAMATIC CLUB, 1903.** Pictured here from left to right are (first row) Wes Eves, Laura Ruckle, Elmer Van Horn, Izora Kraemer, Harry Beck, Mildred Parker, and Edna Parker; (second row) Myra Lawton, Herman Rote, Bess Rich Ruckle, Herbert Miller, and Harry Derrick; (third row) Horace Robbins, Harry Van Horn, Art Eves, Orville Heacock, and Ben Robbins.

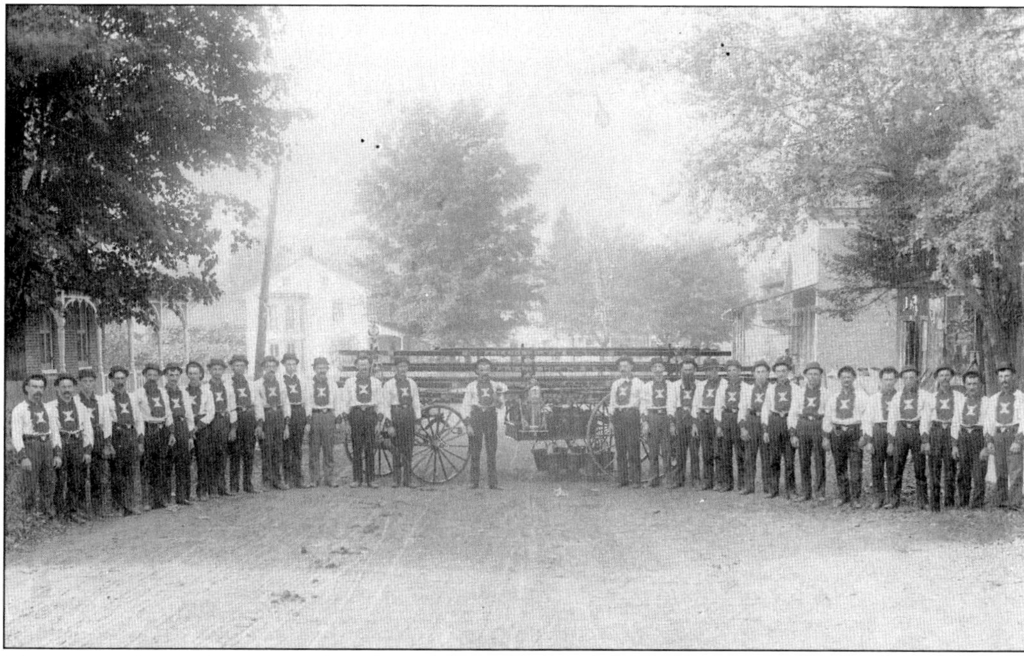

**MILLVILLE FIRE COMPANY, ORGANIZED 1892.** Pictured from left to right are Frank Heller, Frank Patton, Charlie Eves, Wells Shoemaker, Jack Kisner, Ed Eves, Phinny Eves, Pascal Eves, Orville Eves, Will Bogart, Norman John, Boyd Trescott, Gaiton Moore, Lou Lyons, Clem Henrie, Sherm Cole, Lem John, Ulie O'Blosser, Vernon Eves, Grant Johnson, Orville Johnson, Charlie Eckman, Hank Kisner, Joe Lemmons, Sam DeMott, Joe Cole, Russell Smith, and Alf Cole.

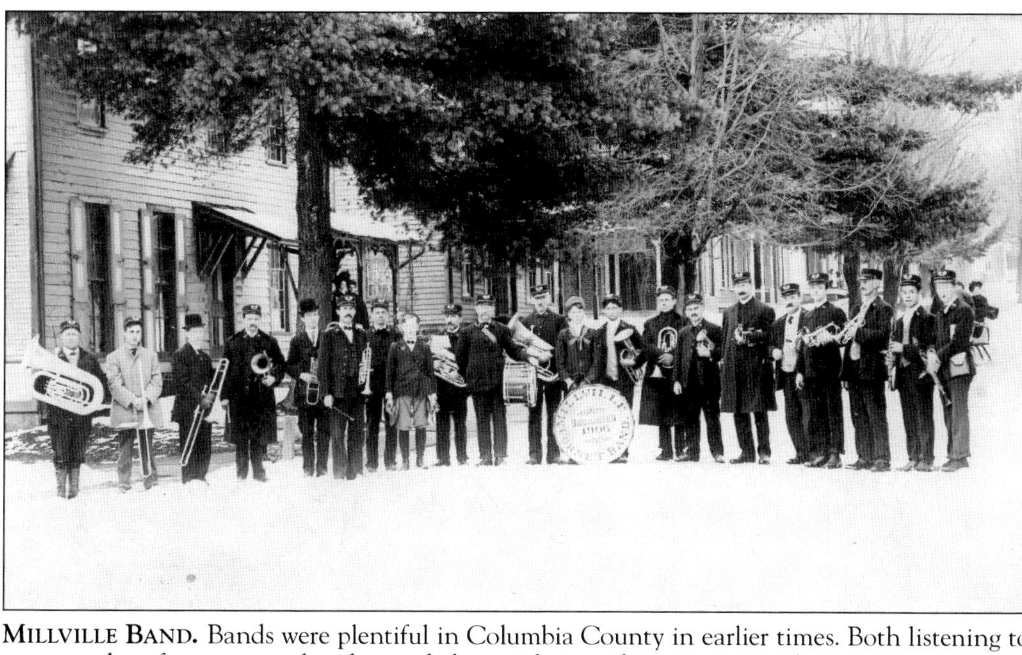

**MILLVILLE BAND.** Bands were plentiful in Columbia County in earlier times. Both listening to music and performing in a band provided many hours of enjoyment to the participants in the days before the spectator sport of television.

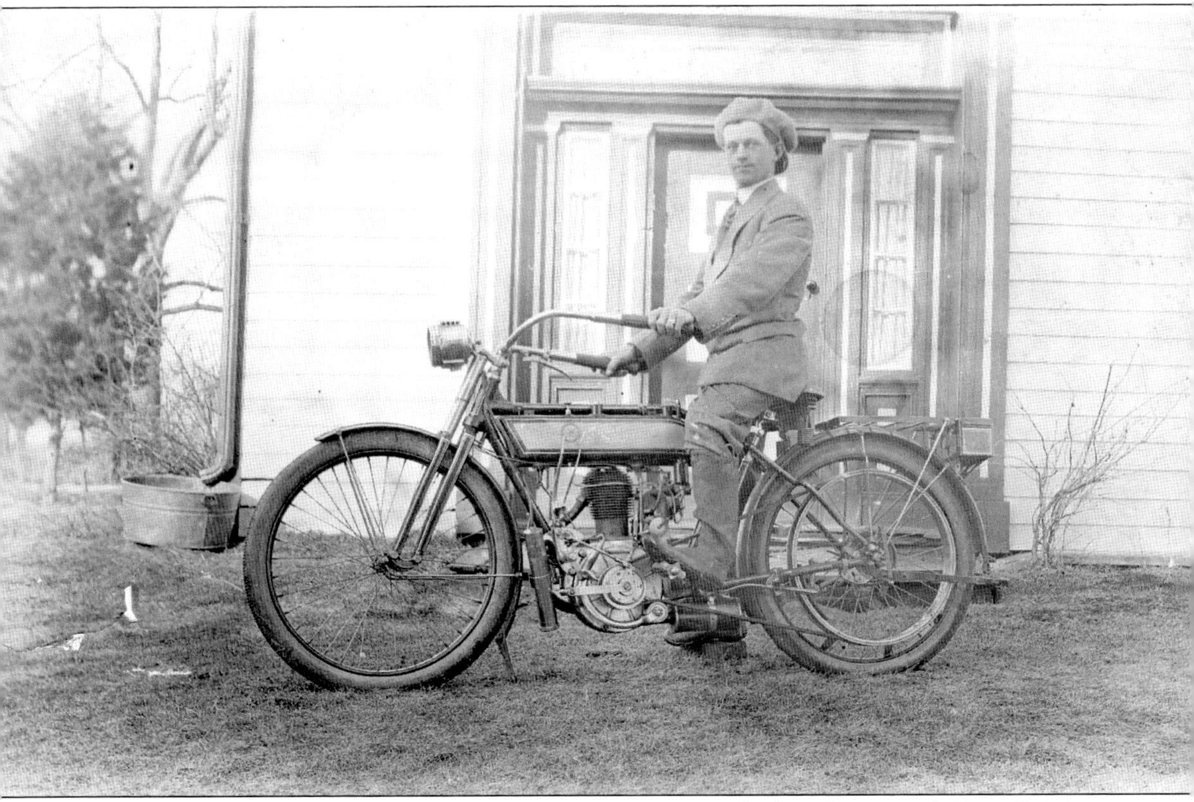

**READING STANDARD MOTORCYCLE.** Jay DeMott of Millville, the son of Elroy DeMott, is shown on his Reading Standard motorcycle. These single-cylinder motorcycles were first produced in 1906 and sold across the country. Jay was born in 1890, died in 1959, and is buried in Millville Cemetery.

# *Three*

# Bloomsburg and Vicinity

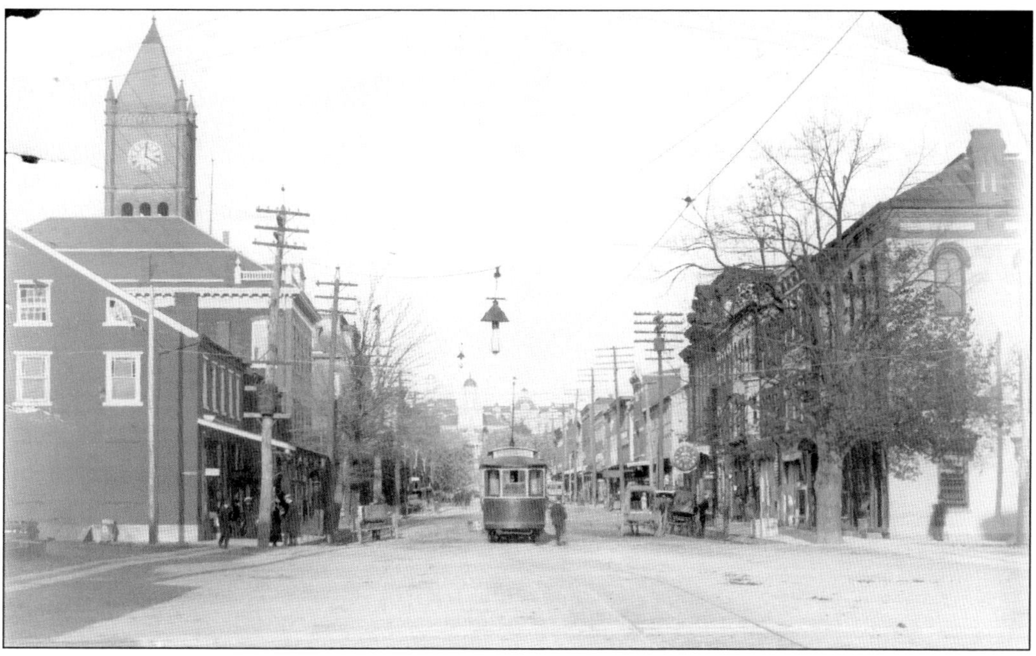

**Main Street, Bloomsburg.** This *c.* 1905 scene looking east on Main Street highlights a trolley car en route to Danville or Catawissa. The trolley system was in operation from 1901 through 1926 and enabled hundreds of people from outlying villages to travel several miles daily for work and shopping.

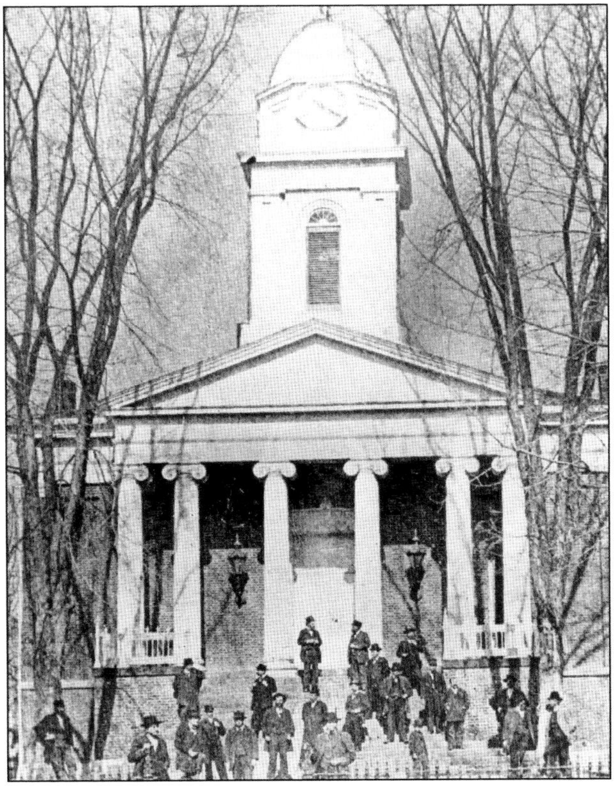

**COLUMBIA COUNTY COURTHOUSE.** The contentious "removal" issue in Columbia County resulted in moving the county seat from Danville to Bloomsburg when the town's citizens agreed to donate the land and erect a courthouse at no cost to the county. The new pillared courthouse opened for business in 1847; its appearance was entirely altered by later additions.

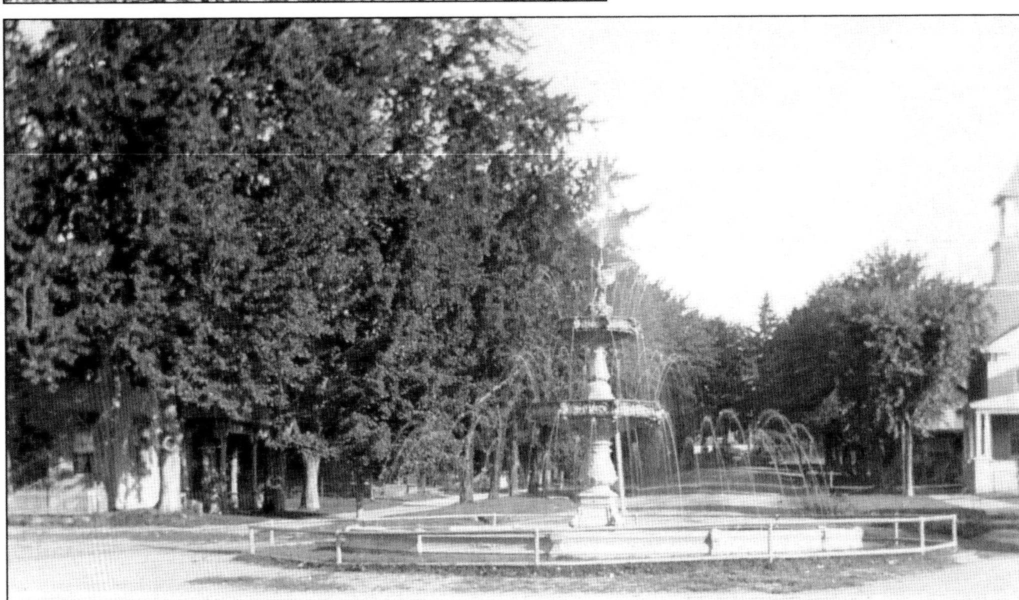

**DAVID STROUP FOUNTAIN.** This fountain, erected in 1892 at Bloomsburg's Market Square, honors local candy shop owner David Stroup, who bequeathed money to the town's waterworks. The current fountain is a restored version of the original, which was dismantled in 1966 but was restored in 1982 by two local residents. In 2005, the original crane sculpture at the top was cleaned, repaired, and replaced on the fountain.

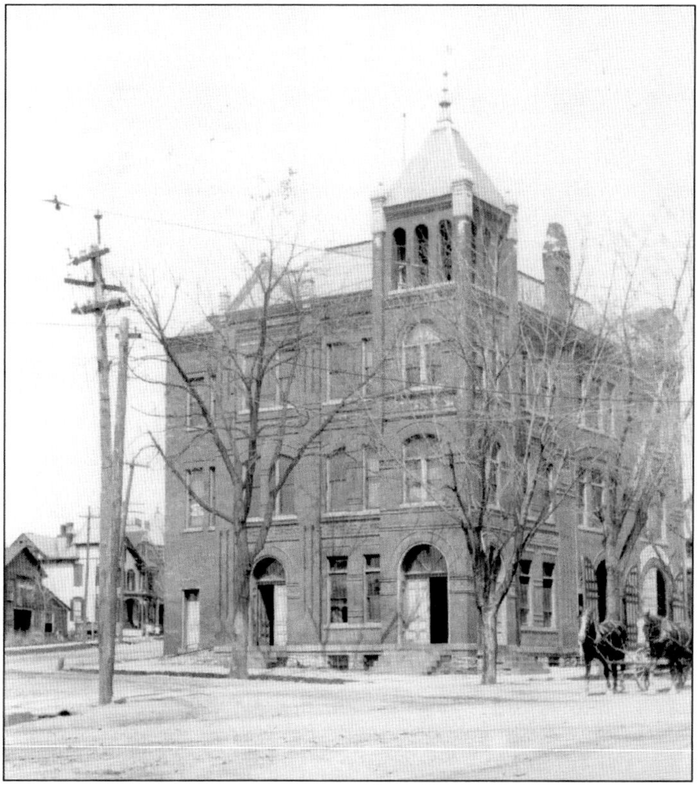

**BLOOMSBURG TOWN HALL.** Before town hall was built, the site housed a blacksmith shop and early lockup. The three-story brick building, erected at a cost of $15,000, was dedicated in 1890 on property originally owned by pioneer settler Daniel Snyder. In its earlier years, the Friendship Fire Company also had its quarters in town hall.

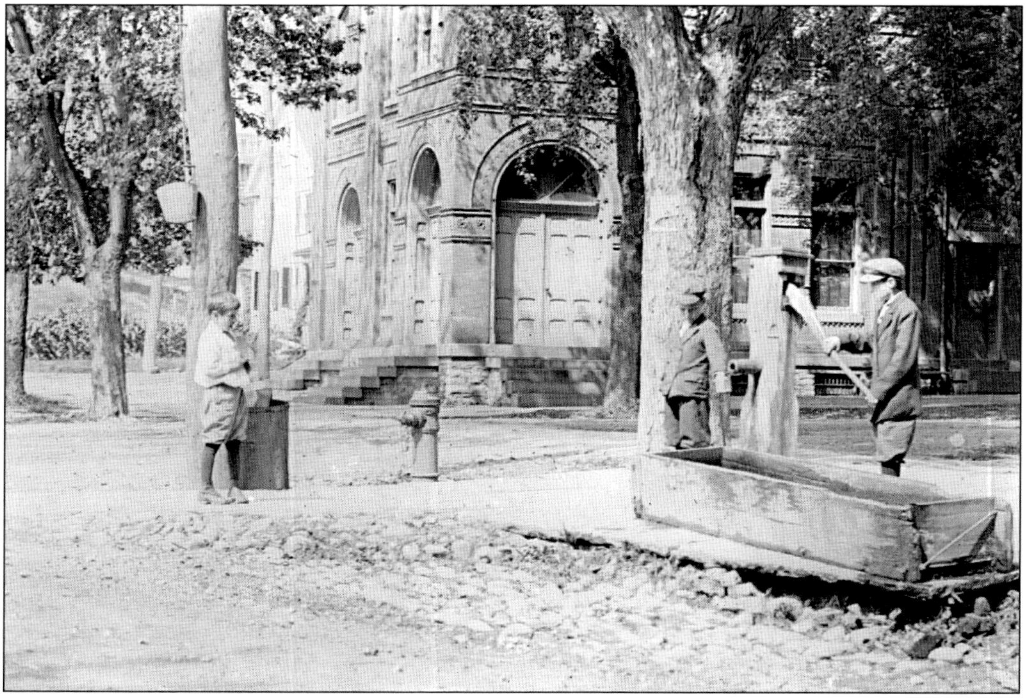

**TOWN PUMP.** This late-1800s photograph shows boys pumping water at the town pump. It was located on East Street at the intersection of Second Street. In the background is town hall.

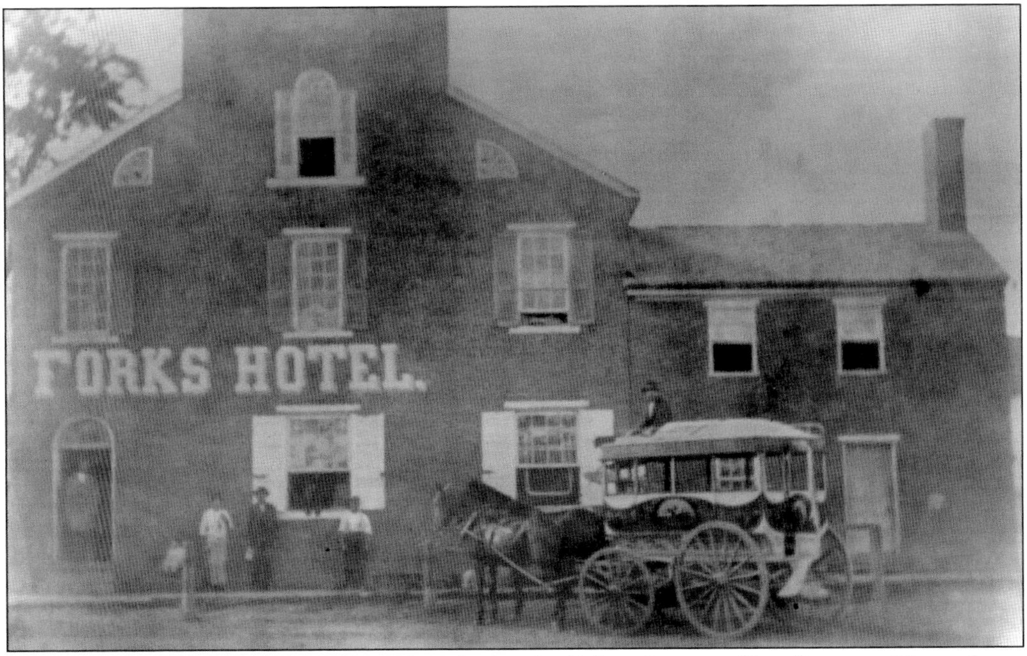


**FORKS HOTEL.** The Forks Hotel stood at the head of Main Street at East Street in Bloomsburg. It was built in 1825 by Daniel Snyder, and for many years, the old settlers resorted there to pass the evening in interchange of stories and reminiscences. The hotel was torn down in 1875 to allow the extension of Main Street up to Institute Hall.

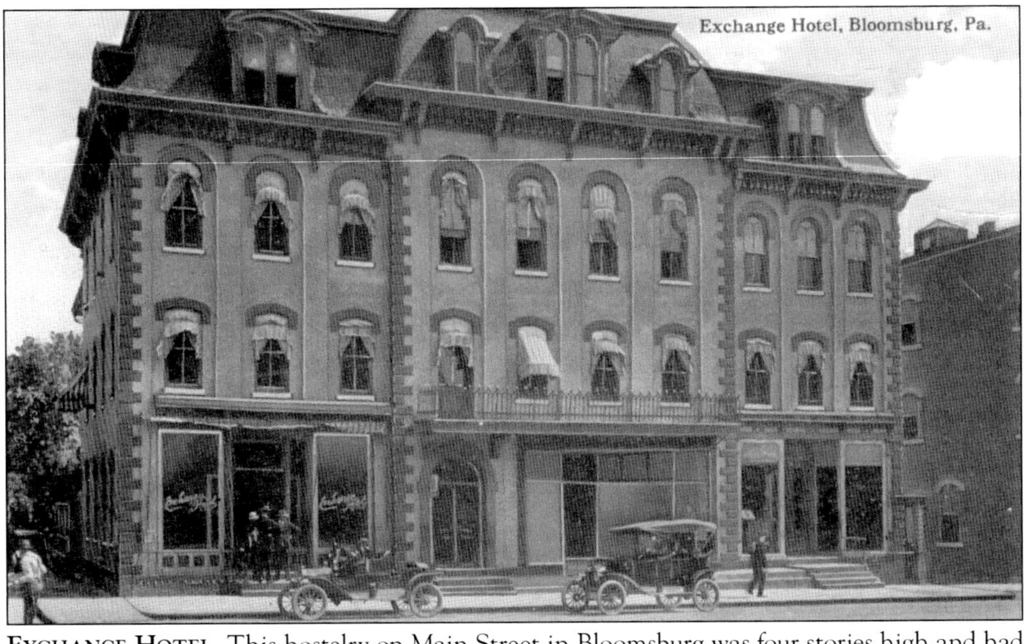


**EXCHANGE HOTEL.** This hostelry on Main Street in Bloomsburg was four stories high and had elegantly appointed offices, sitting rooms, and spacious sleeping rooms. It was known as the Commercial Men's Home. There were 100 nicely furnished sleeping rooms. The hotel's bar was stocked with the choicest brands of imported and domestic wines, liquors, ales, beers, and cigars. The dining room served all delicacies of the season, perfectly prepared.

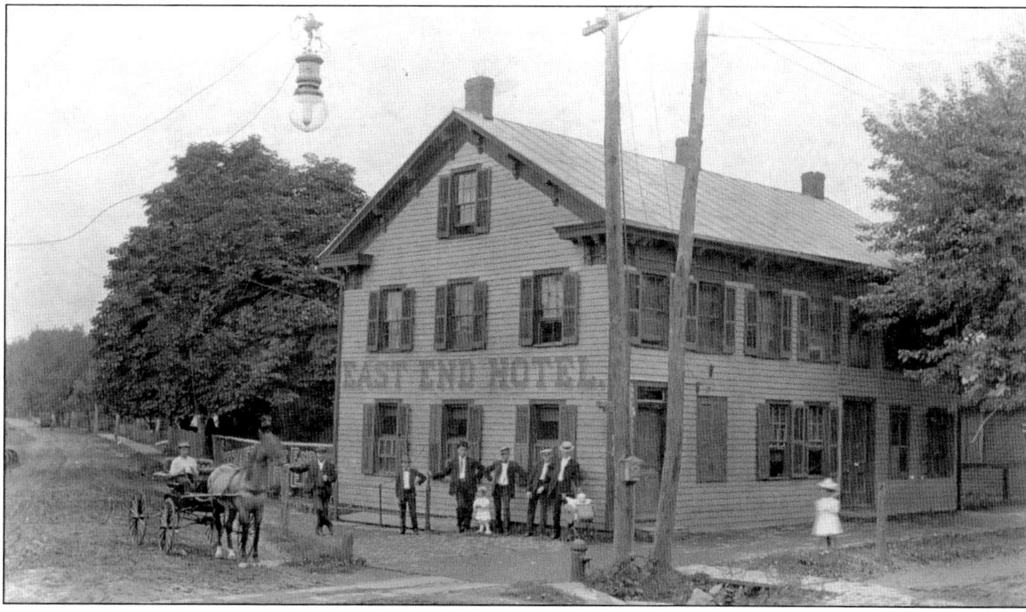


**EAST END HOTEL, C. 1905.** The lad in the buggy is Nevin Dieffenbach. Standing by the hitching post is proprietor Henry F. Dieffenbach. Also pictured from left to right are Daniel Mericle, Hope Furman and her daughter, Edward Strohm, and Louis Coira with one of his children in a carriage. The girl in white at far right is Ruth "Peg" Fry, who paused on her way to Sunday school to get in the picture.

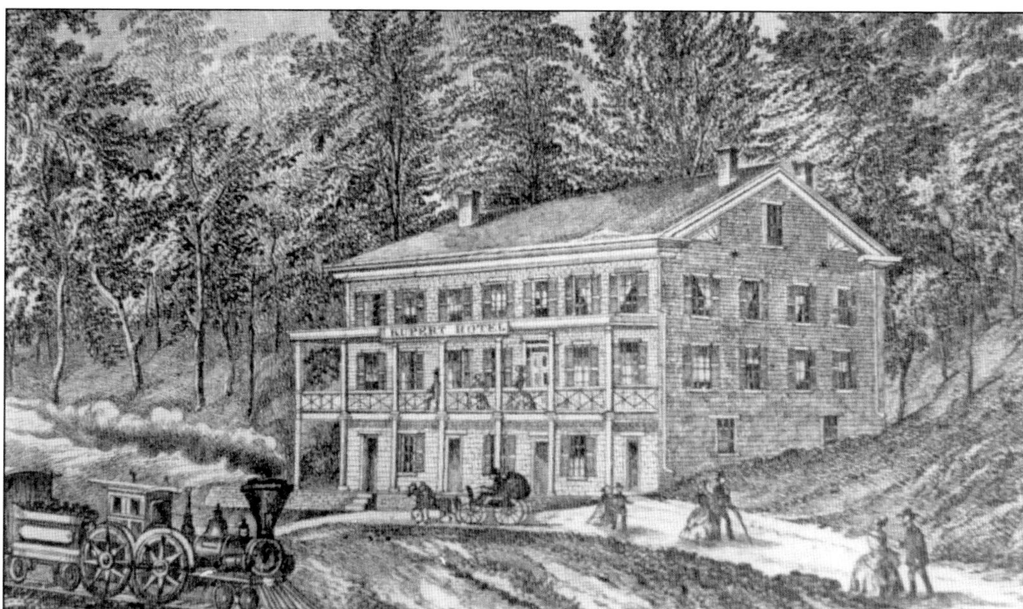


**RUPERT HOTEL.** Built in 1850, this hotel was a fine brick building situated beside the old Catawissa Rupert Road. At one point, it connected to the Rupert railroad depot. Patrons could relax on the verandas while enjoying the sight of the canal boats moving steadily along the North Branch Canal. The hotel went out of business in 1930, became a grocery store, and eventually was demolished.

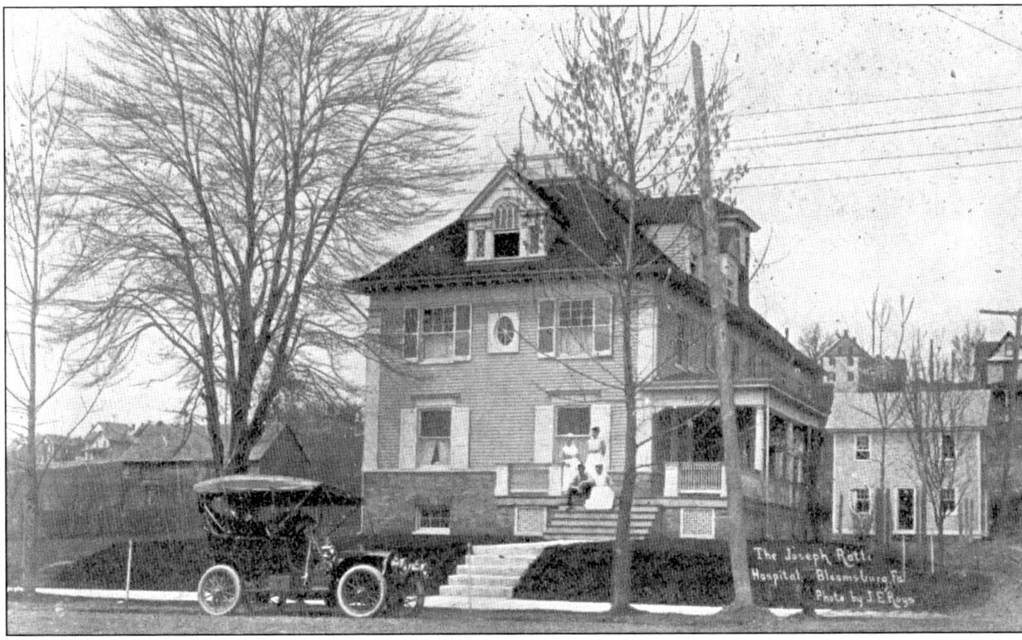


**RATTI HOSPITAL.** Italian immigrant Joseph Ratti, successful manager of the Bloomsburg Silk Mills, provided this building along Fifth Street for the first hospital in Bloomsburg. After his death in 1906, the building was donated to the community. (Courtesy of Sue Koch.)

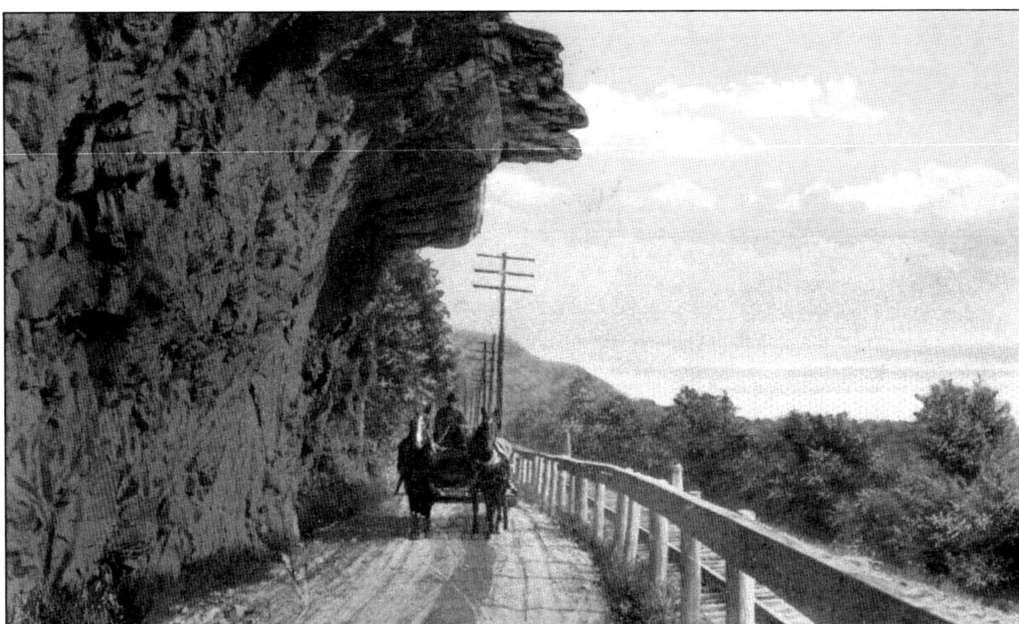

**PROFILE ROCK.** This well-known spot, also known as Indian Head, is a formation of two rock slabs at "the narrows" on the Catawissa-Rupert Road. From the south, the rocks bear a strong resemblance to a Native American profile. The formation was created about 1858 from blasting on the hillside to secure a roadbed for the railroad.

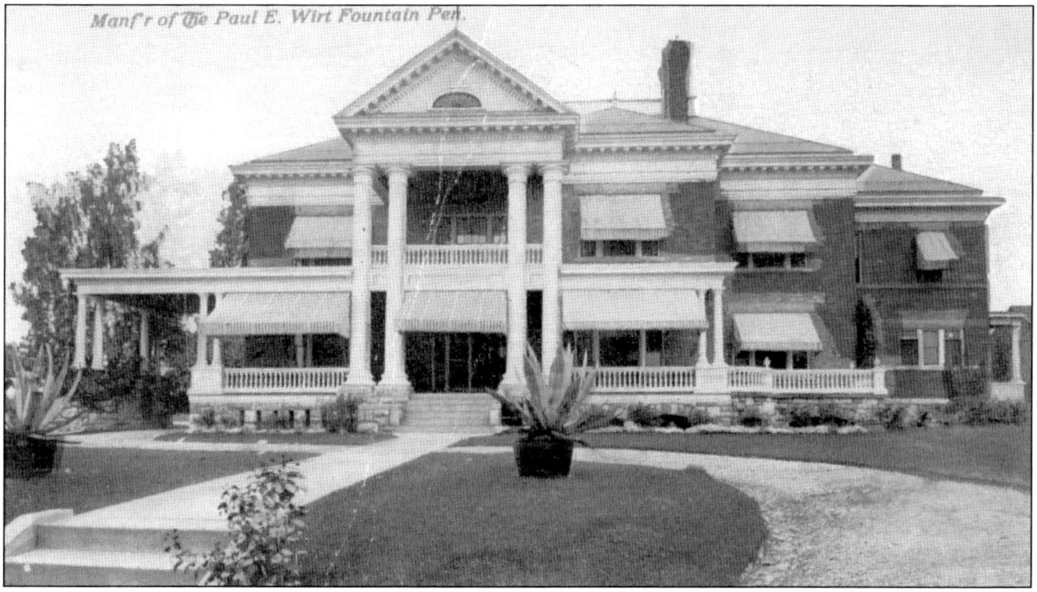


**WIRT HOUSE.** The residence of Paul E. Wirt on East First Street in Bloomsburg was built from the fortune created by the famous Wirt fountain pen in the late 1800s. These famous writing instruments became a necessity to Americans and were carried to the ends of the earth. The mansion has been incorporated into Bloomsburg Health Care Center.

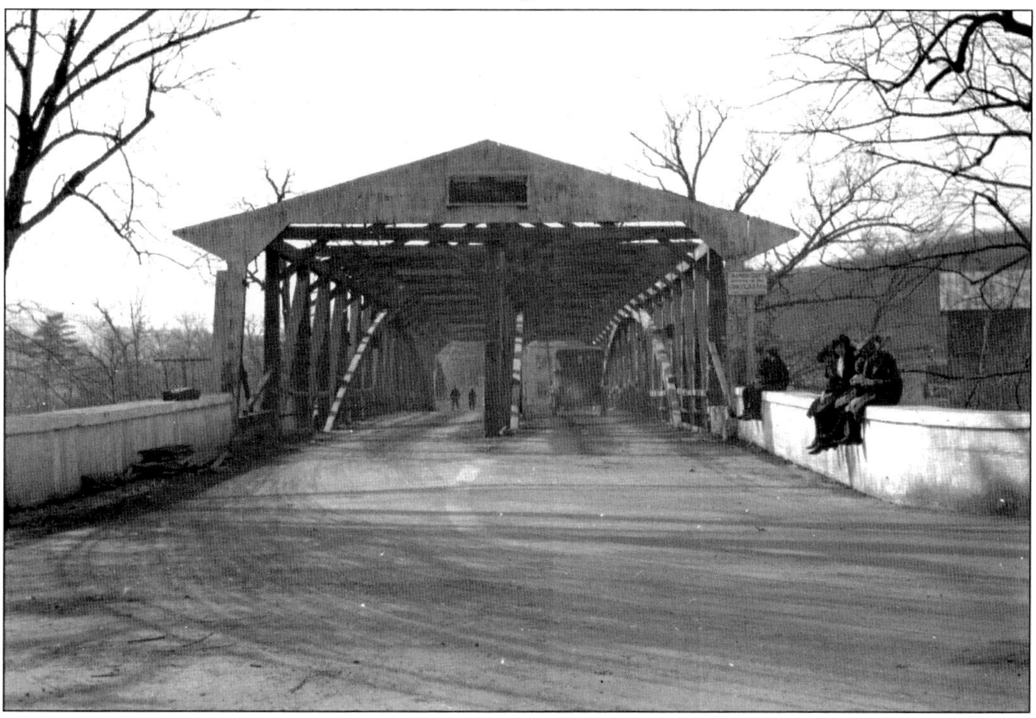

**DOUBLE TRACK BRIDGE.** This covered bridge crossing Fishing Creek at the west end of Bloomsburg was built in 1840. It was called the Double Track Bridge because two wagons could pass each other with a wall separating the lanes. Torn down in 1921 after extensive natural deterioration, it was replaced by a concrete bridge.

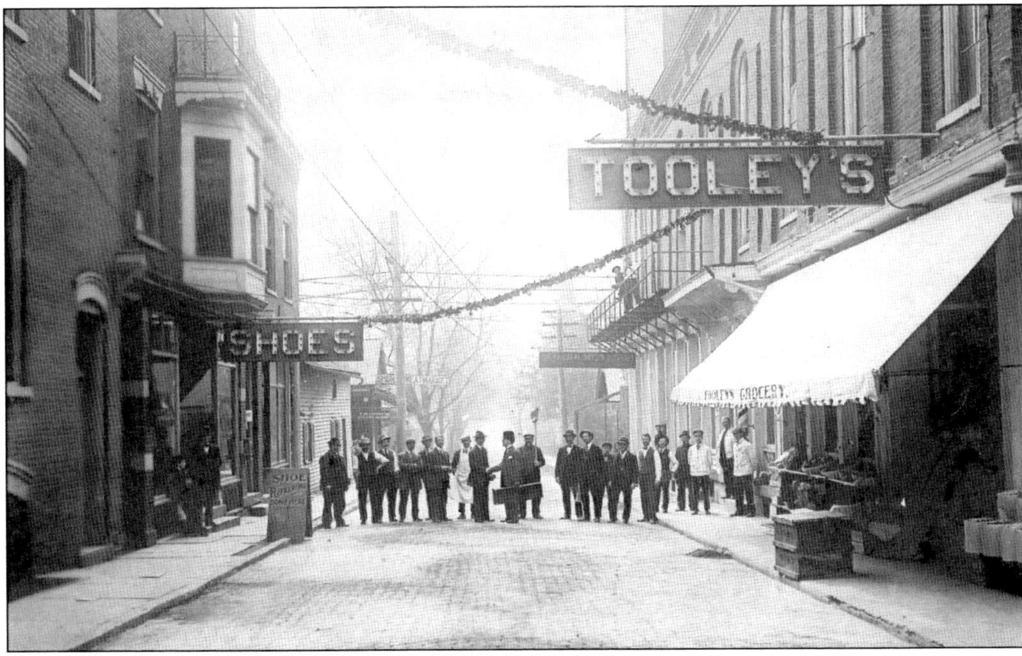


**CENTRE STREET IN BLOOMSBURG, C. 1910.** Looking south from Main Street, the above photograph shows Tooley's Grocery; Bloomsburg Opera House; Shuman's Meat Market; the public library; the Columbia Steam Laundry sign; W. D. Holmes and Son Heating, Plumbing, and Sheet Metal; and a shoe shop. W. A. Watters was proprietor of the steam laundry. The photograph below, dated December 11, 1896, lists the firm's staff on the back: "Steam Laundry Hands: Mrs. Reily, Clara Cole, Dorothy Watters, Will Eastman, W. A. Watters, Heacock ?, signed, W. A. Watters, Bloomsburg Pa."

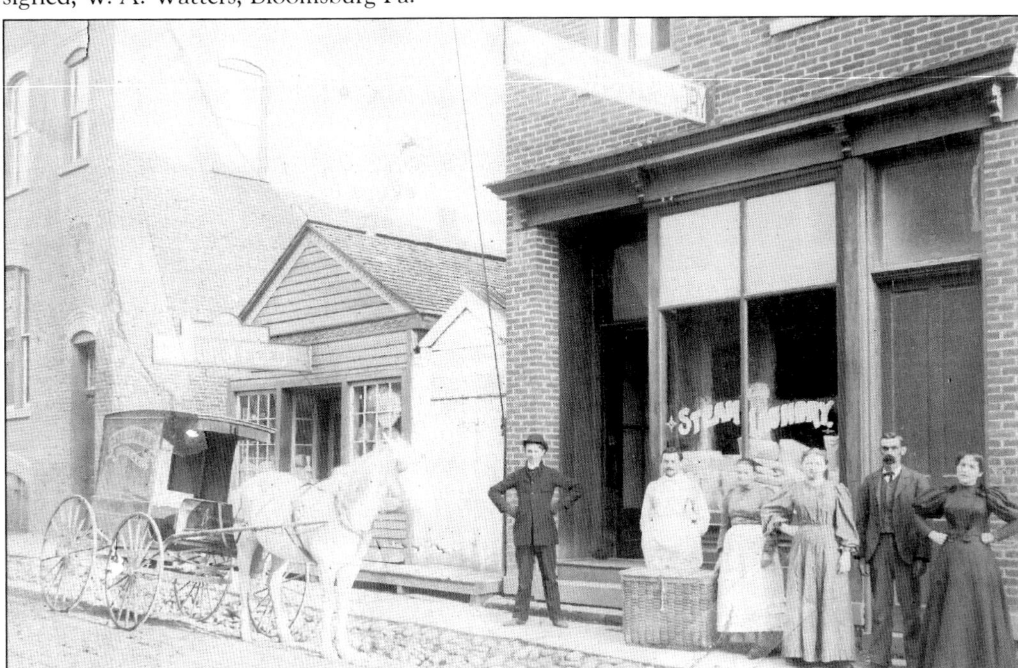

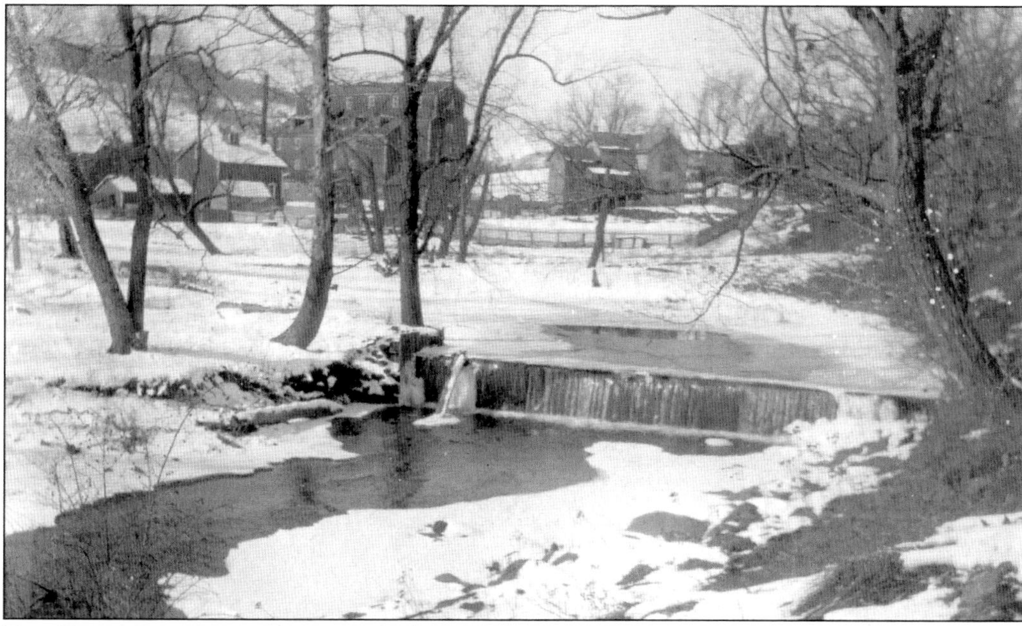

**The Red Mill.** Located in Hemlock Township near Fishing Creek, the Red Mill was built originally by Elisha Barton in 1783. Under six successive owners, the new machinery, electric power, and single-phase motors enabled continuous milling, producing 35 barrels of flour per day. In 1977, the building became a successful antique shop. (Courtesy of Bloomsburg University Archives.)

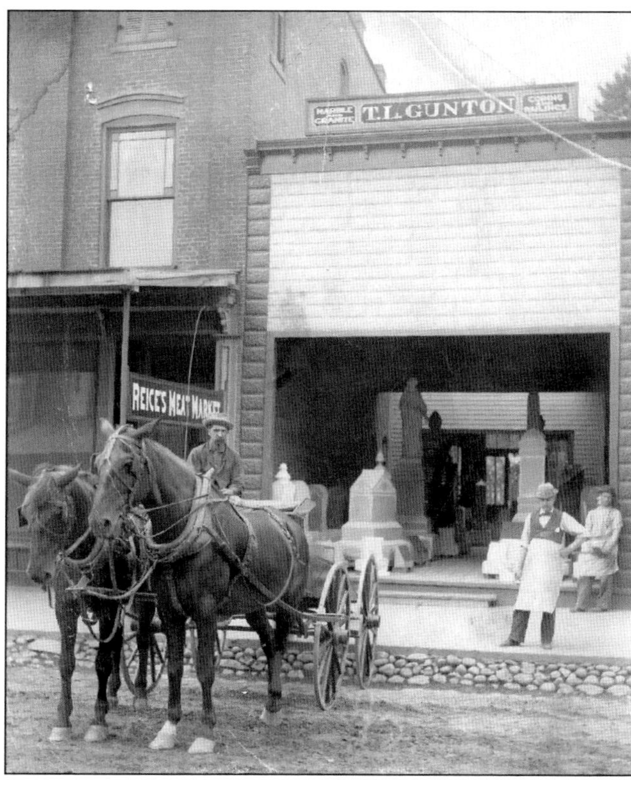


**T. L. Gunton Monument Works.** This *c.* 1900 photograph shows West Main Street in Bloomsburg approximately on the site of the later Morning Press building. Thomas L. Gunton produced monuments and statuary in the latest designs of marble and granite. Also shown is T. L. Reice's meat market.

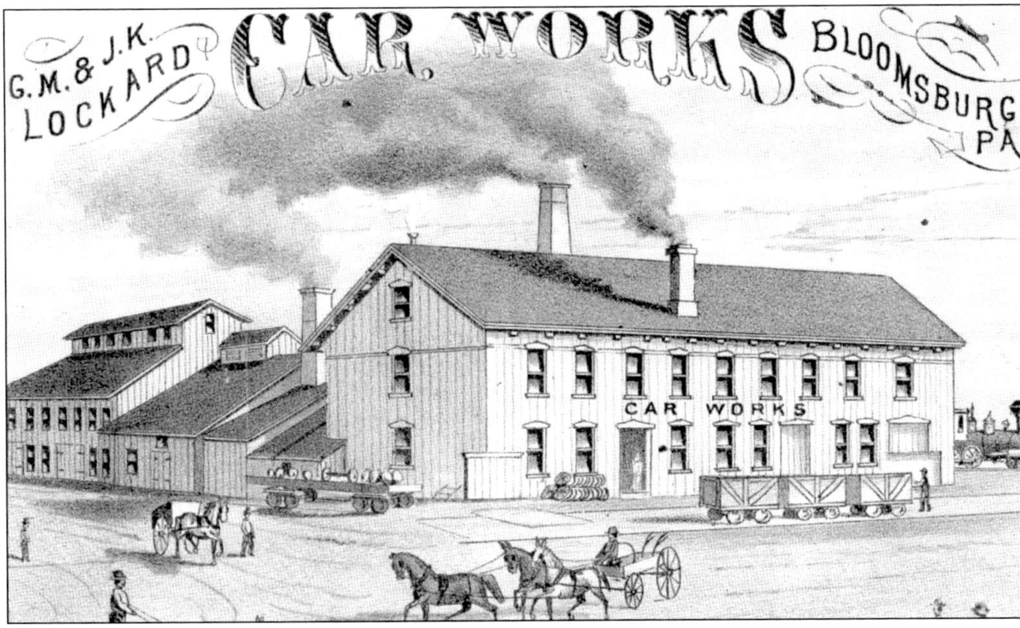


**Bloomsburg Car Manufacturing Company.** Founded in 1863, this manufacturing firm on East Street expanded and changed ownership repeatedly. Production of mine cars began in 1871. After rebuilding from an 1879 fire, the company produced 4,000 twenty-ton railroad cars within the next four years. Production of freight, mine, and rotary dump cars and wheels continued until August 26, 1930, when a devastating fire destroyed the plant.

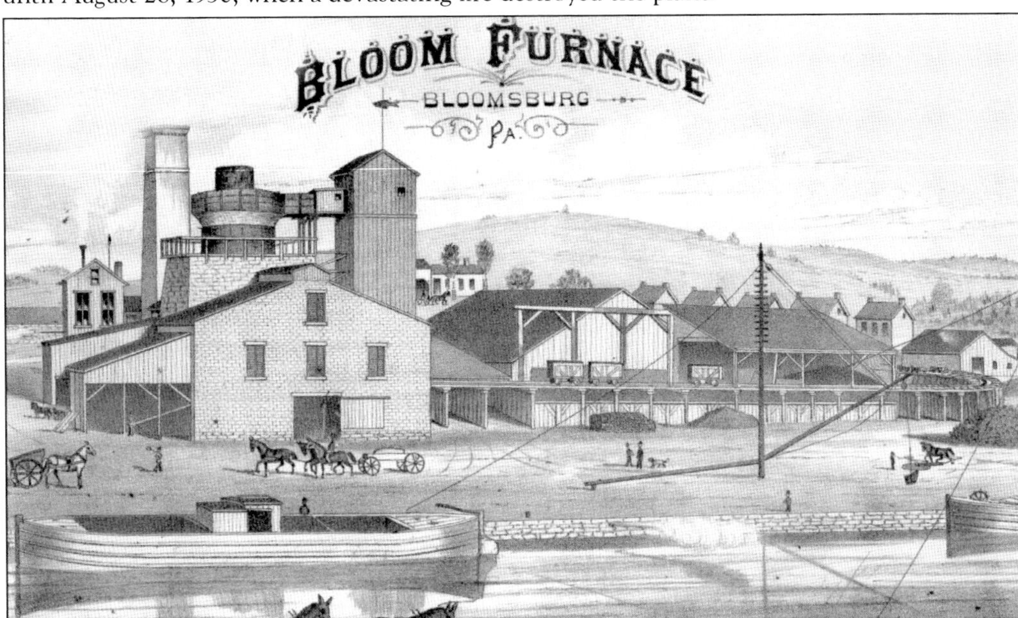


**Bloom Furnace.** Iron furnaces and foundries were the main industries in Bloomsburg during the latter half of the 19th century. At the peak, there were two furnaces and at least five foundries in Bloomsburg. One of these was the Bloom Furnace owned by William Neal and Sons, located alongside the North Branch Canal. In 1856, this furnace processed 5,669 tons of ore into pig iron.

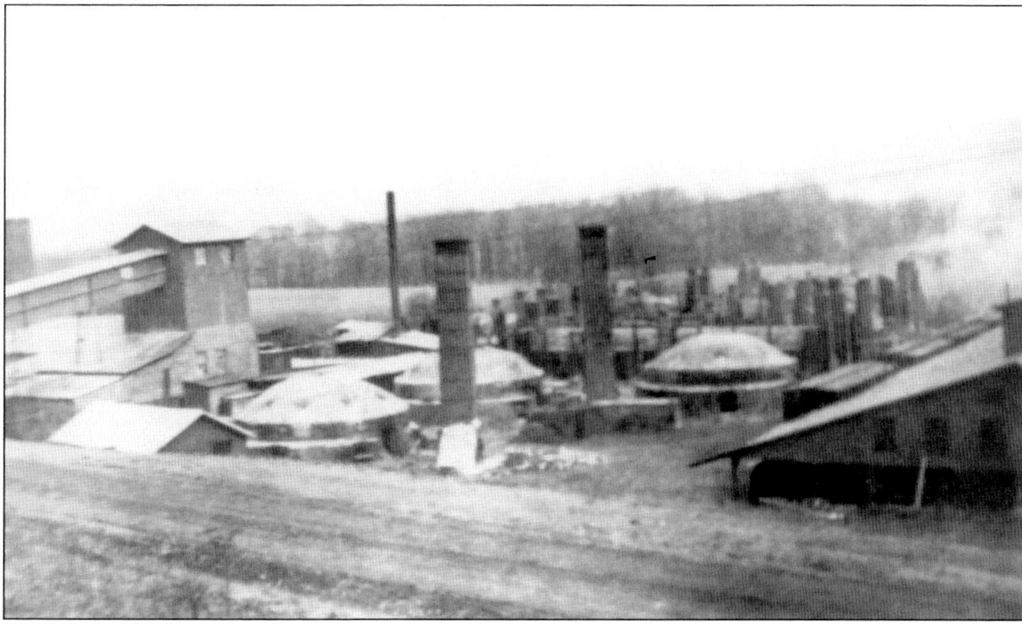

**BLOOMSBURG BRICK COMPANY.** Chartered on April 12, 1910, the Bloomsburg Brick Company was located on East Fifth Street near the boundary of Bloomsburg and Scott Township, later the site of the Dillon greenhouses. It could produce six million bricks per year. A minor fire in 1914 caused limited damage, but a second fire on November 16, 1923, caused extensive damage, and the business closed.

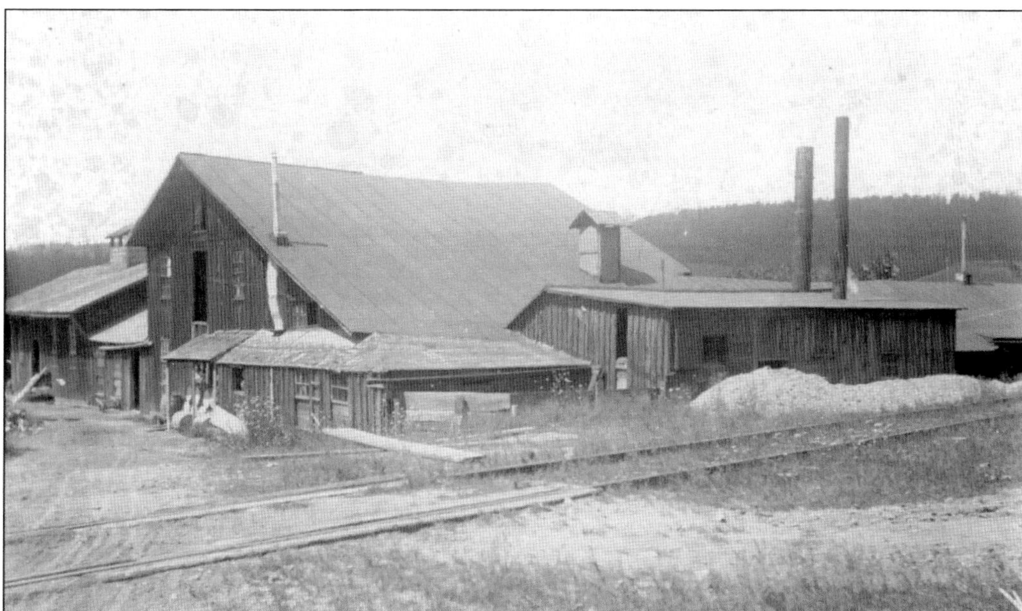

**BLOOMSBURG PAPER MILL.** This photograph, dated 1910, shows one of five buildings of the paper mill that was located not in Bloomsburg but was a mile west of Lightstreet along Fishing Creek. At one time, the plant had the capacity to produce three tons of paper daily. Two sets of tracks connected the plant to two railroads, the Bloomsburg and Sullivan and the Susquehanna, Bloomsburg and Berwick.

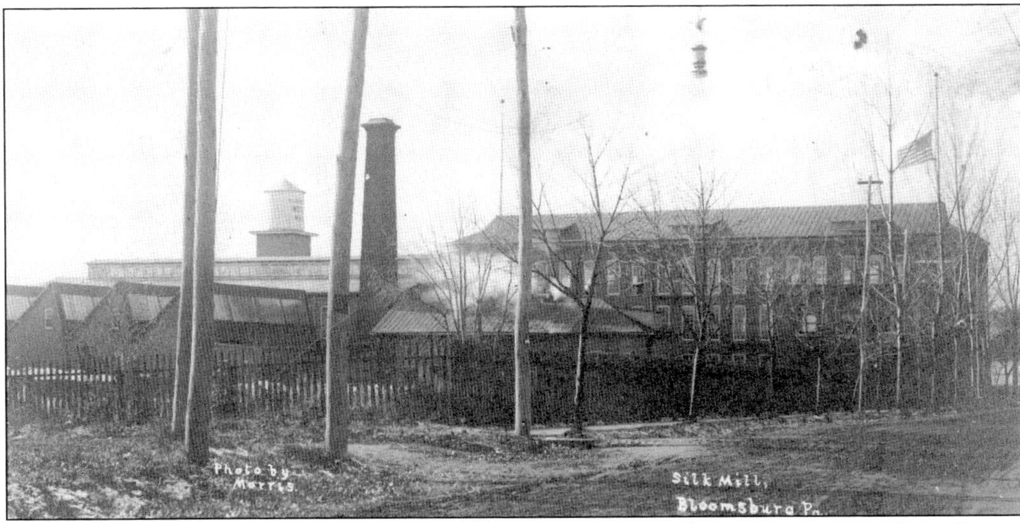


**BLOOMSBURG SILK MILL.** In 1888, the Bloomsburg Board of Trade began searching for industries to replace the dying iron industry. In 1890, experienced manager Joseph Ratti was brought in, and by 1897, the mill employed 280 workers. The production of woven silk for umbrellas and silk ties ended in 1933, and the firm, renamed Bloomsburg Mills, began producing synthetic fabrics. The firm closed in 2009 after 120 years of manufacturing.

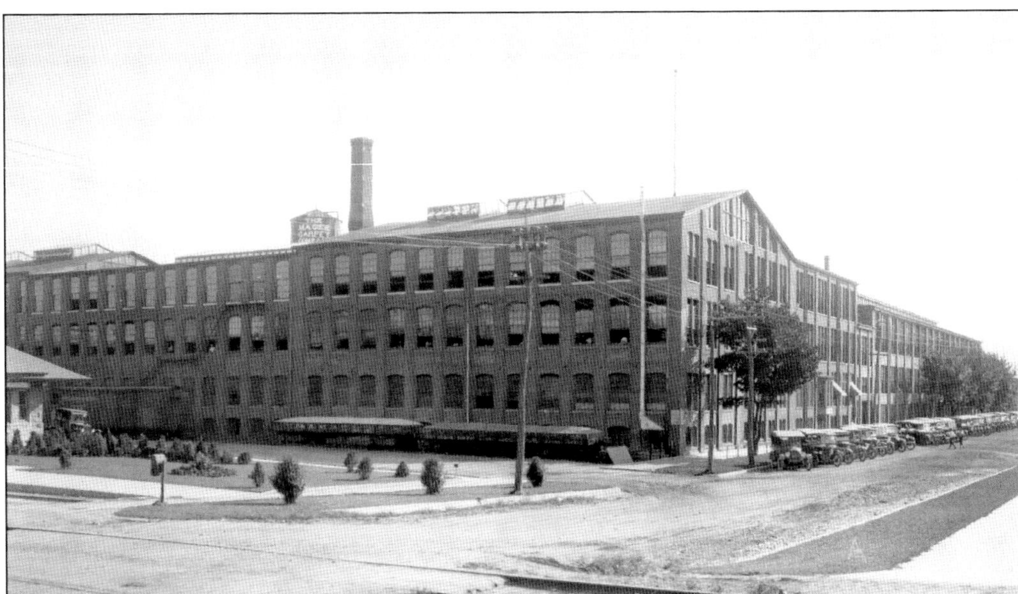

**MAGEE CARPET COMPANY.** Enticed by the Bloomsburg Board of Trade, James Magee II relocated his carpet manufacturing business from Philadelphia to Bloomsburg in 1890. Over the years, Magee has been a major manufacturer of residential, commercial, and automotive carpet, employing more than 2,000 workers at its peak. After a 1997 merger with a Swiss company, the firm is known today as Rieter Automotive Systems and ships automotive carpet worldwide.

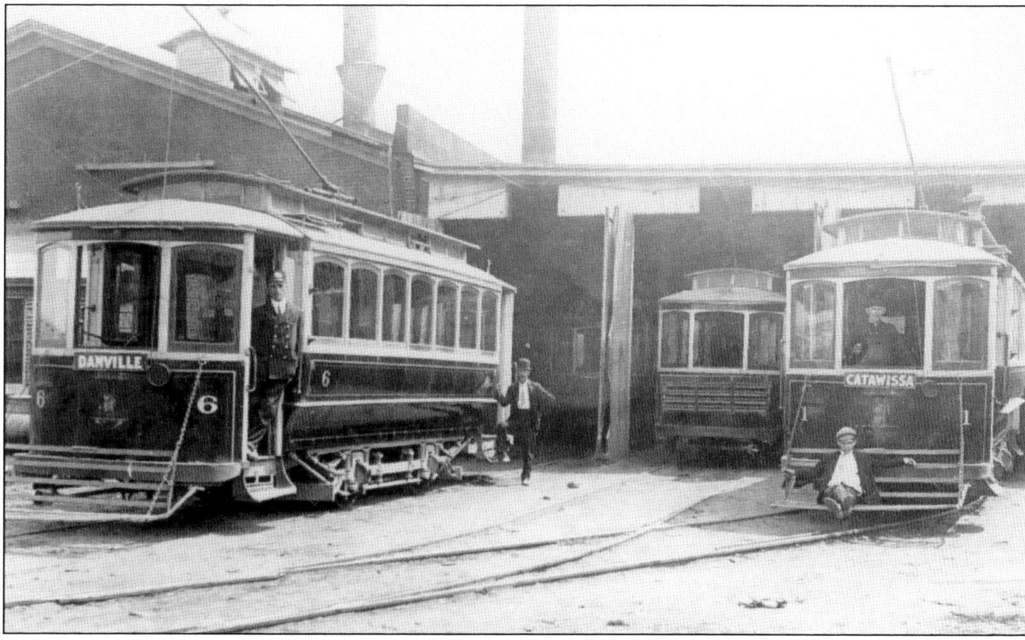


**TROLLEY SYSTEM.** The Columbia and Montour Electric Railway Company served Berwick, Bloomsburg, Catawissa, Danville, and the villages between those towns. The firm built a carbarn (above) in Bloomsburg in 1901 on the site of the former McKelvy and Neal iron furnace; it featured the powerhouse on the left and carbarn at right. In 1910, the trolley firm began buying electricity from outside sources, and by 1915, the entire building had been converted into a repair facility. West of Bloomsburg (below), trolley workers pose around a snow sweeper near Grovania, possibly after the storm of March 1, 1914. Snow clearing was the most physically demanding job one could have while working for the trolley company. Some years, 50 to 75 men were needed to clear 5-to-10-foot drifts that went on for miles. (Courtesy of Bloomsburg University Archives.)

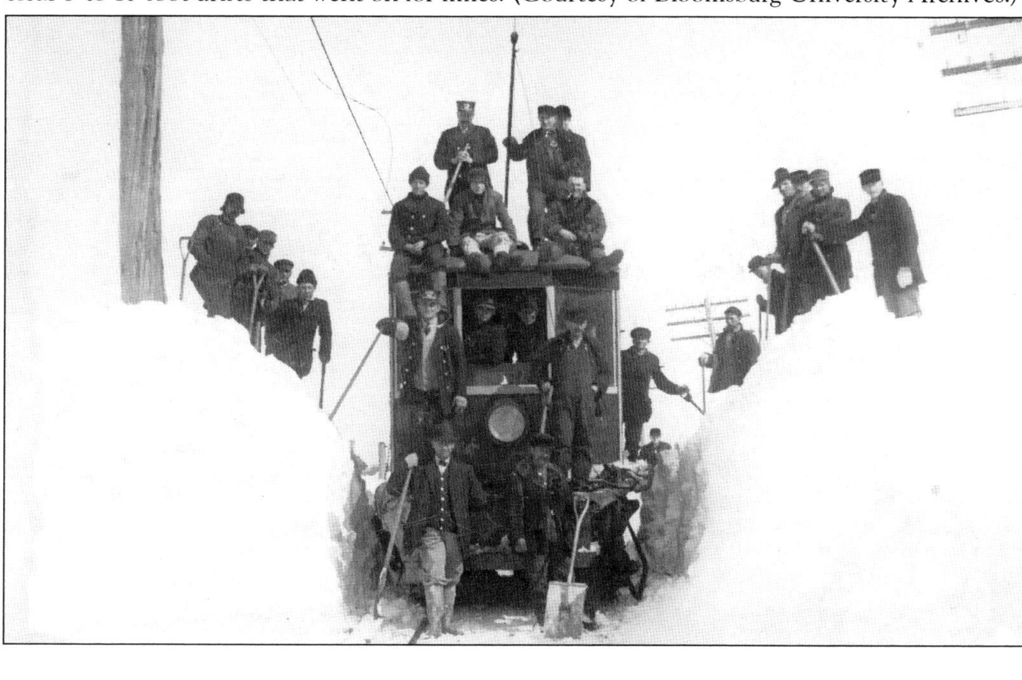

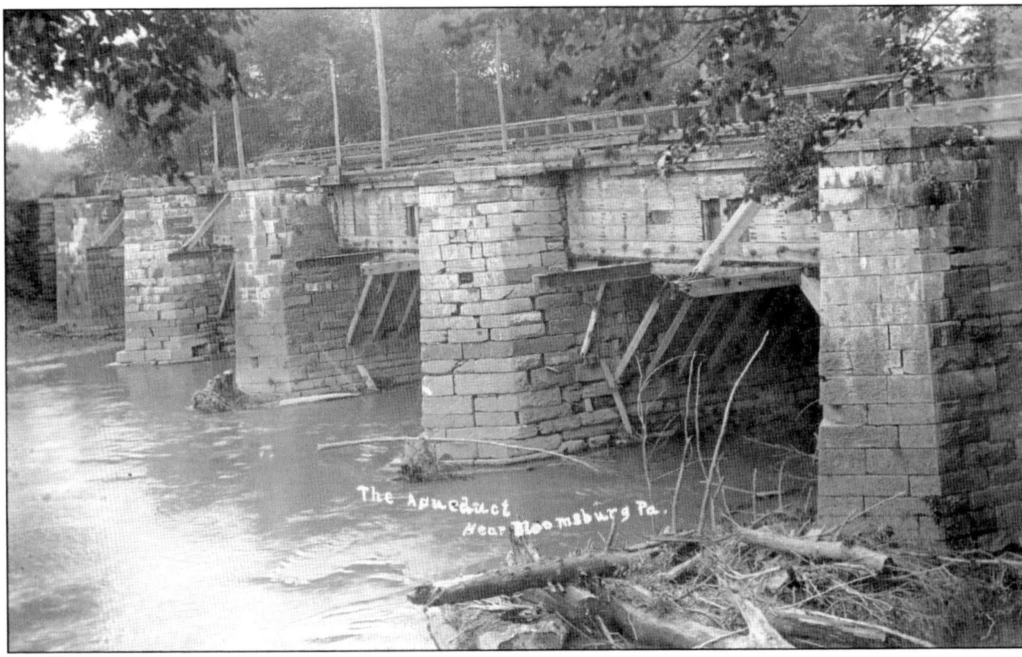


**AQUEDUCT BRIDGE AT RUPERT.** The Aqueduct Bridge of 1830 at Rupert was built to carry the North Branch Canal across Fishing Creek. The small doors were used to drain excess water. Later the canal was drained, and trolley cars ran along the bridge floor and continued to use this aqueduct until it was replaced by a steel bridge in early 1917. (Courtesy of Donald Brewer.)

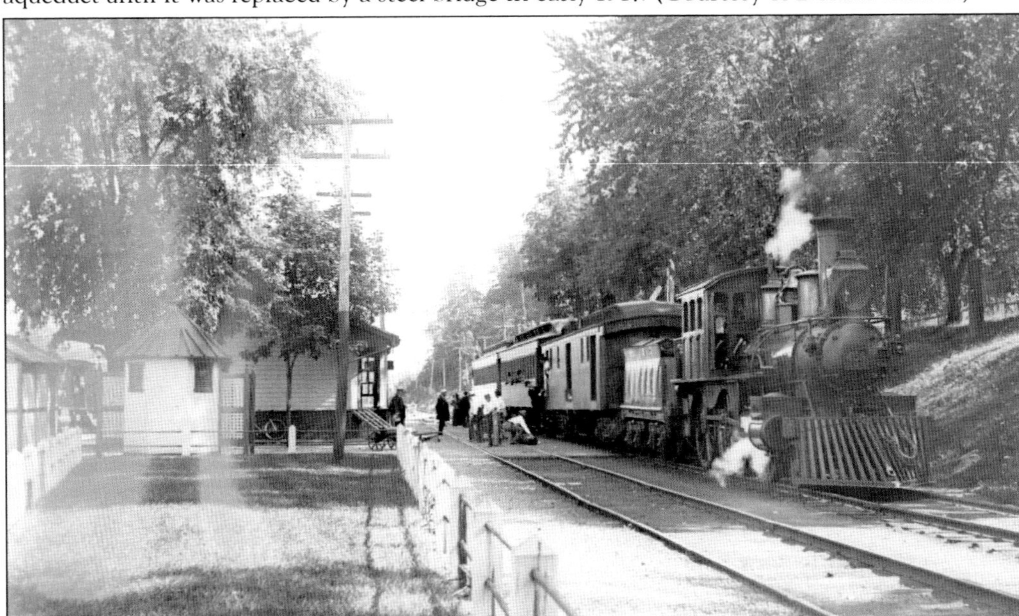

**RUPERT TRAIN STATION.** In the mid-1850s, Rupert became important as having the region's only railroad depot on the north side of the Susquehanna River. Until 1889, Rupert was the nearest point from Bloomsburg to reach the Philadelphia and Reading Railroad. A horse-drawn omnibus met all passenger trains, and travelers had a memorable dusty ride to town in the rumbling coach.

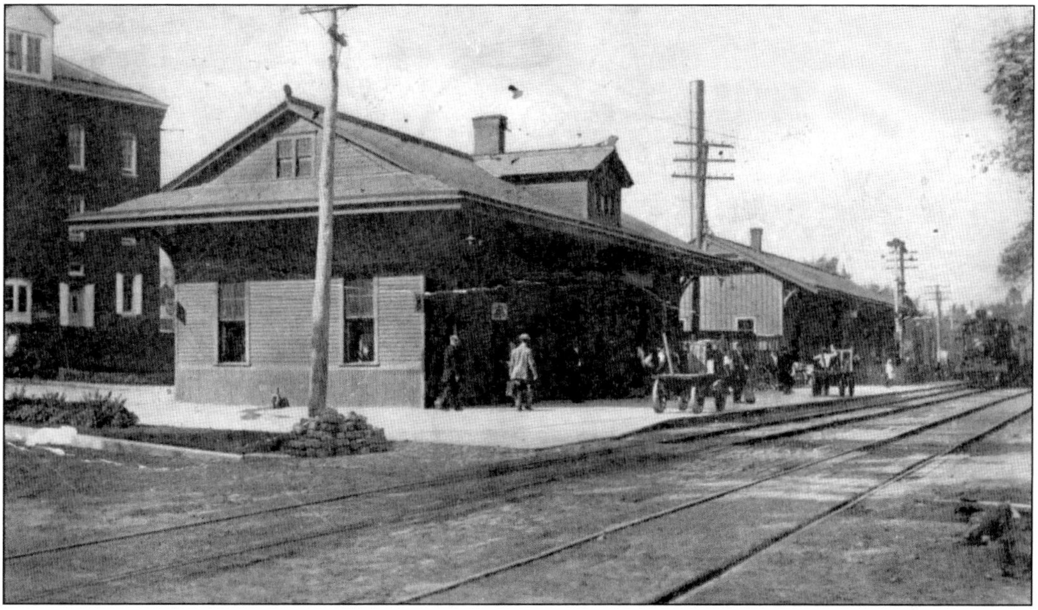

**DELAWARE, LACKAWANNA AND WESTERN RAILROAD STATION.** In the late 19th century, Bloomsburg was served by five railroads. A branch line of the Delaware, Lackawanna and Western Railroad connected riverside communities from Scranton to Northumberland; its station at Market and Seventh Streets is shown here.

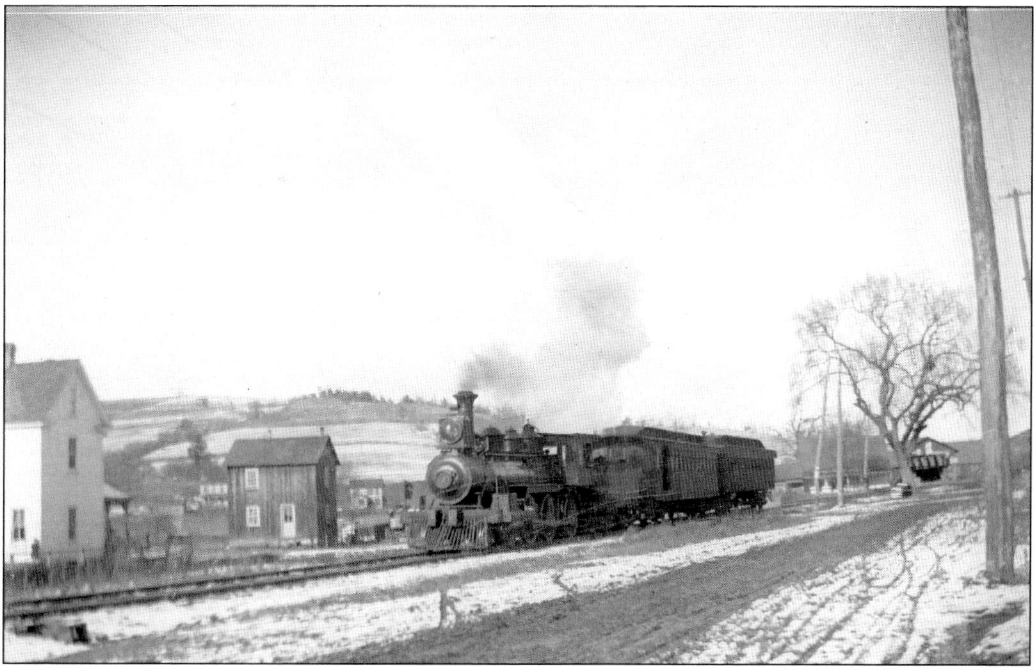

**BLOOMSBURG AND SULLIVAN RAILROAD.** The Bloomsburg and Sullivan Railroad, completed in 1888, ran north from Bloomsburg through Fishing Creek valley for 29 miles, with stops at Lightstreet, Orangeville, Forks, Stillwater, and Benton before reaching the village of Jamison City on the edge of Sullivan County. In this photograph, a passenger train arrives in Bloomsburg along Railroad Street, approaching the station at Fifth Street.

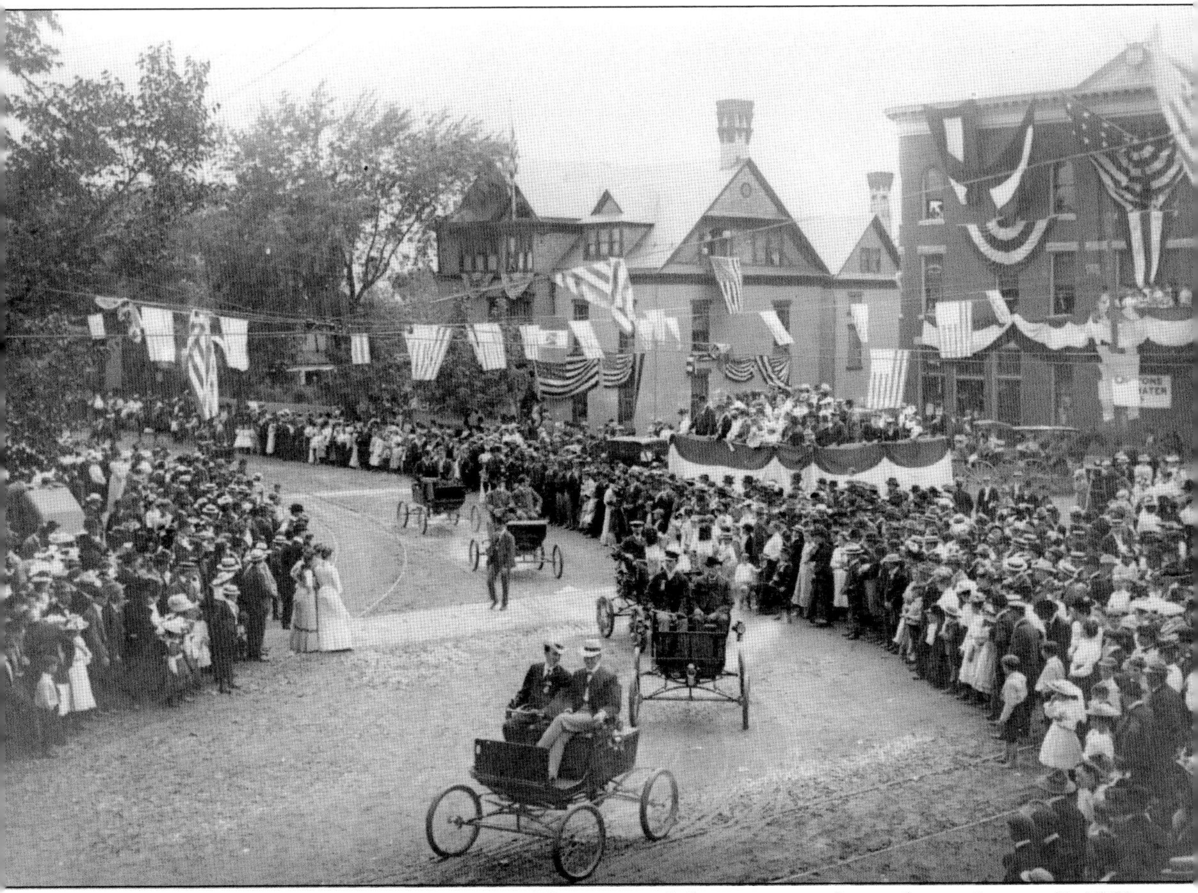

**Bloomsburg Centennial Parade.** This view of the centennial parade on August 8, 1902, shows horseless carriages turning onto Main Street at Market Square. The five steam-powered automobiles are driven by Carl Wirt (first car), J. E. Roys (second), Dr. H. Bierman (third), Charles Funston (fourth), and Mr. Schmeck (fifth). In the center of the photograph is the John L. Moyer residence, which was torn down around 1931 for the construction of a new post office.

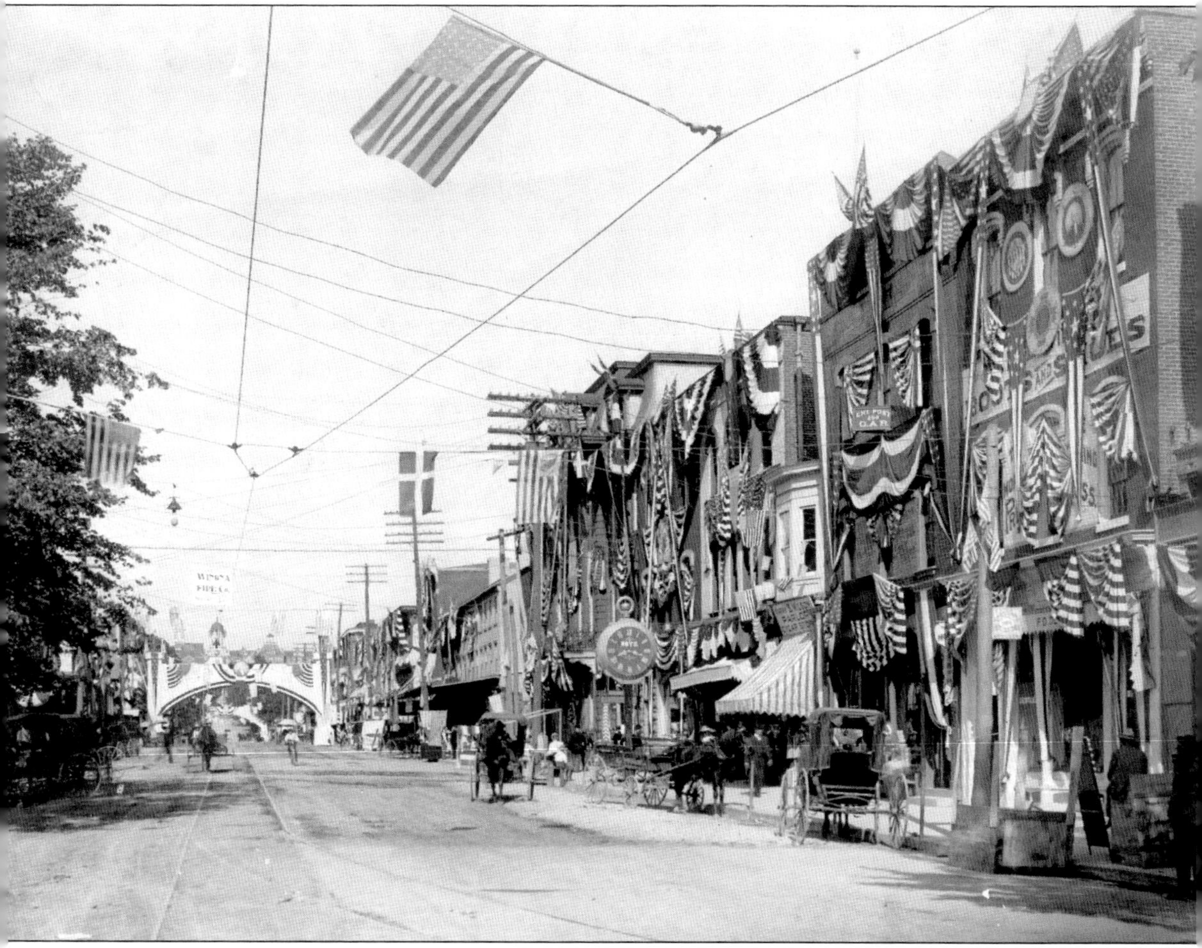

**BLOOMSBURG CENTENNIAL CELEBRATION.** Bloomsburg was founded in 1802 by two brothers from Northampton County, Ludwig and John Adam Eyer. Their village grew slowly, but by 1902, the town included a dozen varied industries that provided steady employment. The centennial festivities included a lengthy ceremony at Market Square, with speeches, musical performances, and drill demonstrations watched by a large, appreciative crowd.

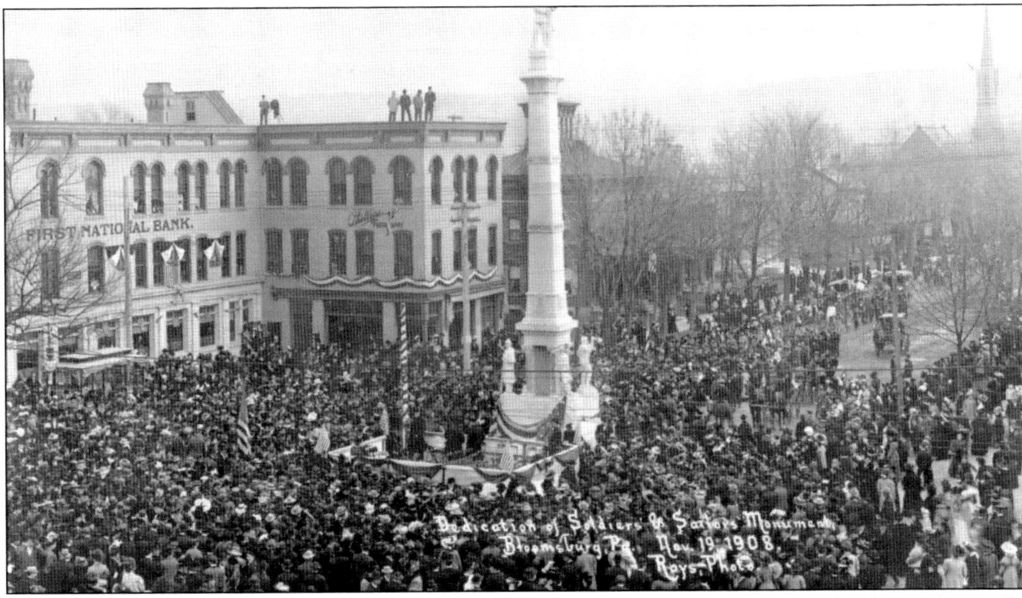


**DEDICATION OF CIVIL WAR MONUMENT.** On November 19, 1908, people throughout the county came to Bloomsburg to participate in a patriotic celebration to dedicate the Soldiers' and Sailors' Monument and commemorate the county's contribution to the Union cause in the Civil War. On this festive occasion, which coincided with the 45th anniversary of Pres. Abraham Lincoln's Gettysburg Address, all the town industries closed at noon and students were dismissed from school.

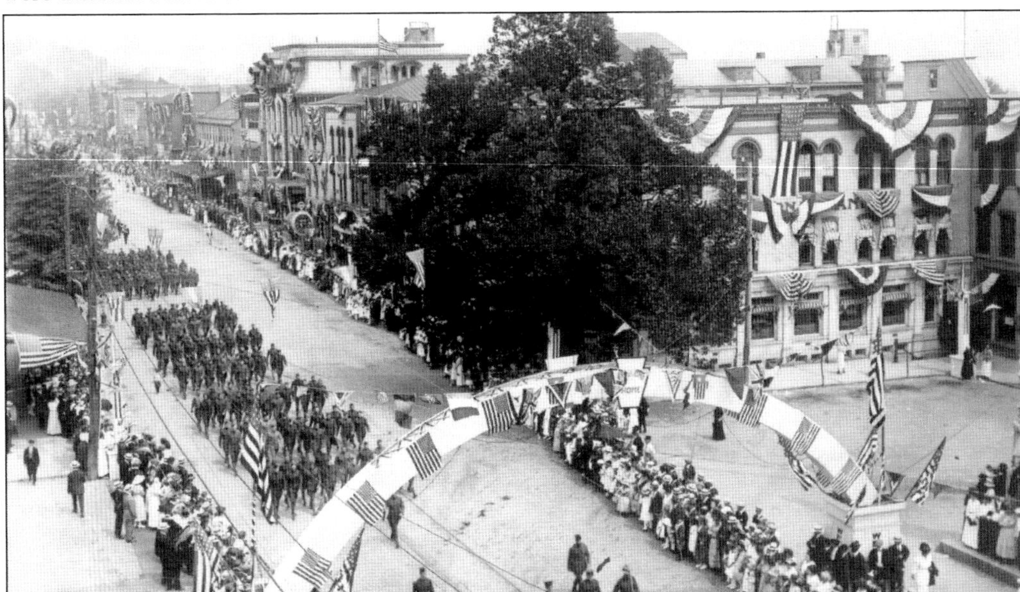

**WELCOME HOME PARADE.** Thousands flocked to Bloomsburg for a two-day celebration on August 8 and 9, 1919, to honor those who served in World War I. Activities included band concerts, baseball games, wrestling, boxing, bike races, horse races, fireworks, and more. A parade included 750 servicemen and nurses, floats, bands, Red Cross volunteers, and 70 Civil War veterans. The newspaper claimed, "It was a sight such as Bloomsburg has never seen."

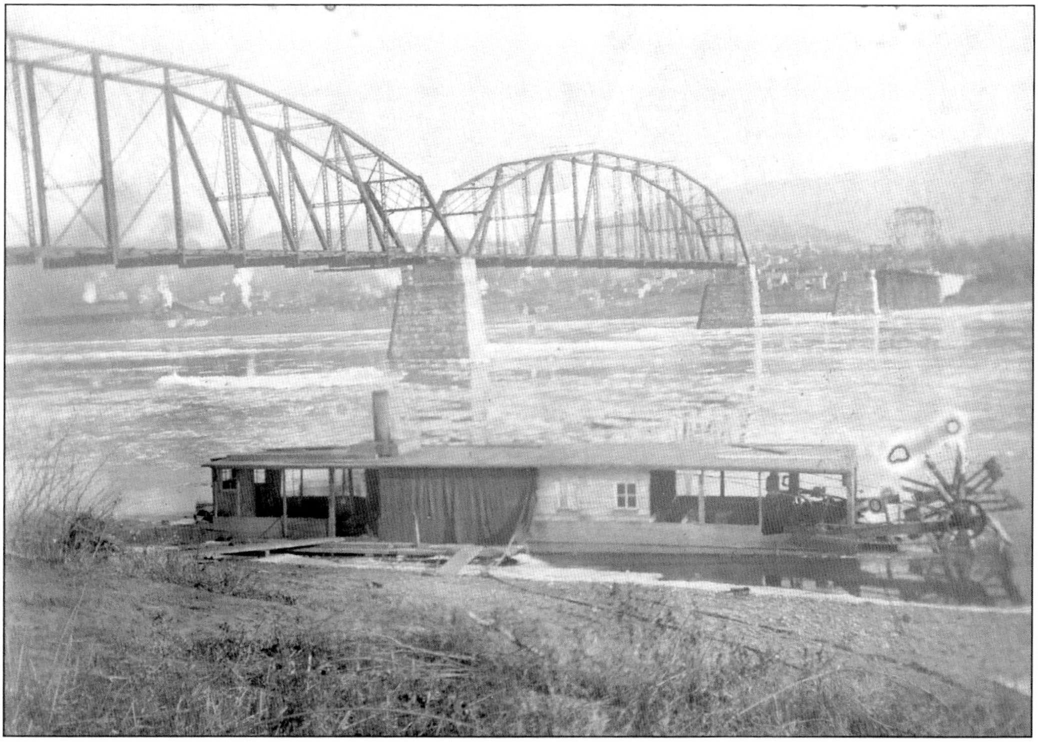

**FLOOD OF 1904.** The March 1904 flood of the Susquehanna River is the highest on record, with the floodwaters reaching 32.7 feet. In 1972, Hurricane Agnes's floodwaters reached a height of 31.2 feet. In 1904, when sections of the East Bloomsburg Bridge were swept away, a ferryboat named the *Mary Ann* was brought in to provide passage across the river until the bridge could be rebuilt. The flood inundated large areas of Bloomsburg, including Ninth Street, shown below. The entire length of Ninth Street to Market Street was underwater. Boats were used to rescue those who remained in their homes.

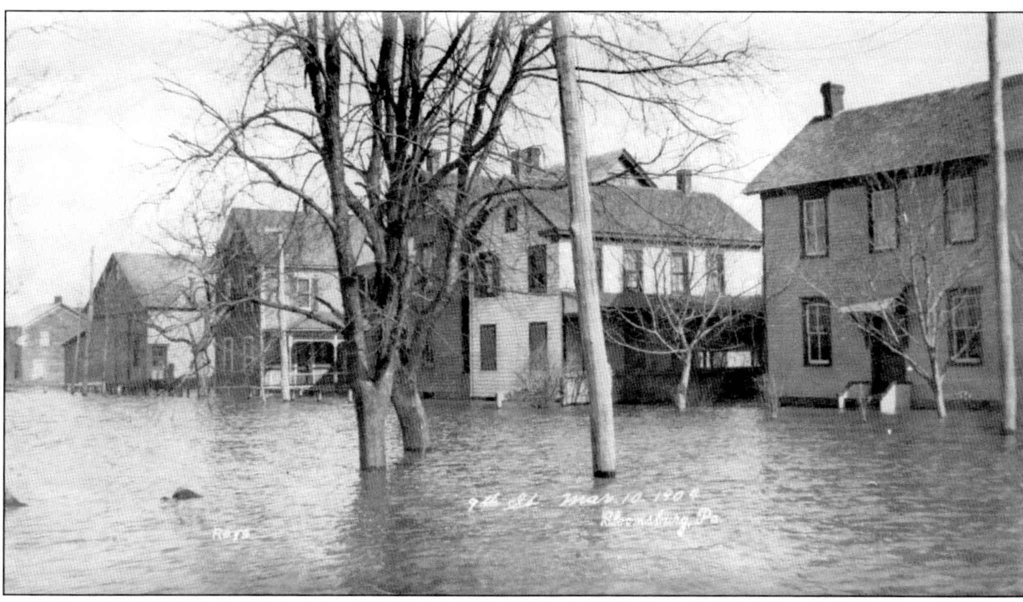

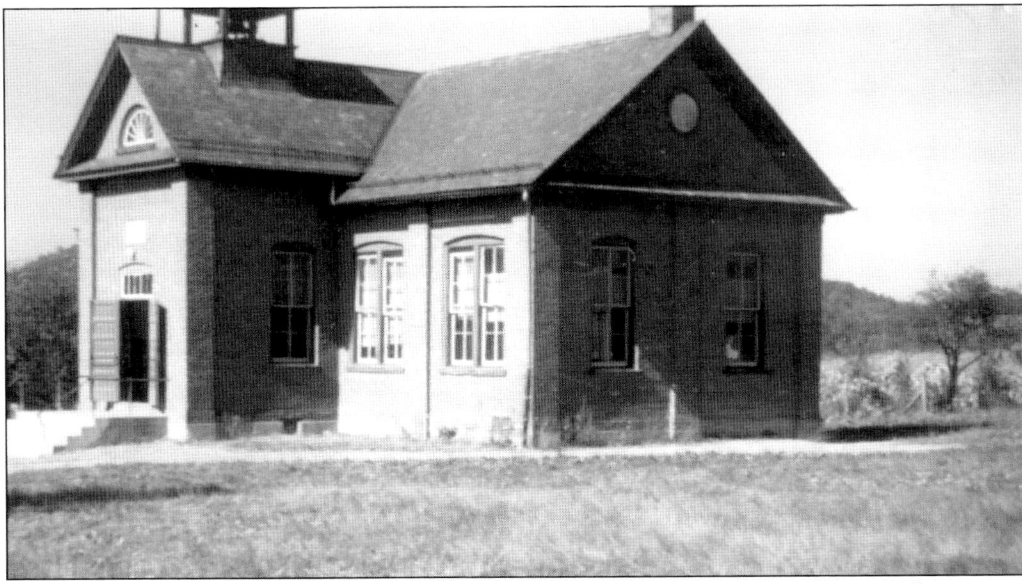

**BUCKHORN SCHOOL.** This village school was built in 1875 and 1876 at a cost of $3,000 and furnished for $195. The school had two large rooms and held first through eighth grades. A round wood-burning stove heated the building. Three outhouses served as bathrooms: two for the girls and a "two seater" for the boys. The school closed in 1956 after 51 years of service.

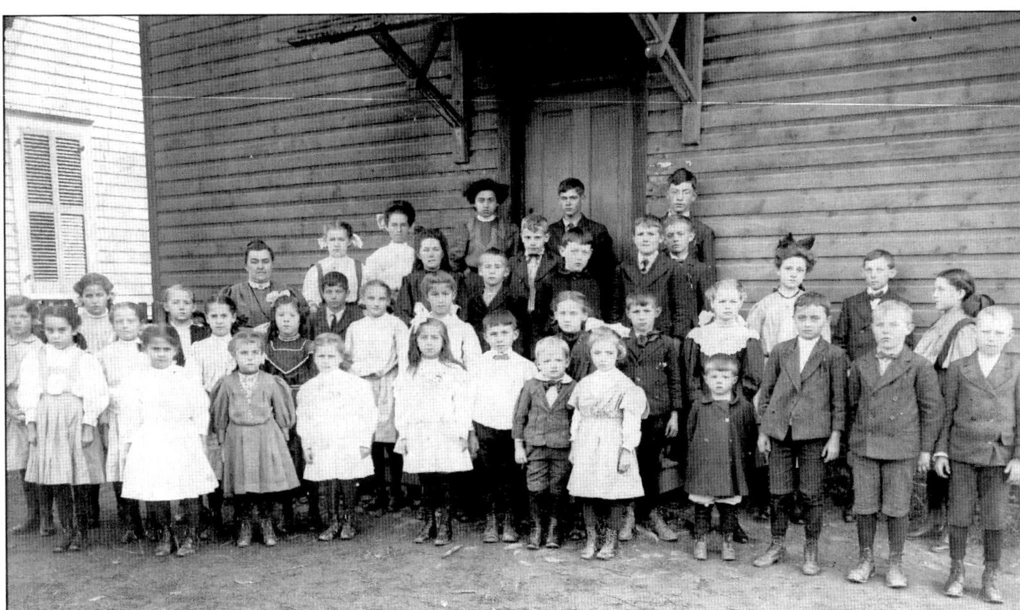

**FERNVILLE SCHOOL.** This 1908 photograph shows students attending Fernville School in Hemlock Township across Fishing Creek from Bloomsburg. Opened in 1893, the school included only the first four grades.

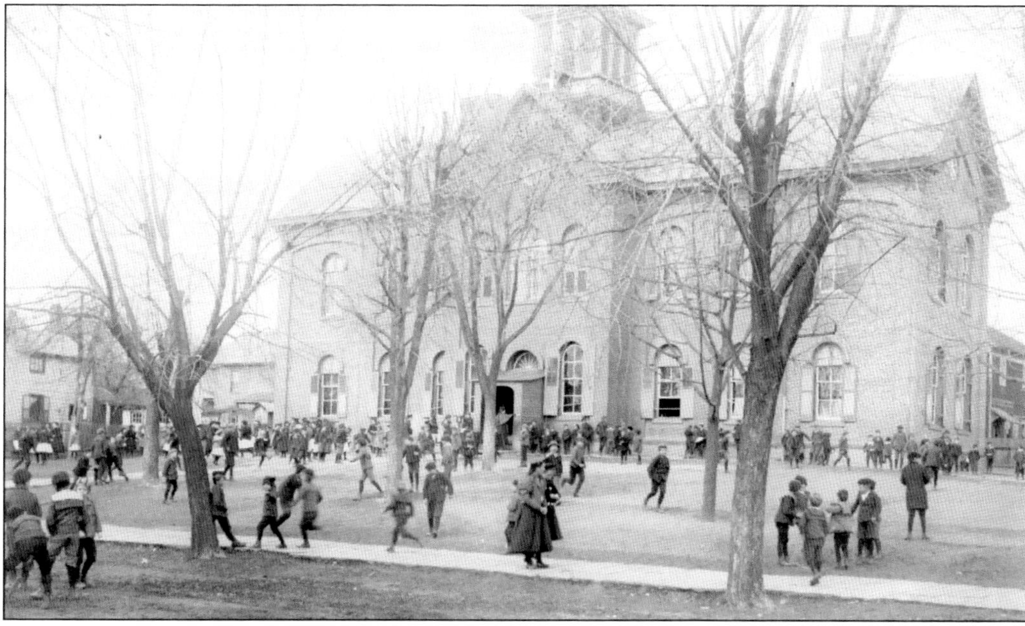

**FIFTH STREET SCHOOL IN BLOOMSBURG.** Erected in 1870, this two-story brick building with two wings could hold up to 1,000 children. A very modern school for its time, it housed a library, was heated with steam, and had the latest school furniture. It closed in 1953, served for two decades as a youth center, and then was torn down in the 1980s to make way for the Bloomsburg Child Development Center.

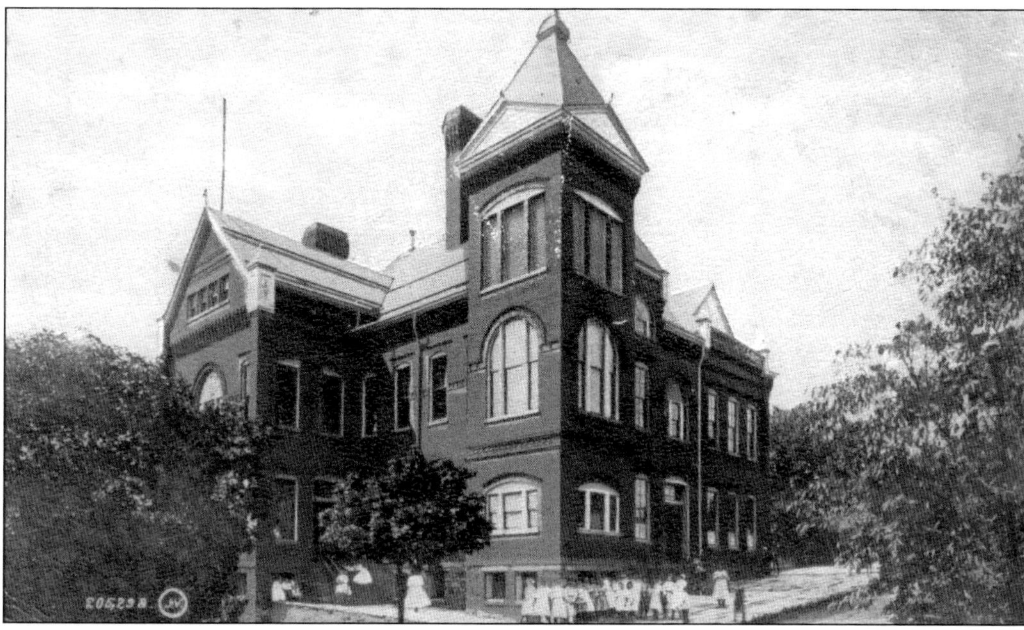

**BLOOMSBURG HIGH SCHOOL, C. 1920.** The first Bloomsburg High School at the corner of First and Center Streets was completed in 1889. Sixty-five students marched in procession from the old Third Street School to the new high school. Several ceremonies were held to mark the event. Fire destroyed the building on October 23, 1923, but it was rebuilt across the street on the site of the Lutheran and Reformed Cemetery, which was moved.

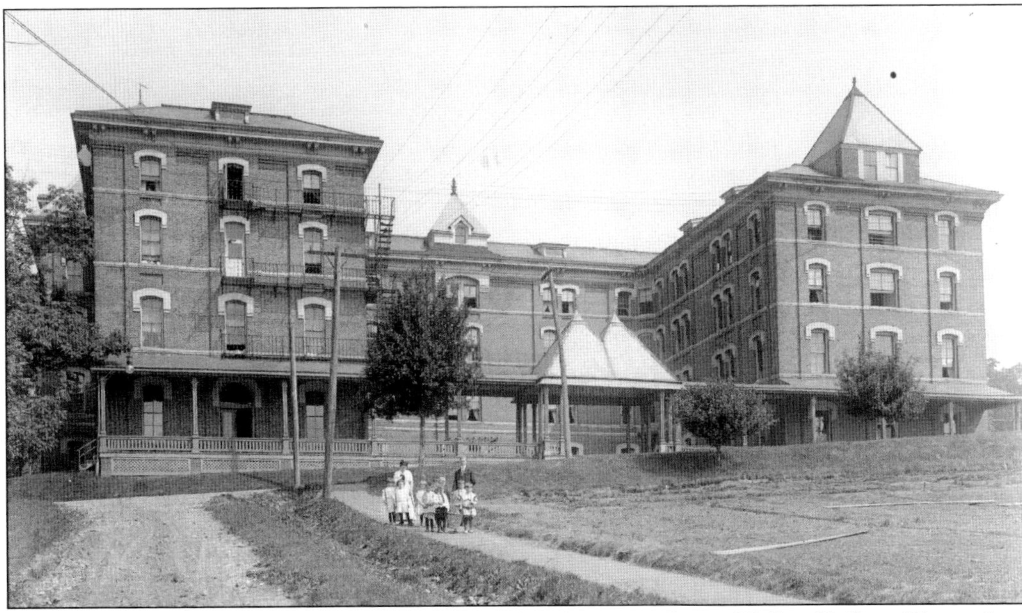

**THE LONG PORCH, 1898.** The original, wooden long porch on Waller Hall at Bloomsburg Normal School was added onto the building in 1890; it was replaced with a prominent brick colonnade in 1949. The porch quickly became a popular place for students and served as a focal point for alumni until the entire building was torn down in January 1975. (Courtesy of Bloomsburg University Archives.)

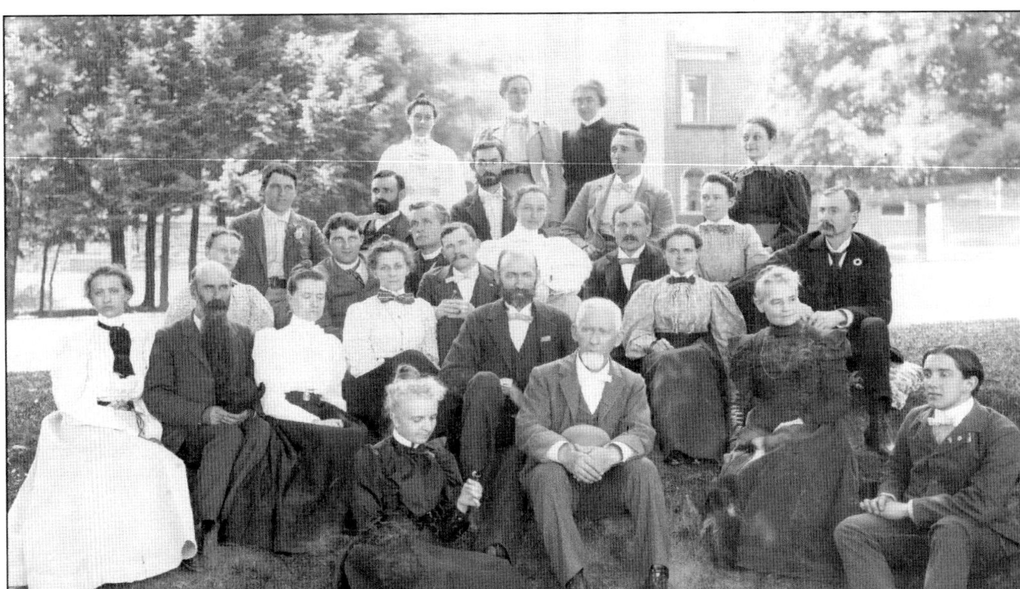

**NORMAL SCHOOL FACULTY, SUMMER 1893.** In the center with a beard and balding head is Judson Welsh, principal of the Bloomsburg Normal School from 1890 to 1906; he was a native of Orangeville and an 1876 normal school graduate. Above him to the left is Daniel Hartline, who taught manual training and the sciences, and below to the right is William Noetling, instructor in pedagogy. (Courtesy of Bloomsburg University Archives.)

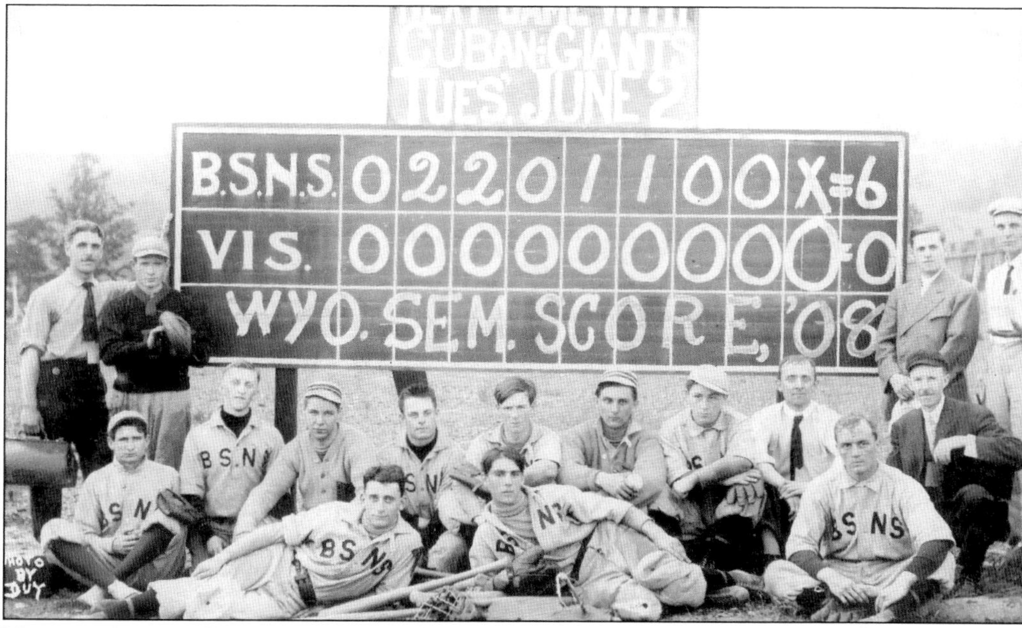


**NORMAL SCHOOL BASEBALL TEAM.** The team poses following a victory over their biggest rival, Wyoming Seminary of Kingston, on May 29, 1908. Baseball began at the normal school in the 1880s, enjoyed great success over the years, and by 1908 was coached by B. F. Bryant (standing, far left). The next opponent was the Cuban Giants, a touring African American professional baseball team. (Courtesy of Bloomsburg University Archives.)

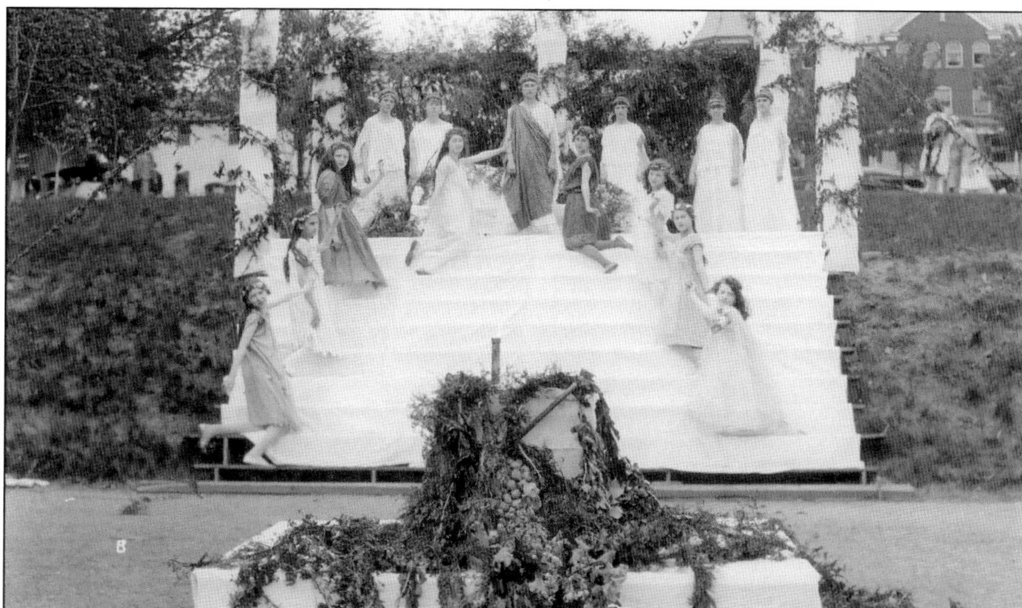

**MAY DAY, 1917.** The goddess Diana, portrayed by Evalyn Quinney as the queen of May, presides over dances and chariot races during the May Day ceremony on May 31, 1917. This rite, dedicated to the celebration of spring, was held on the Bloomsburg campus from 1910 to 1963, most often with training school children and on the terraced lawn, which is the current site of Kehr Union. (Courtesy of Bloomsburg University Archives.)

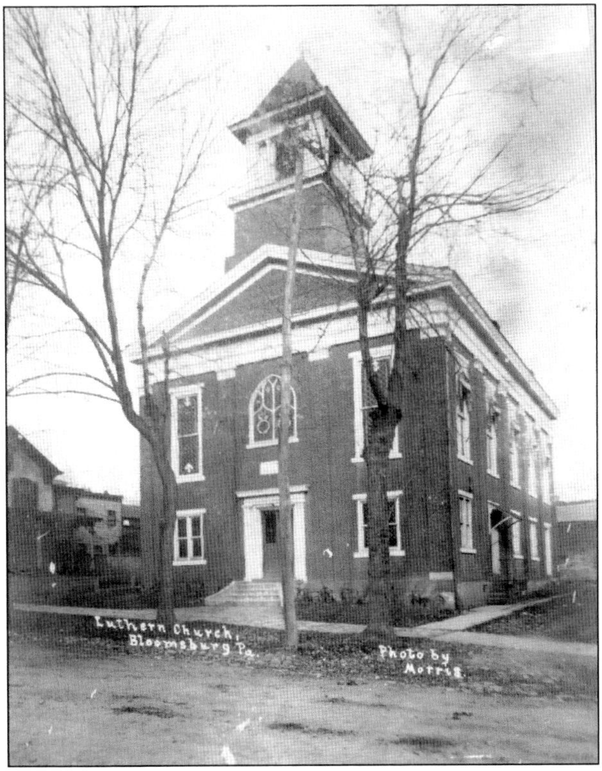


**ST. MATTHEW LUTHERAN CHURCH.** This church began as the German-speaking Union Church made up of St. Paul's Evangelical Lutheran Church and the Reformed Church, located at First and Center Streets on a lot bought from town founder Ludwig Eyer in 1808. The Reformed congregation built its own church in 1854. The Lutherans established a separate church, St. Matthew's, on Market Street in 1857. The present St. Matthew's opened on November 15, 1925.

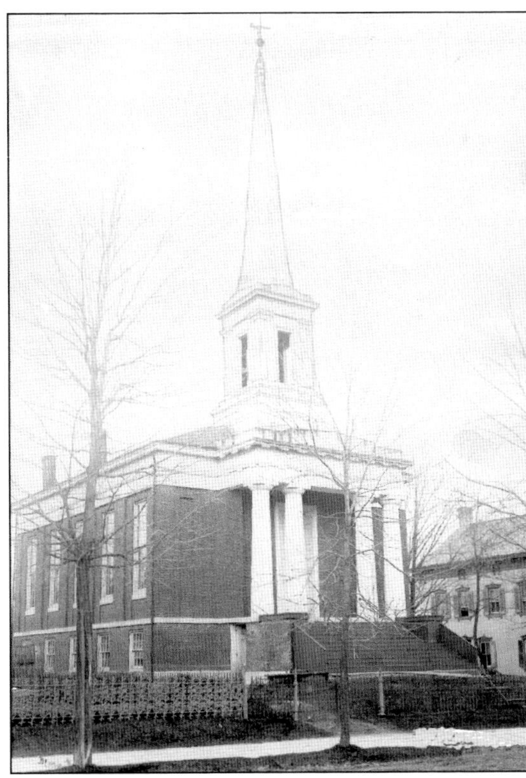

**FIRST PRESBYTERIAN CHURCH.** The first worship site of Presbyterians was on West Third Street in 1817, where Rev. David J. Waller, a citizen of prime importance in the early development of Bloomsburg, served 33 years as pastor. In 1846, the congregation purchased property at Third and Market Streets and erected this church designed by the architect who, in the same year, designed the original county courthouse.

**AFRICAN METHODIST EPISCOPAL CHURCH.** In 1870, the African Methodist Episcopal congregation in Bloomsburg built and dedicated this church on the corner of Jefferson and First Streets. To support this endeavor, people in the white community provided funds and donations of building materials. One hundred years later, due to declining membership, the church closed, and the building was torn down in 1980.

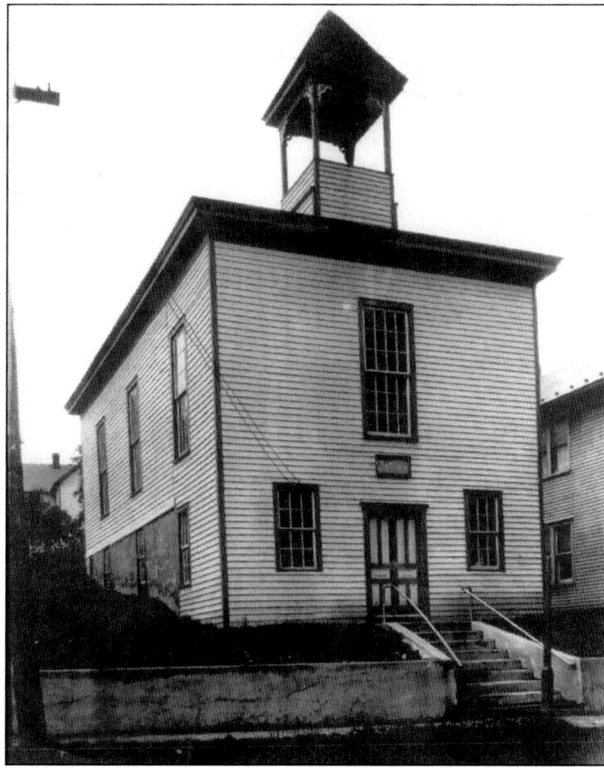

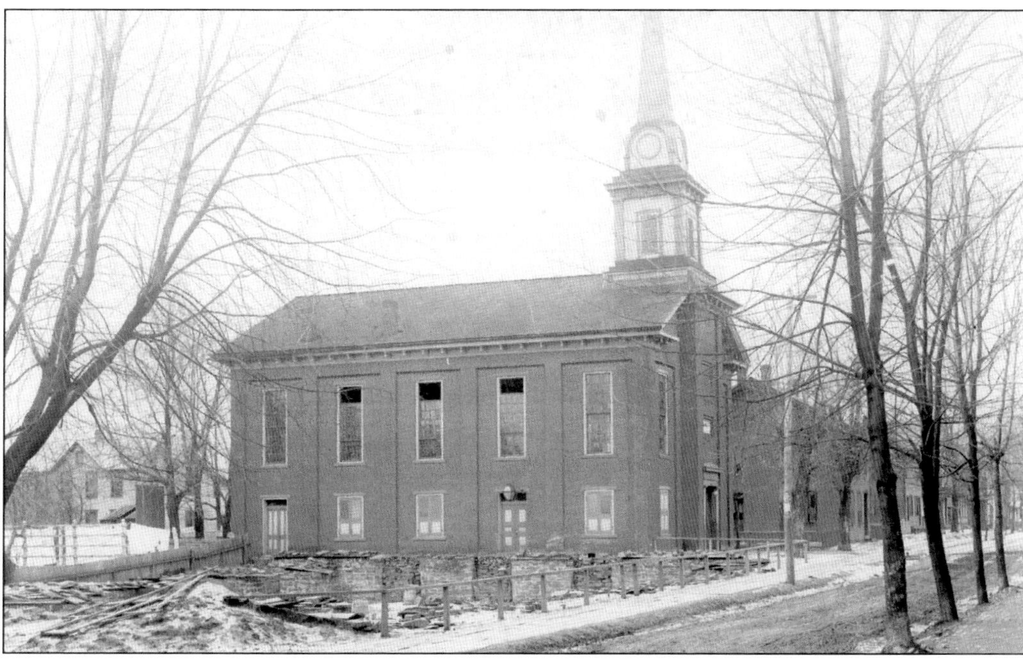

**FIRST METHODIST EPISCOPAL CHURCH.** Built in 1857 on the corner of Third Street and Murray Avenue, this was the second building to house this congregation. The first was built in 1837 at a cost of $540. The third was built in 1897 and is still in use today, currently known as Wesley United Methodist Church. Note the unpaved streets in the photograph.

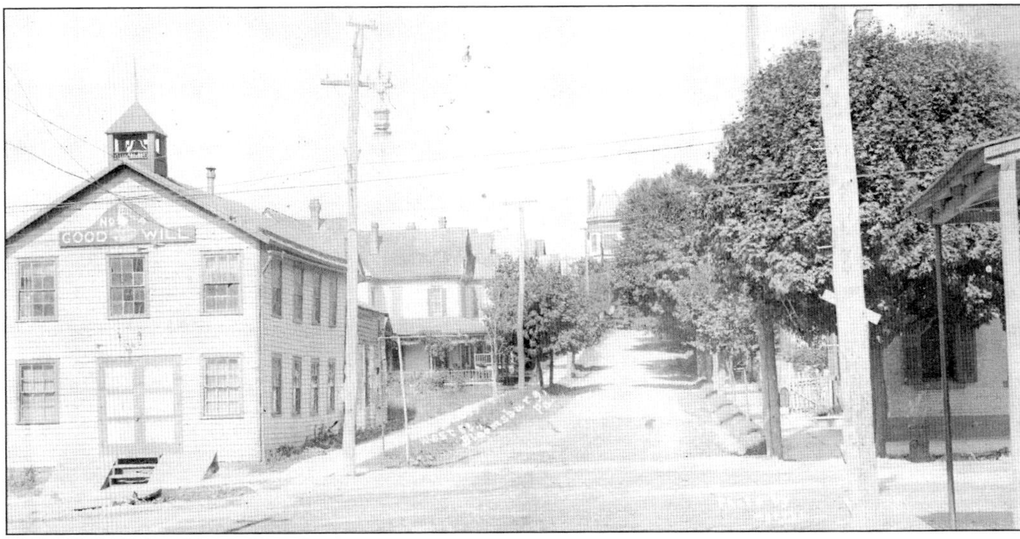


**GOOD WILL FIRE COMPANY.** The Good Will Fire Company at Main and West Streets was chartered in December 1898 and introduced firefighting with chemicals to the town. The organization functioned only until 1900. A small faction eventually formed another company known as the Liberty Fire Company.

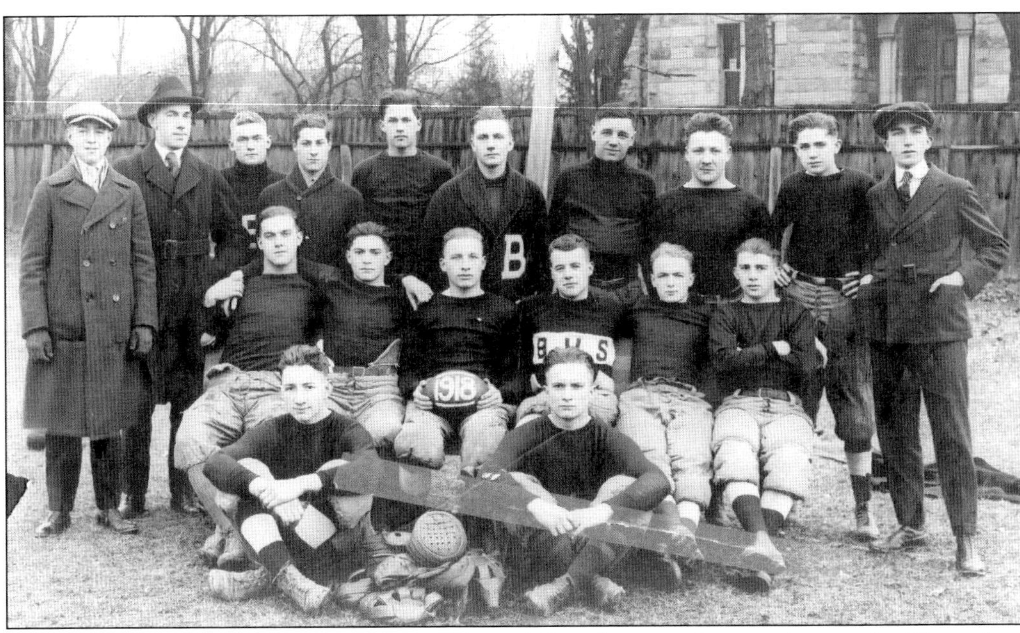


**BLOOMSBURG HIGH SCHOOL FOOTBALL TEAM.** This photograph was taken at the Bloomsburg Athletic Park at Seventh and Iron Streets in 1918. The jail is in the background. Future local magnate Harry L. Magee is shown in the second row with "BHS" across the front of his shirt.

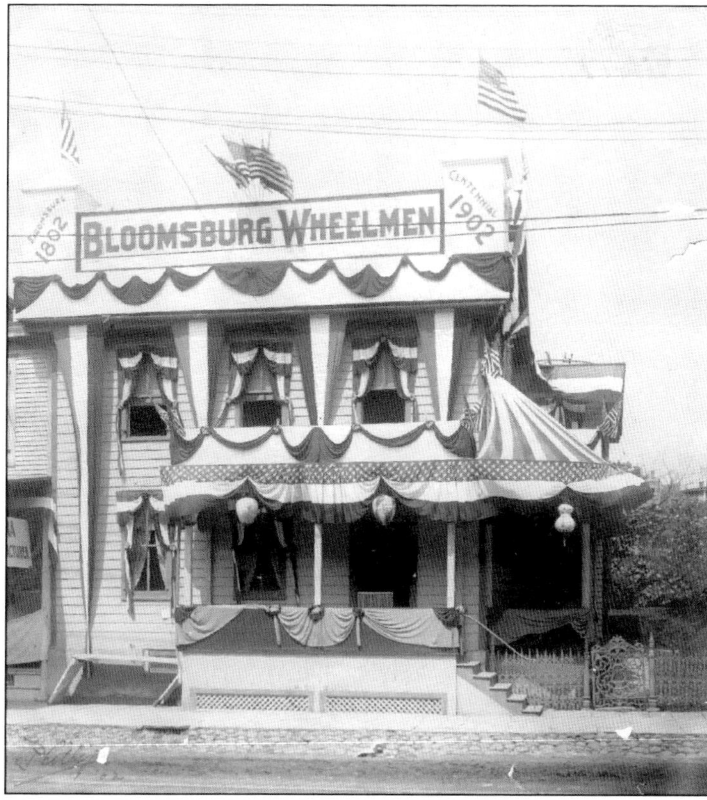


**BLOOMSBURG WHEELMEN'S CLUB.** In addition to bicycling, Bloomsburg's oldest social club also sponsored euchre, pool, basketball, and baseball for its members. The club's membership was over 100 at first, but so dwindled that in 1912, it moved to two rooms in the Wirt building and one year later disbanded and donated the funds on hand to the Bloomsburg Hospital.

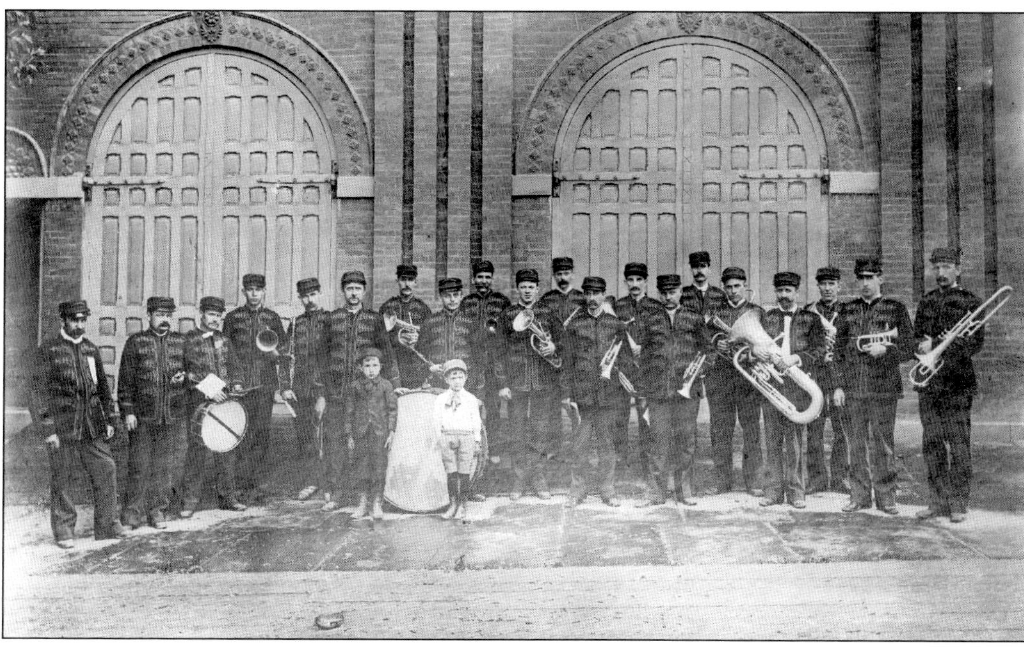

**BLOOMSBURG BAND.** The band poses in 1893 in front of the Friendship Fire Hall located in the town hall building.

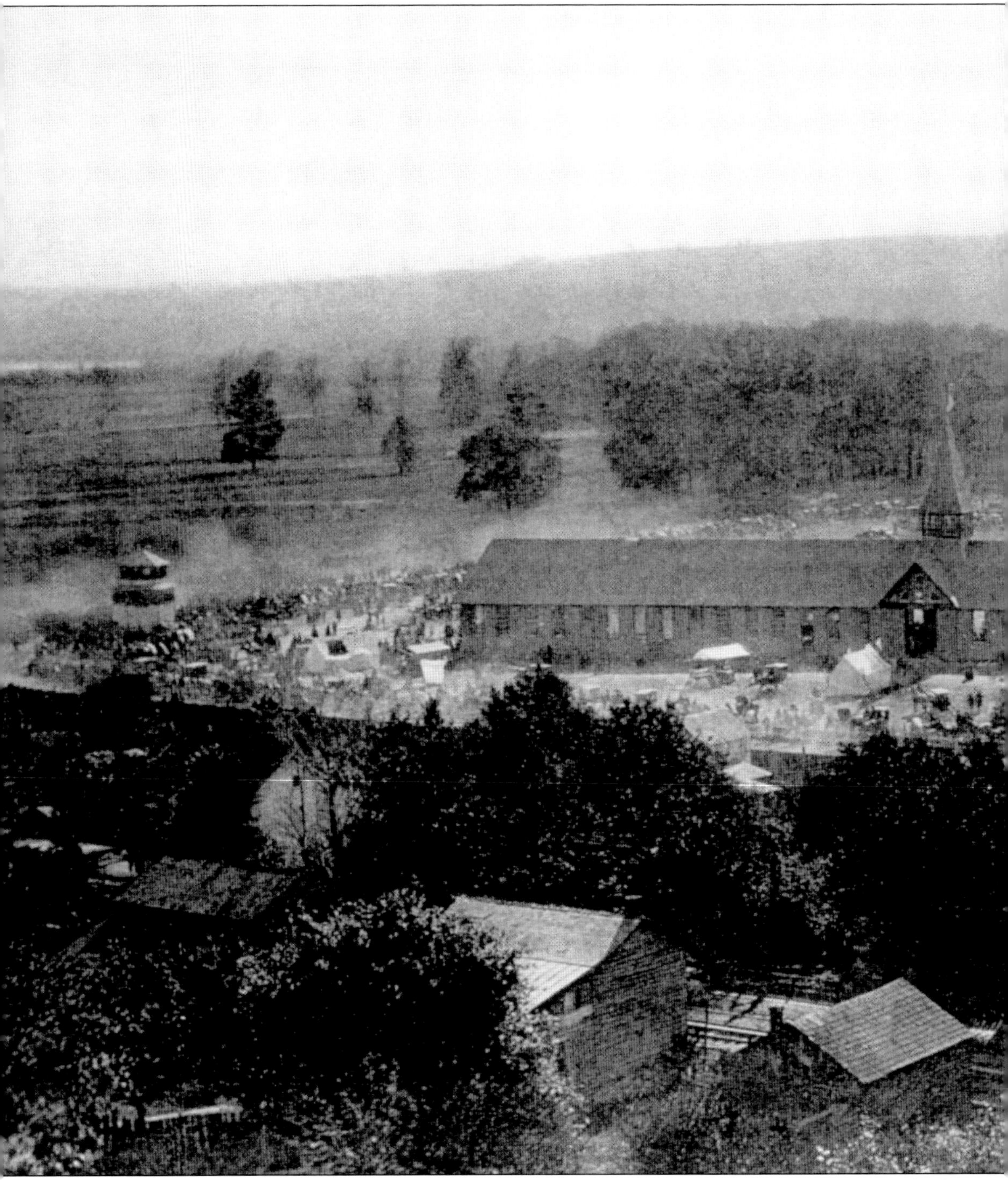

**BLOOMSBURG FAIRGROUNDS, BEFORE 1892.** This view of the fairgrounds from before 1892 looks west from the elevated vantage point of the Third Street School. Inside the squarish racetrack is the large, steepled stables and exhibit building. The infield is crowded with fairgoers' buggies. In the foreground between houses along Railroad Street is the track of the Bloomsburg and Sullivan Railroad. The Bloomsburg fair's official name is the Columbia County Agricultural,

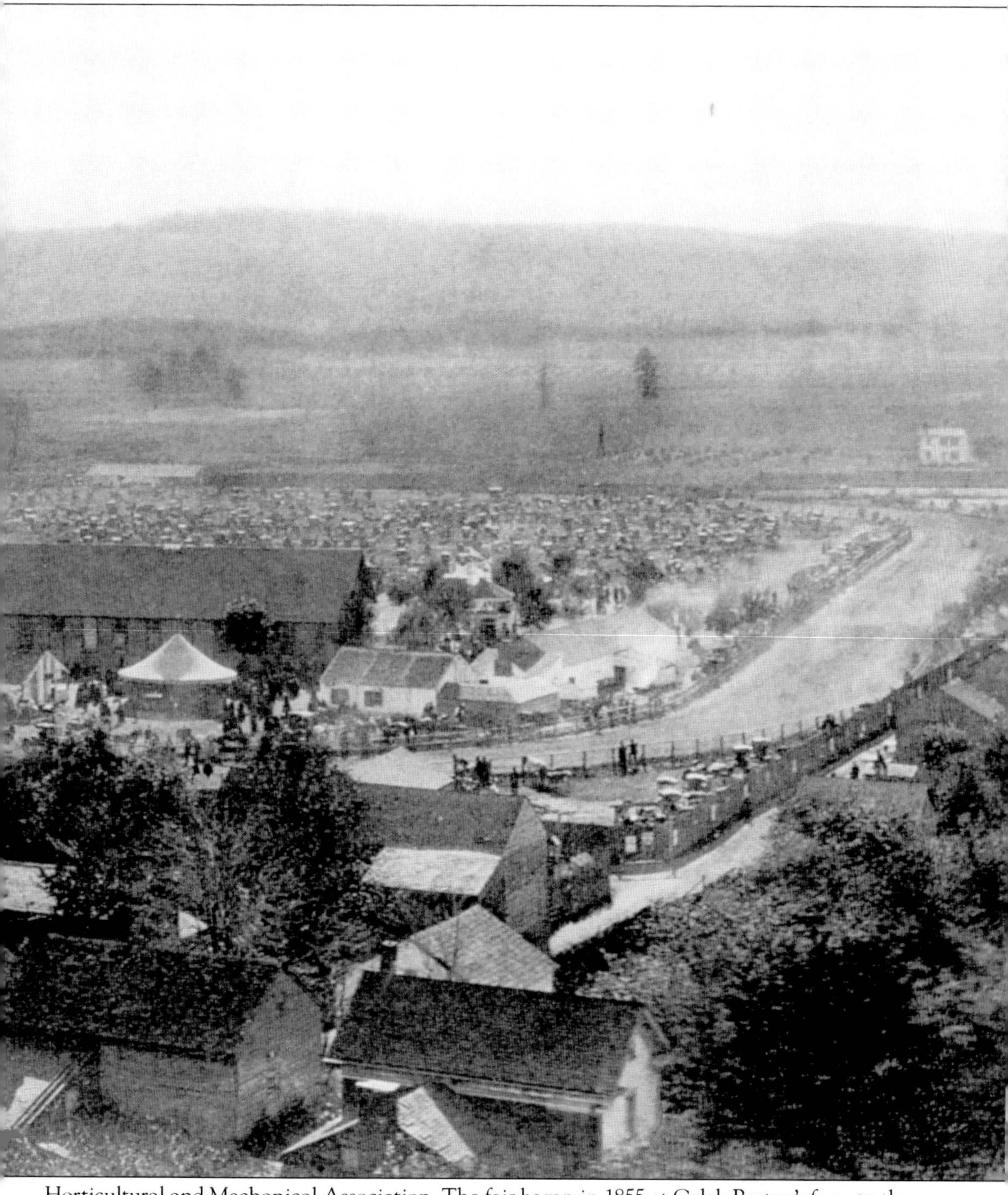

Horticultural and Mechanical Association. The fair began in 1855 at Caleb Barton's farm to the west of Bloomsburg and has been observed at that location most years since. The fair expanded steadily in area and attendance until 2000, when the exhibition was attracting more than a quarter million visitors each year.

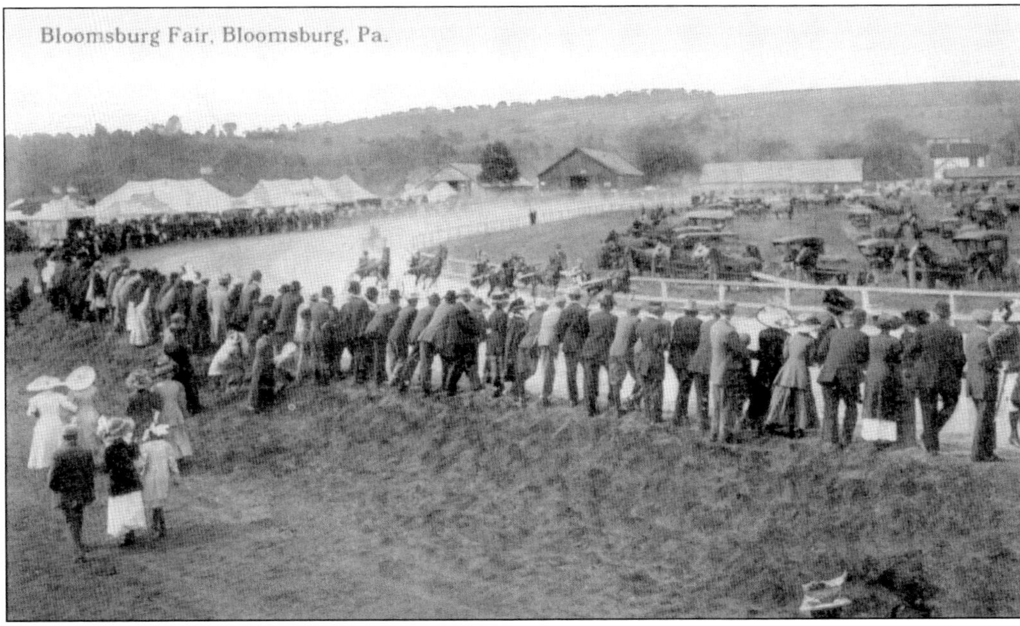


**BLOOMSBURG FAIR RACETRACK, 1900.** Racing in some form has been a part of the fair's entertainment almost since the first one was held in 1855. This has primarily been harness racing, but until 1900, it also included foot and bicycle races. A wooden grandstand that held 2,000 people was built in 1892, but hundreds of spectators continued to ring the track to get a closer look at their favorite horse.

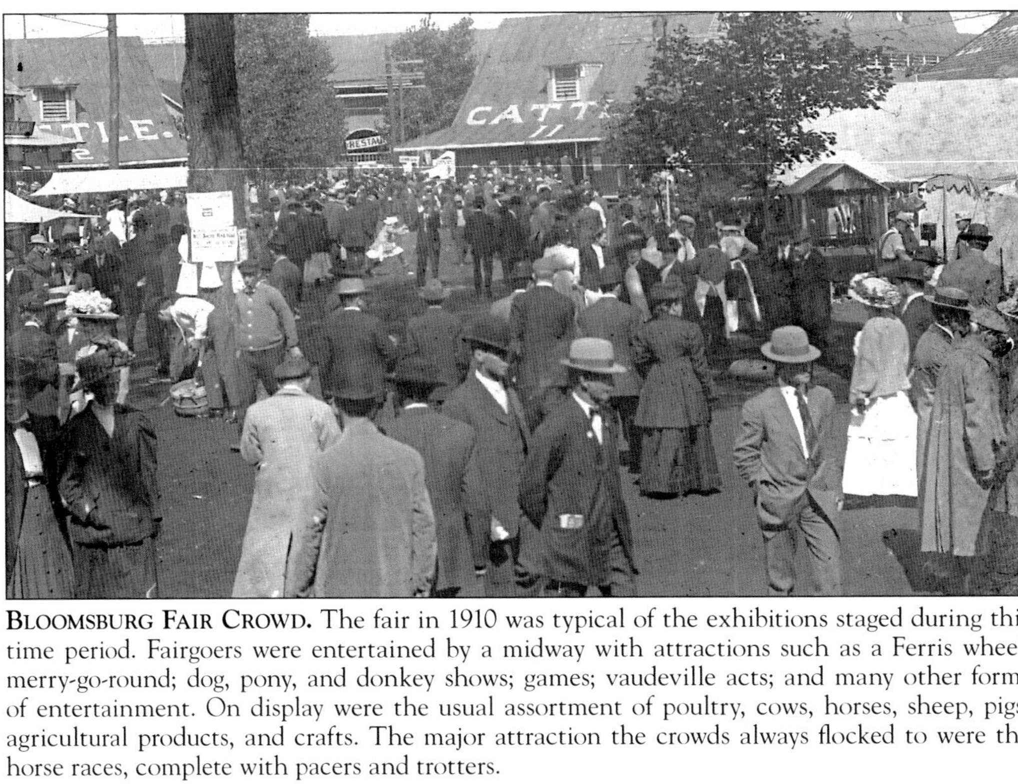

**BLOOMSBURG FAIR CROWD.** The fair in 1910 was typical of the exhibitions staged during this time period. Fairgoers were entertained by a midway with attractions such as a Ferris wheel; merry-go-round; dog, pony, and donkey shows; games; vaudeville acts; and many other forms of entertainment. On display were the usual assortment of poultry, cows, horses, sheep, pigs, agricultural products, and crafts. The major attraction the crowds always flocked to were the horse races, complete with pacers and trotters.

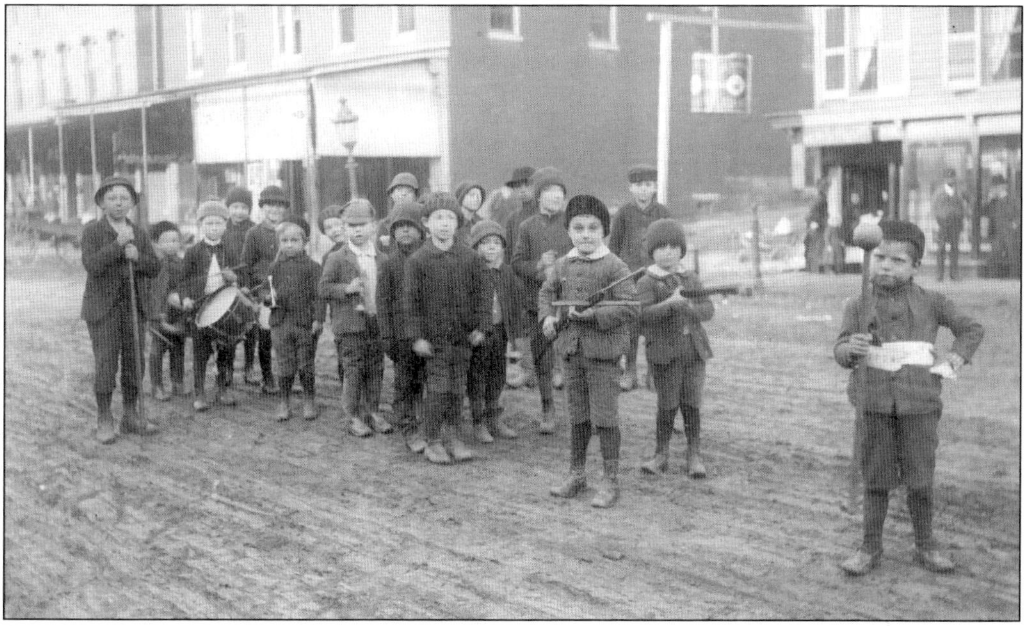

**The Iron Street Gang.** The Iron Street Gang parades at the corner of Main and Iron Streets around 1890. Weldie Fisher serves as drum major, while the two boys behind him carry toy rifles, and others have horns and drums. Fisher worked as a barber until his death in 1934 and was followed by his son and grandson in a 100-year-plus tradition of barbering in Bloomsburg. (Courtesy of Charles Fisher.)

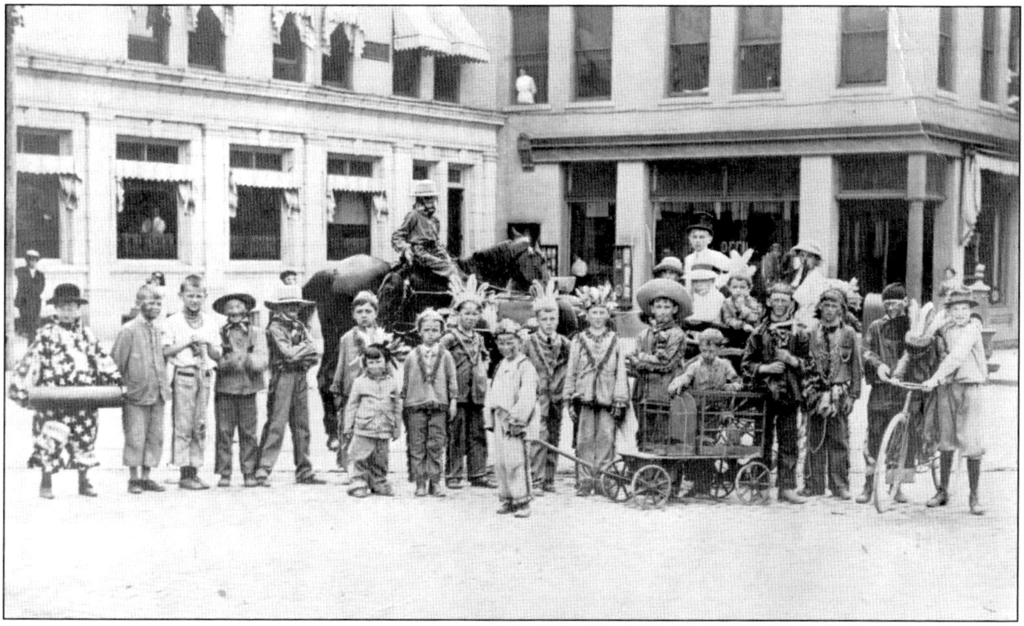

**Cowboys, Native Americans, and Clowns Galore.** Neighborhood children composed the Keller Brothers Circus that gathered crowds on West Fourth Street in Bloomsburg in 1907. Among the performers were future industrialist James Law, Dr. Charles Gennaria, and Dr. Charles Keller. On the horse is Harry Rinker, and on the wagon with a high hat is George J. Keller, a future professor at the state normal school, wild-animal trainer, and circus performer.

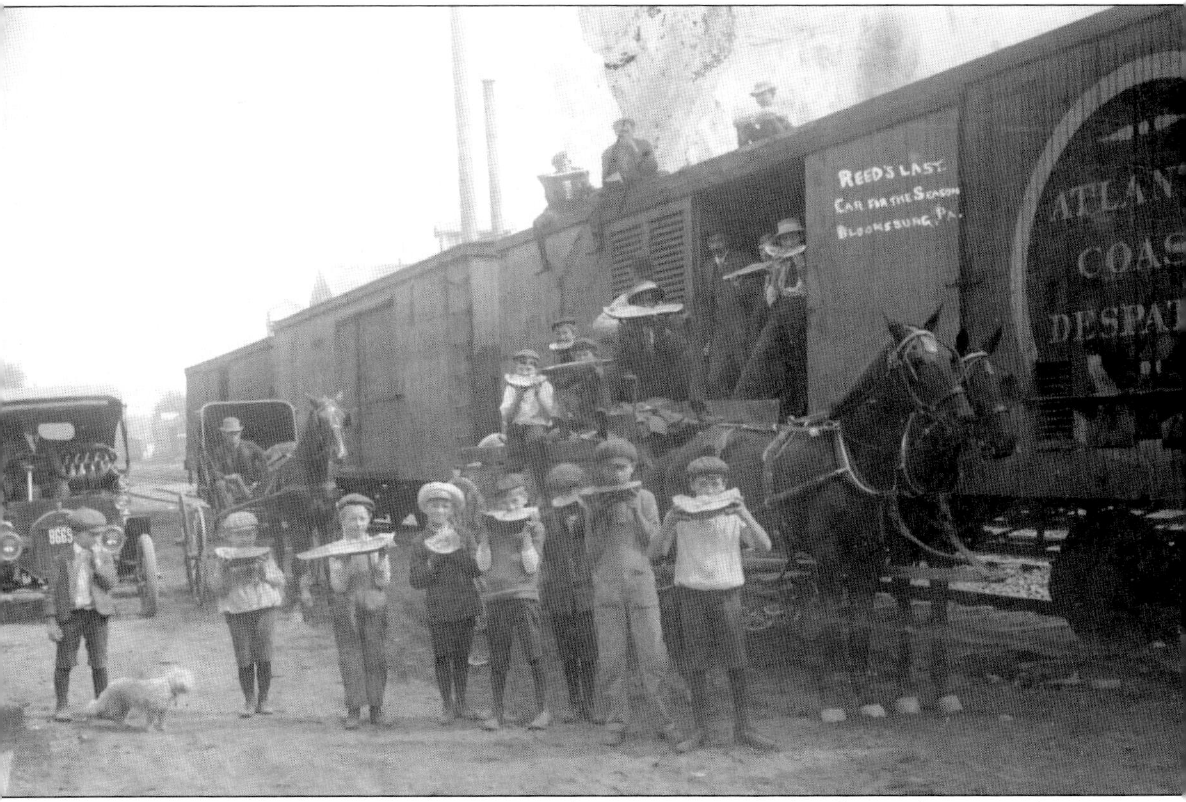


**SAYING GOOD-BYE TO SUMMER.** Young boys enjoy watermelon from a boxcar with a sign reading, "Reed's Last Car for the Season Bloomsburg PA." William Scott Reed was a traveling salesman who moved to town at the dawn of the 20th century and was well remembered for the carloads of watermelons he brought to the local market. These served as treats not only for the boys in town but also for the Bloomsburg Wheelmen when members went off to meetings at Columbia Park. Reed lived for many years on West Fifth Street and worked almost up until the time of his death in 1942 at the age of 88.

*Four*

# Berwick and Briar Creek

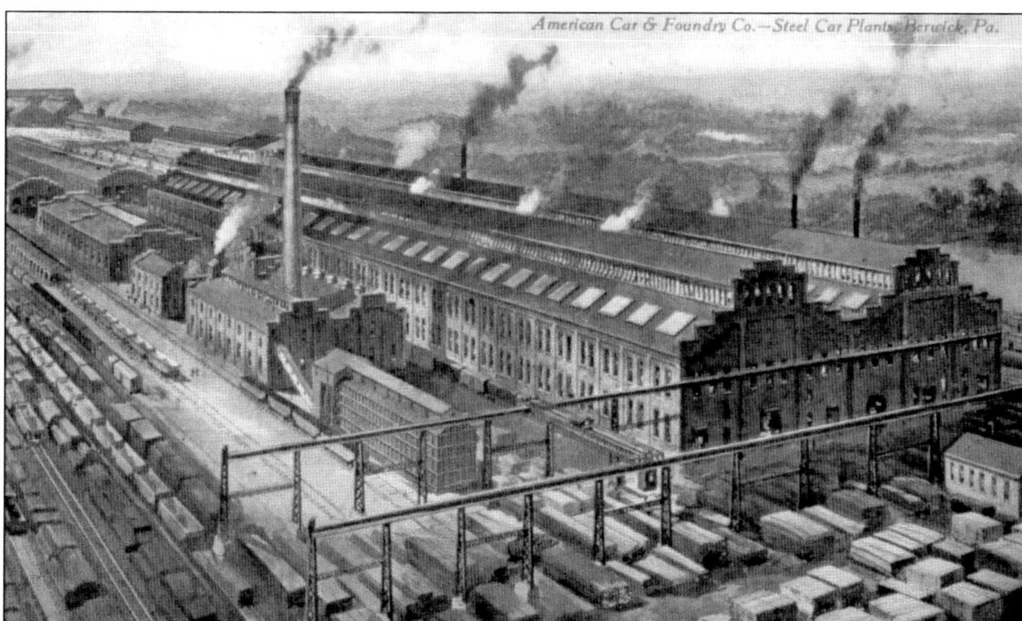


**American Car and Foundry Company, Berwick.** Founded by Mordecai Jackson in 1840, the firm that became Berwick's largest employer originally manufactured agricultural implements. By 1860, the company began to manufacture mining and railroad cars, and by 1899, it had become the largest manufacturer of railcars in the eastern United States. In 1907, it employed 5,700 workers. When the firm ceased operation in the early 1960s, the borough's economy was devastated.

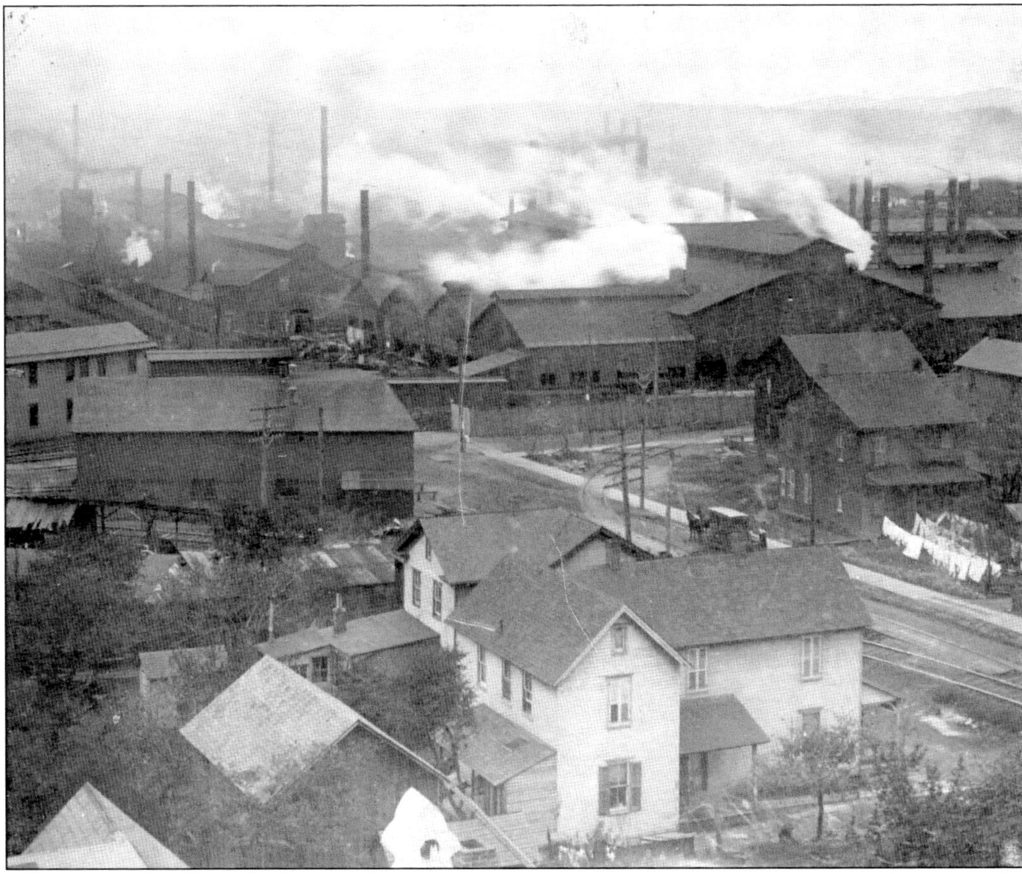

**Berwick's Largest Industry.** The rolling mill at the American Car and Foundry Company in Berwick in the early 1900s is shown in the above photograph. By World War I, the plant began to manufacture military hardware. It excelled at producing tanks for World War II. The company had its own security force, pictured in the photograph below.

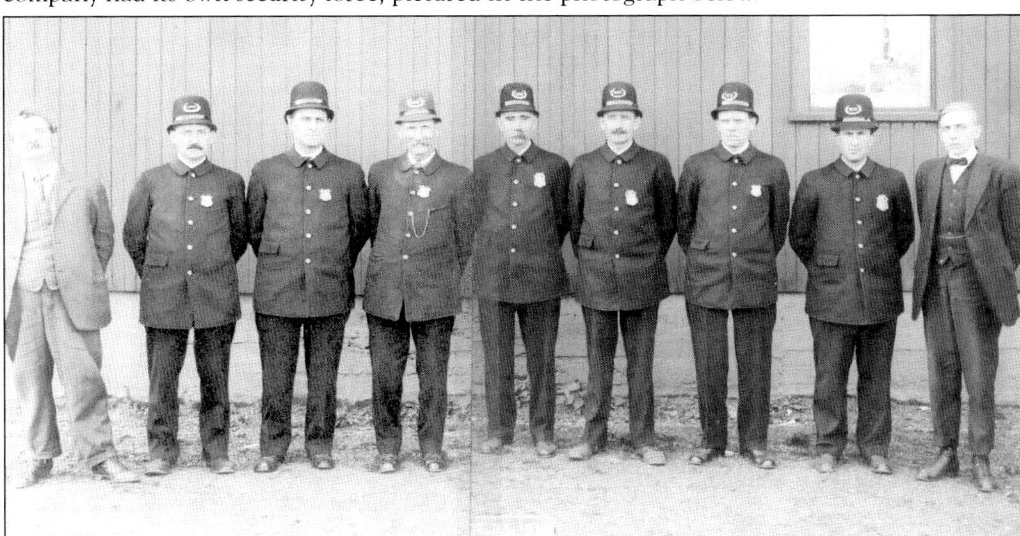

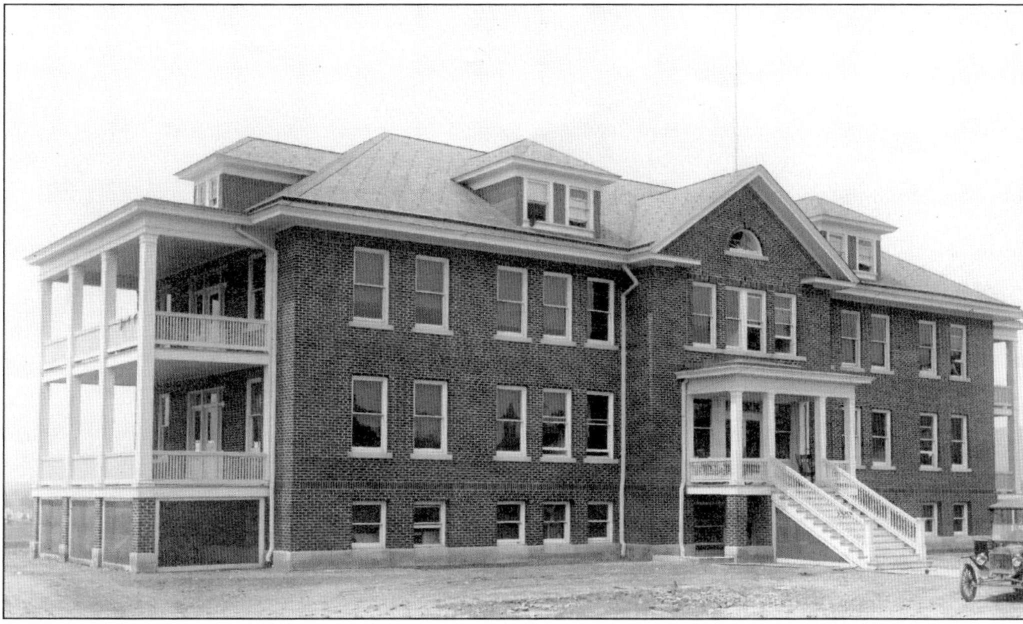

**OLD BERWICK HOSPITAL.** The old Berwick Hospital was actually the second hospital. Faced with bricks manufactured in Bloomsburg, the building was completed in 1913 at a cost of $28,000. Many individuals and groups donated funds to make the new hospital a reality, and numerous workmen donated a day's wages. The hospital operated a training school for nurses, 10 of whom graduated in 1915. Today the building houses apartments.

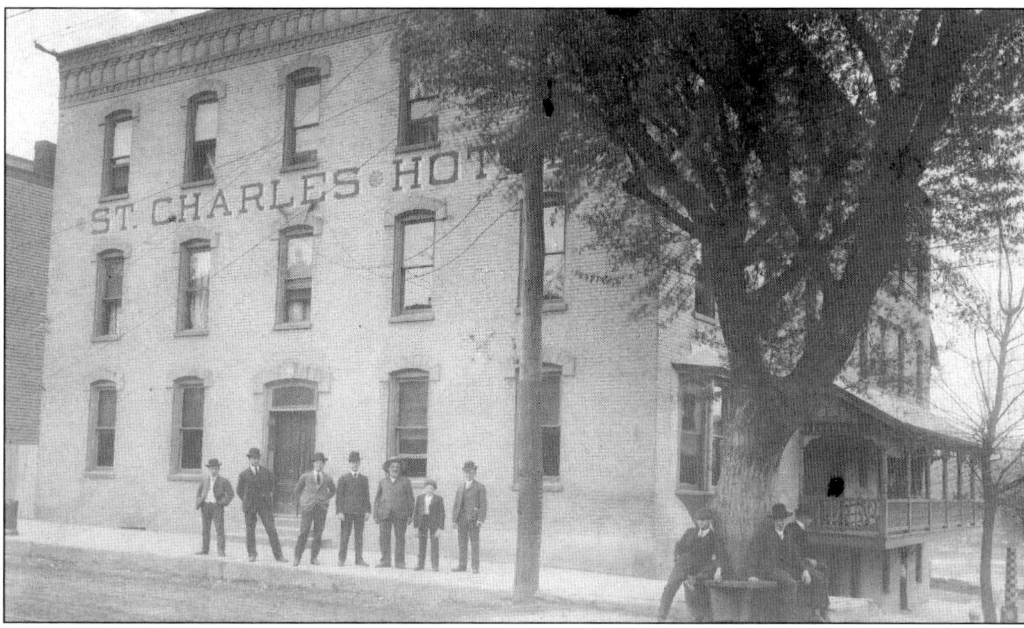


**ST. CHARLES HOTEL.** Berwick was a choice location for inns because it was the terminus of the Nescopeck Turnpike and the beginning of the Tioga and Susquehanna Turnpike. This hotel was on a prime site at Front and Market Streets. When the trolleys came, the St. Charles Hotel was at the intersection of the Danville, Bloomsburg and Berwick electric railway and the Berwick-Nescopeck trolley.

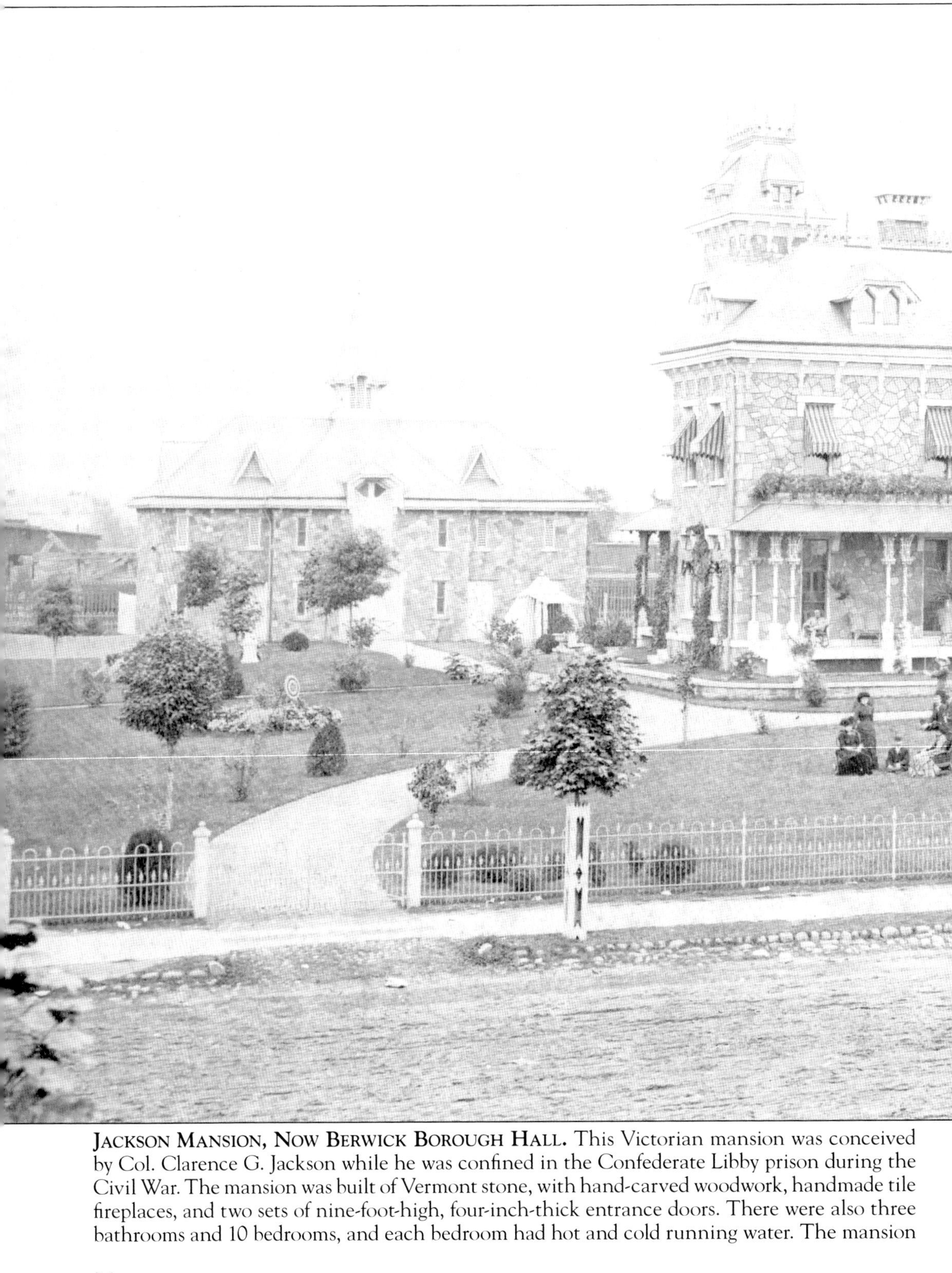

**JACKSON MANSION, NOW BERWICK BOROUGH HALL.** This Victorian mansion was conceived by Col. Clarence G. Jackson while he was confined in the Confederate Libby prison during the Civil War. The mansion was built of Vermont stone, with hand-carved woodwork, handmade tile fireplaces, and two sets of nine-foot-high, four-inch-thick entrance doors. There were also three bathrooms and 10 bedrooms, and each bedroom had hot and cold running water. The mansion

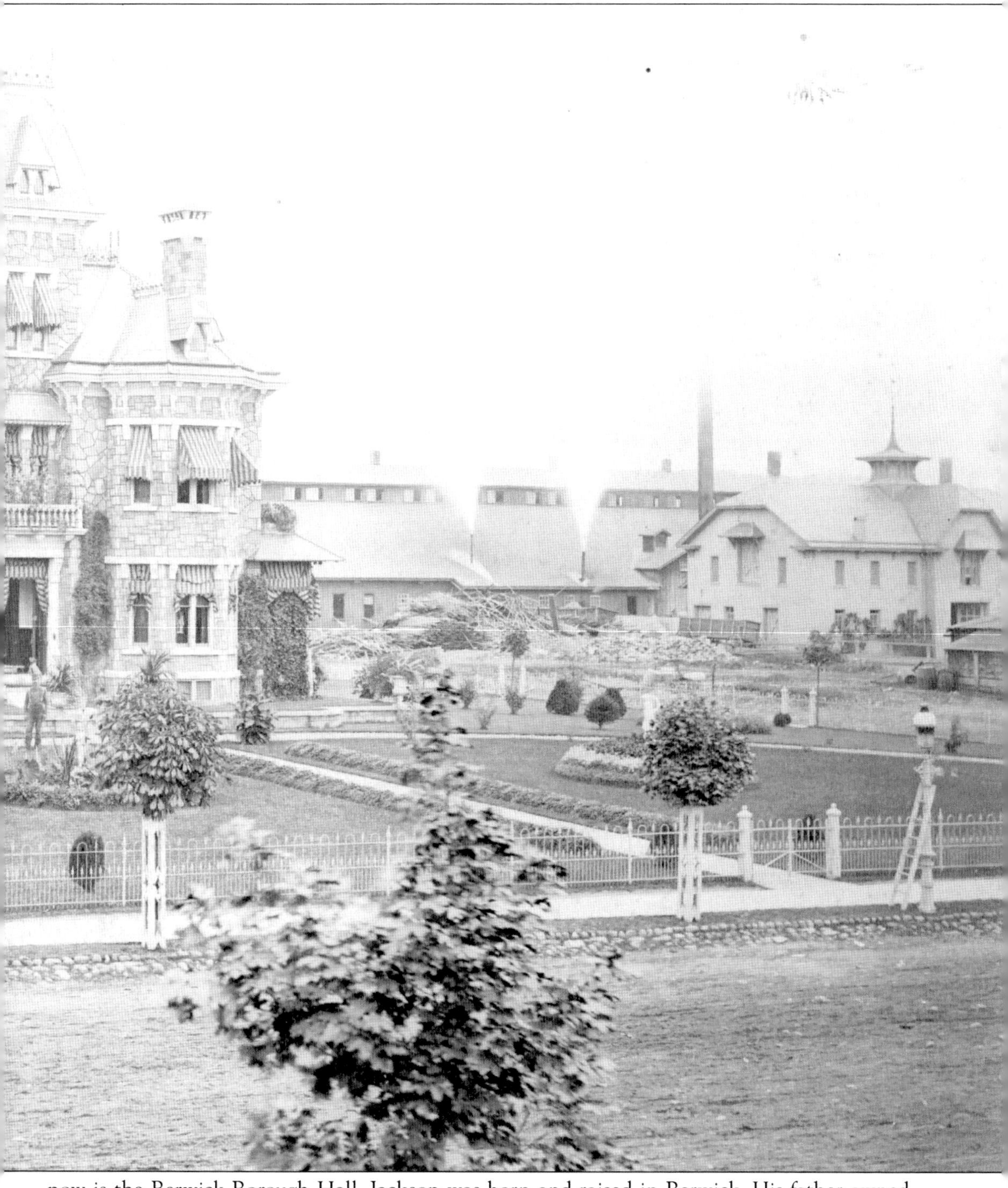

now is the Berwick Borough Hall. Jackson was born and raised in Berwick. His father owned a foundry on Third and Market Streets and in 1849 merged with William Woodin, who had a furnace and foundry in Foundryville. This merger firm was the predecessor of the American Car and Foundry Company.

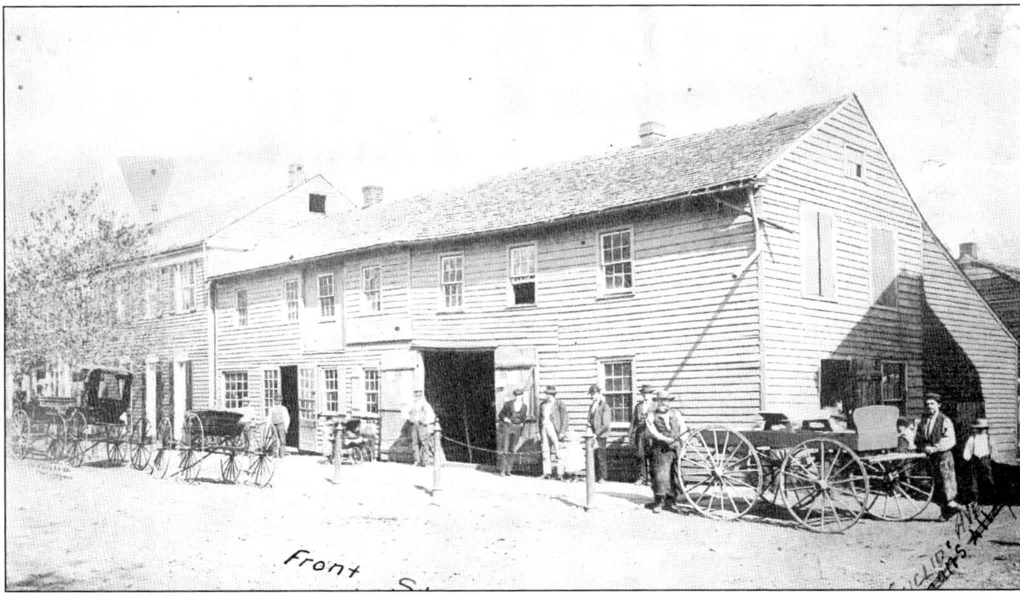


**FRANTZ CARRIAGE MAKER, 1870.** Madison Frantz owned this business located at Front Street and Euclid Avenue in Berwick. According to his nephew Lewis Frantz, Madison Frantz was still working at his trade when he died at the age of 90. Both wheel making and blacksmithing were essential skills in the carriage and wagon industry.

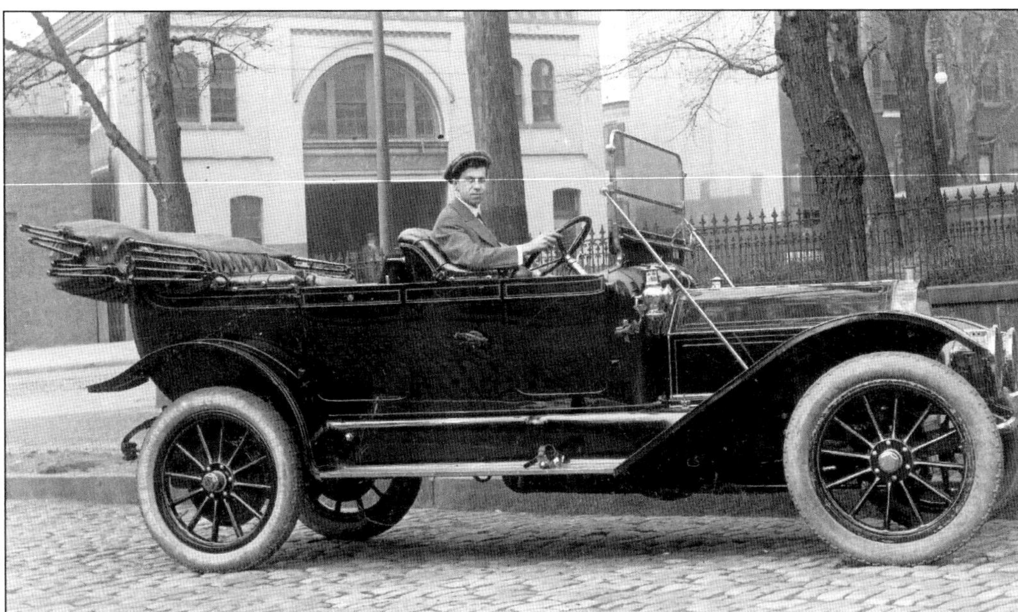

**MULTIPLEX AUTOMOBILE.** This is one of a dozen Multiplex cars built between 1911 and 1913 at the Multiplex plant at 600 Fowler Avenue in Berwick. Engineer Clarence Crispin designed and built the cars at this facility. He approached the American Car and Foundry about producing the cars, but the board of directors declined, as they were of the opinion that automobiles would not catch on. Crispin discontinued the venture. The driver is Charlie Bower.

**WRIGHT'S LIVERY STABLE.** William B. Wright's livery stable was located at Reagan's Alley and Mulberry Street in Berwick. It was one of several livery stables in operation in Berwick prior to 1914.

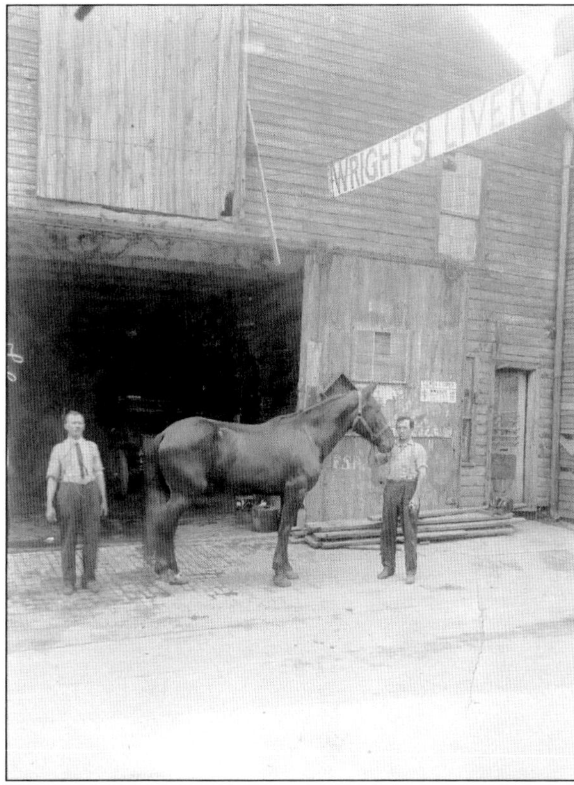


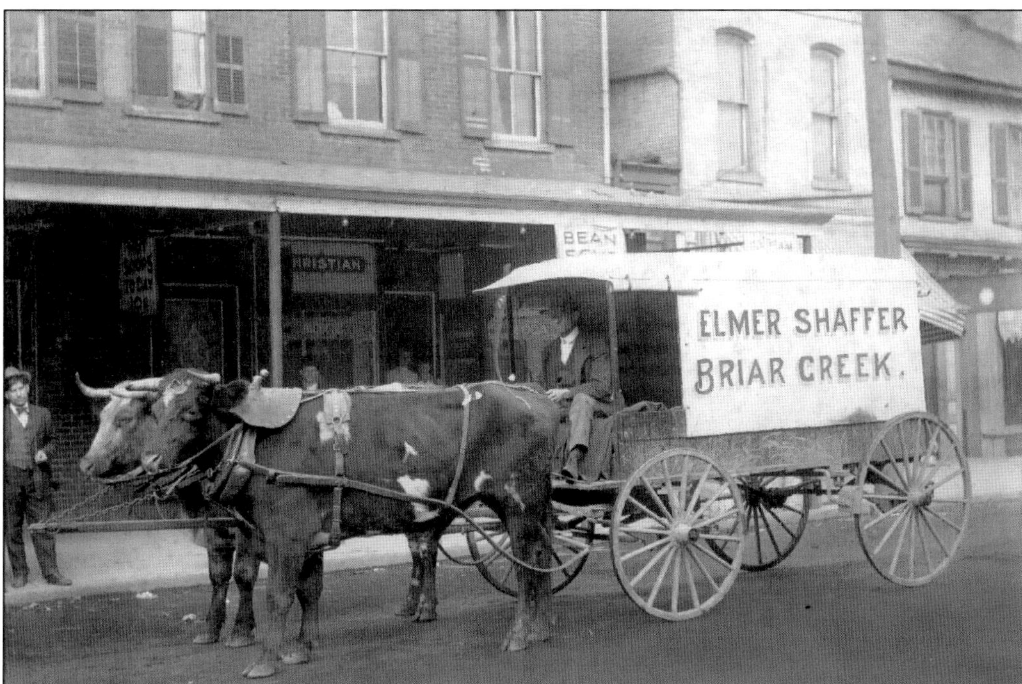


**FARM OXCART.** Oxcarts carried heavy loads. This one belonged to farmer Elmer Shaffer of Briar Creek.

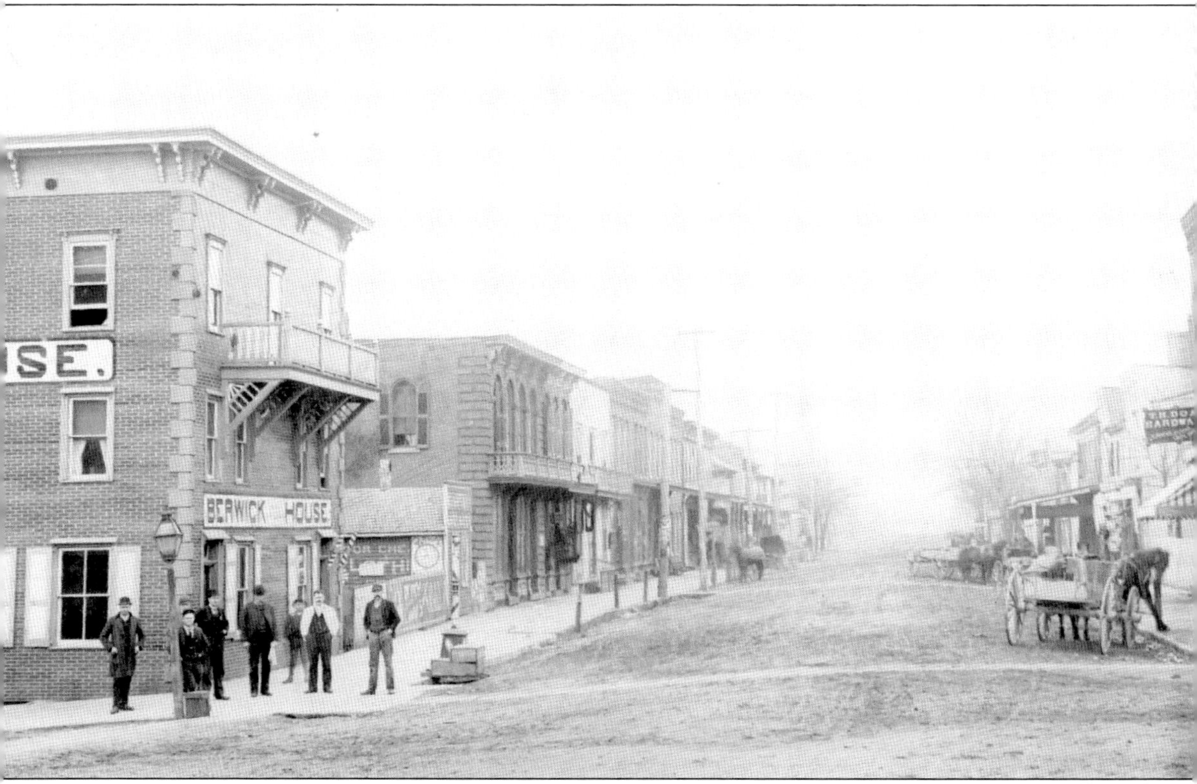


**FRONT AND MARKET STREETS, C. 1900.** This early street scene shows the Berwick House on the left, which later became the Morton Hotel. Note the unpaved streets and several horse-drawn vehicles. The sign on the extreme right reads, "T. H. Doan, Hardware."

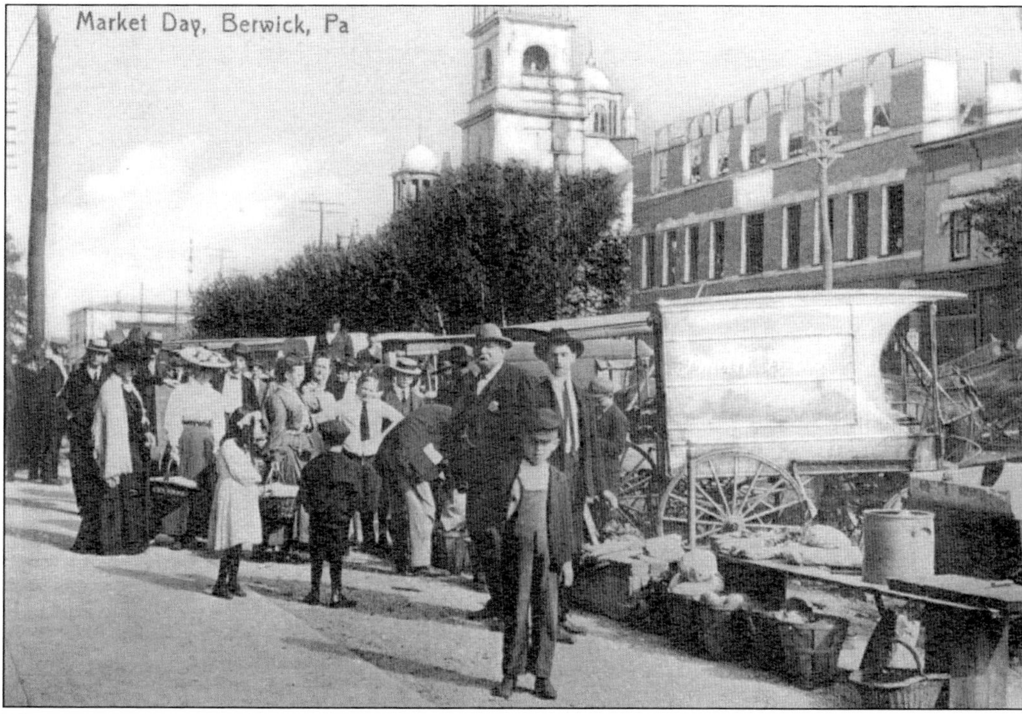


**Market Day.** Berwick's Market Street on Market Day bustles with local farmers selling their produce around 1905. Visible in the background is the Masonic building under construction.

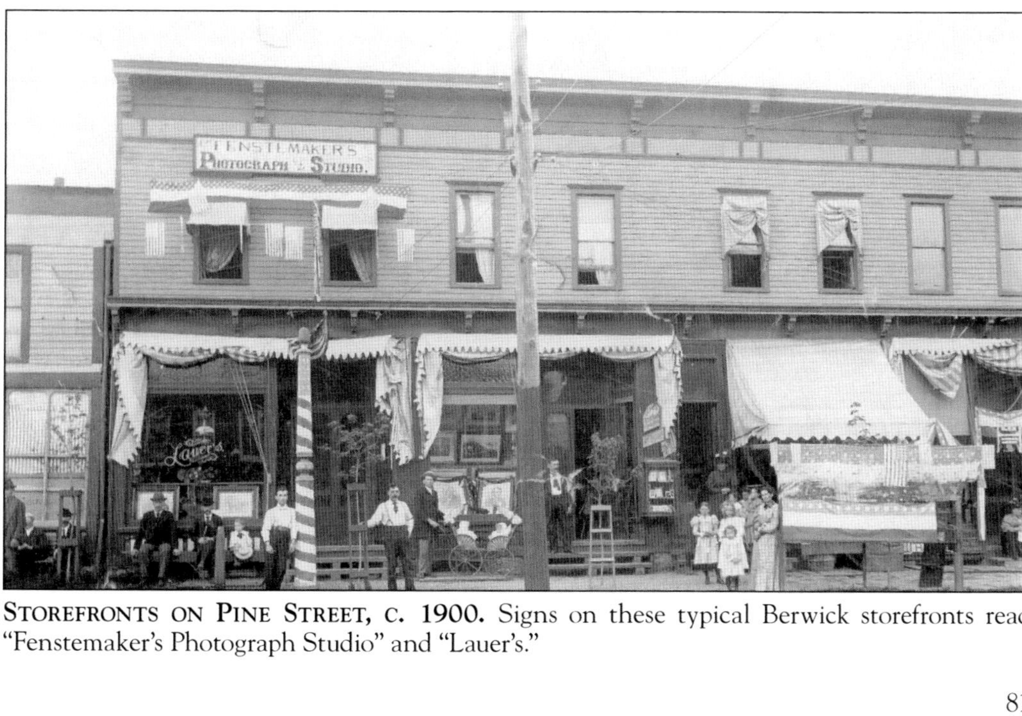


**Storefronts on Pine Street, c. 1900.** Signs on these typical Berwick storefronts read "Fenstemaker's Photograph Studio" and "Lauer's."

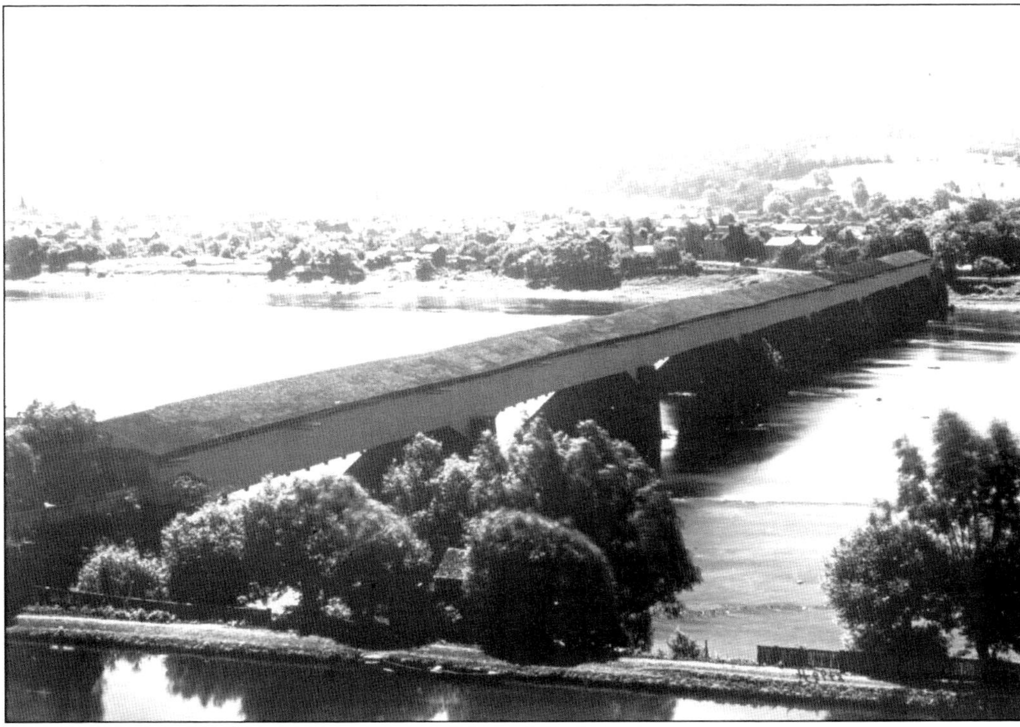

**BERWICK-NESCOPECK BRIDGE.** A privately owned bridge crossed the Susquehanna River, connecting Berwick and Nescopeck. It opened in 1815 and was swept away by a flood in 1836. The bridge pictured above, built in 1837 and also privately owned, was carried away by another flood and ice jam in March 1904. The North Branch Canal can be seen at the bottom of the photograph above. The replacement bridge of iron arches, shown under construction in the photograph below, was erected by the York Bridge Company and completed in 1906. Many years later in the 1990s, it was replaced with a new bridge of a modern concrete-span design.

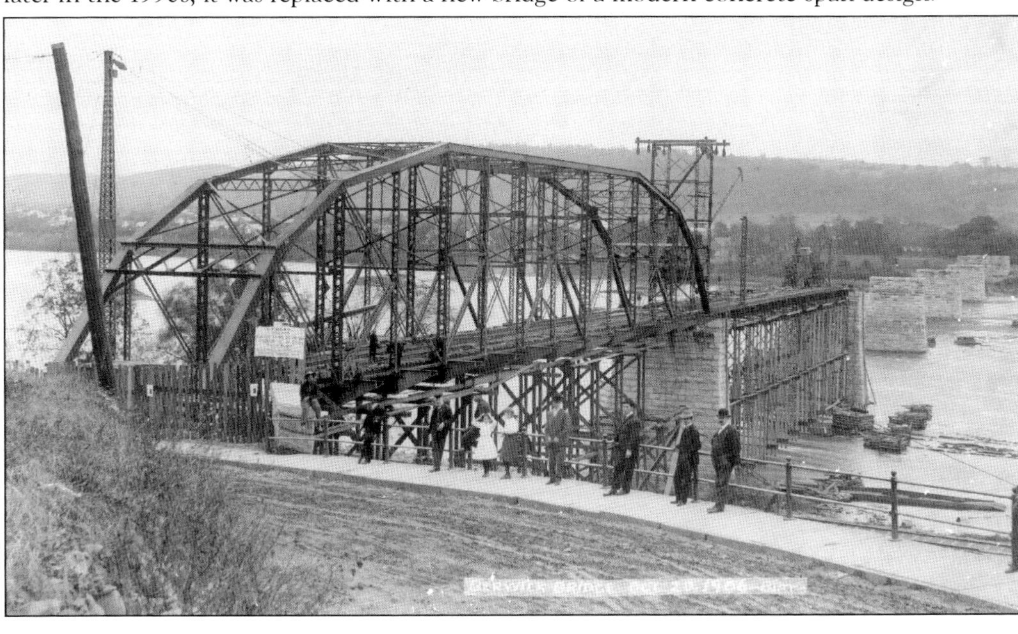

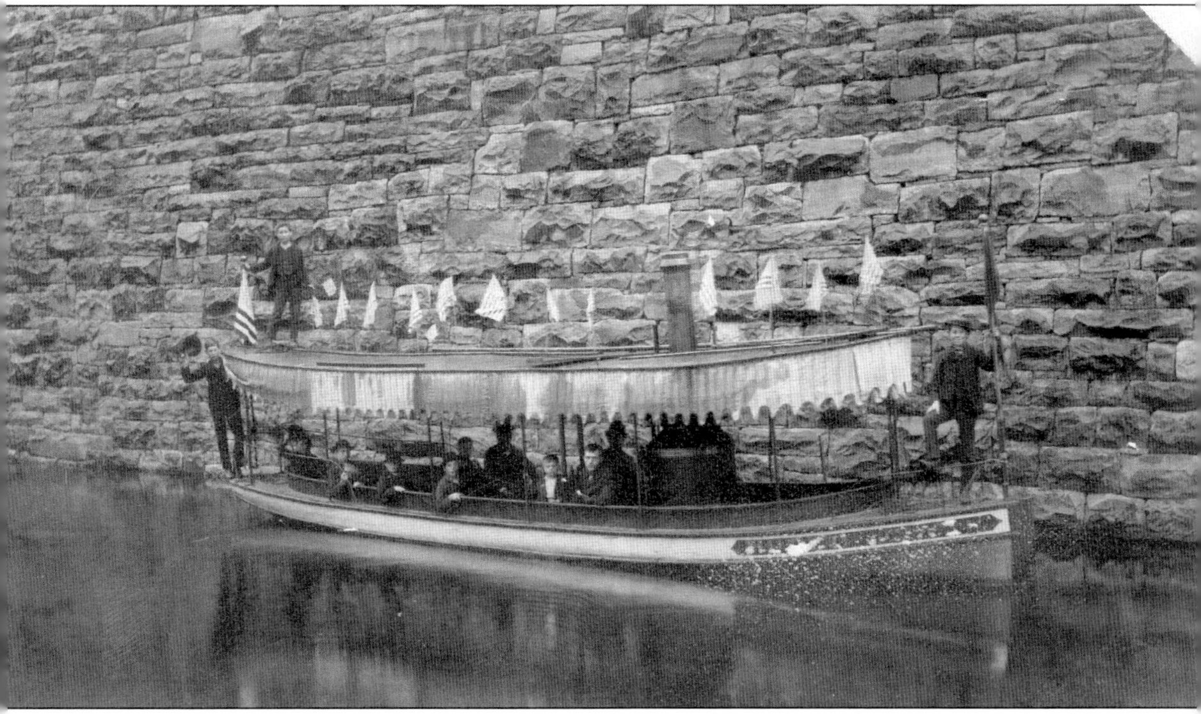

**THE *HUDSON OWEN*, C. 1890.** Alonzo J. Sult ran his steamboat, the *Hudson Owen*, on the old Berwick canal for excursions and pleasure trips.

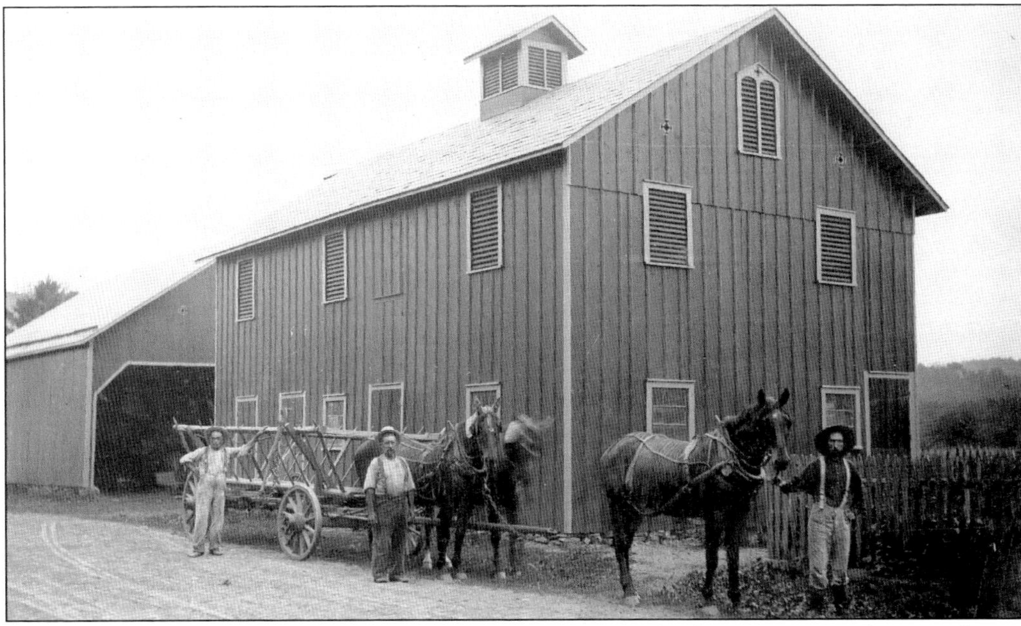

**Farm Wagon and Horses.** This work team in front of a barn in Berwick around 1900 represents the main industry of that era. At that time, the principal farm products in Columbia County were wheat, oats, buckwheat, corn, rye, and potatoes. Pennsylvania ranked first in buckwheat among grain-producing states, and this section of the state was tops in buckwheat. Apple growing and swine farming were also popular in Columbia County.

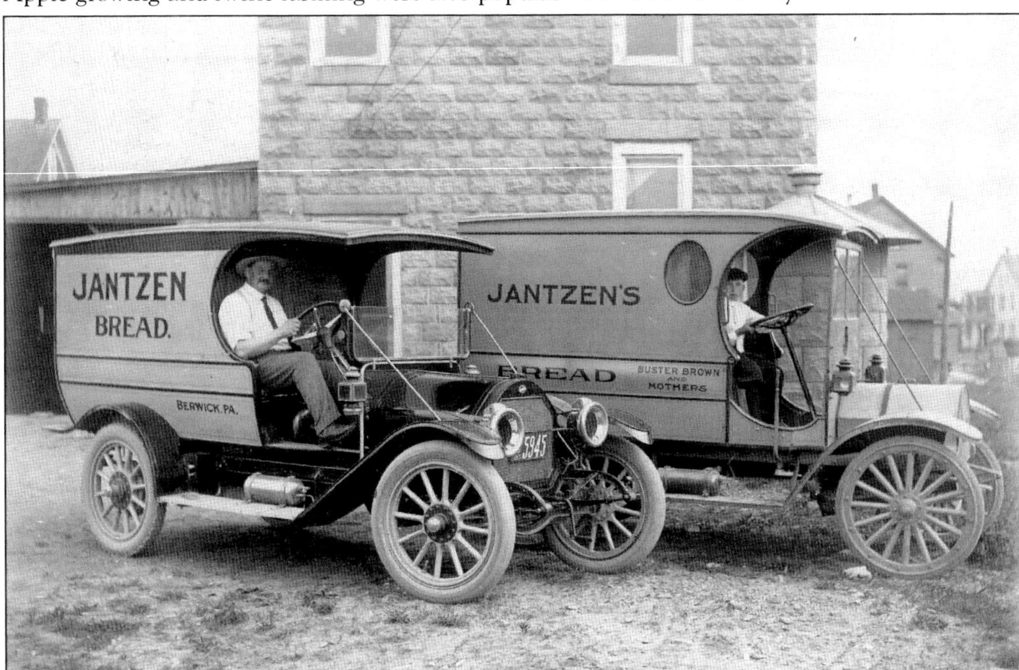


**Jantzen Bakery Trucks, 1913.** William C. Jantzen established his bakery in 1905. In 1908, with business expanding, the company moved to the building in the background at 1348 Spring Garden Avenue. In the early 1920s, there were four bakeries in Berwick.

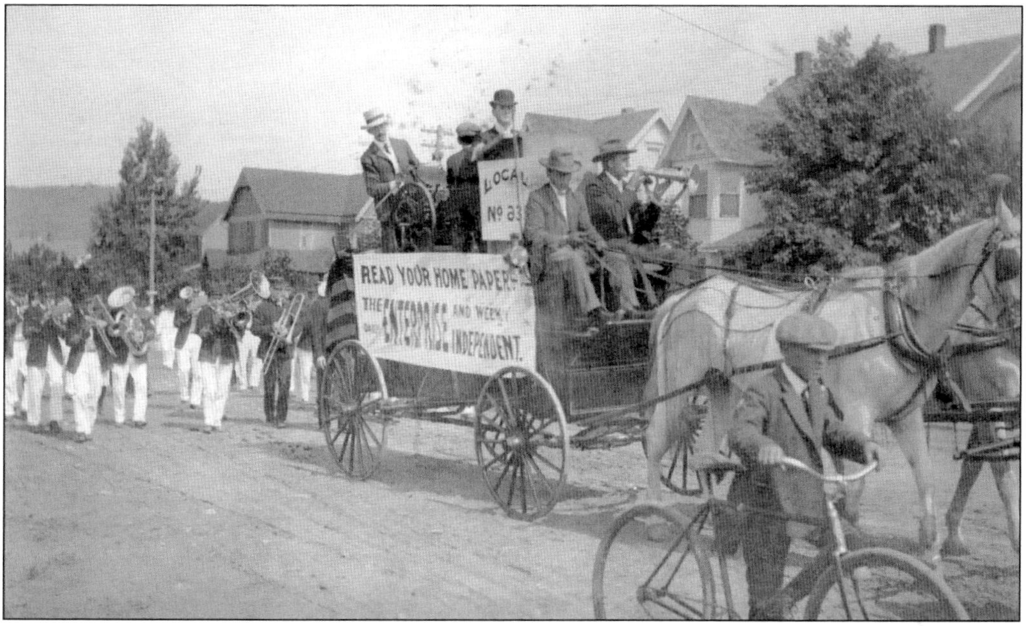


**NEWSPAPER FLOAT.** This advertising float exhorts, "Read Your Home Papers; The Daily Enterprise and Weekly Independent." A surprising number of newspapers were published in the early days of the county. The *Independent* was started by Charles B. Snyder in 1871. It was sold in 1879, and the name was changed to the *Berwick Independent*. Eventually the *Berwick Daily Enterprise* emerged in 1903.

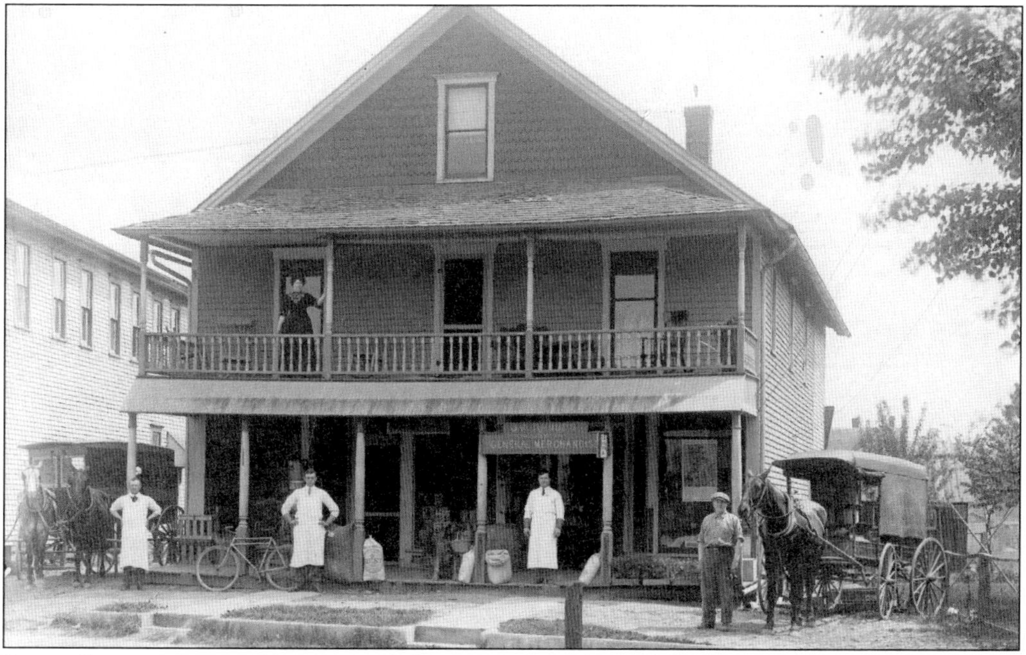

**JASON RHODES STORE.** Residents of the community depended on a general store, such as this one on Orange Street, for those items that they did not make or grow at home. Horse-drawn delivery trucks were common. At times, the stores also served as community gathering places where local news and most likely some gossip was shared.

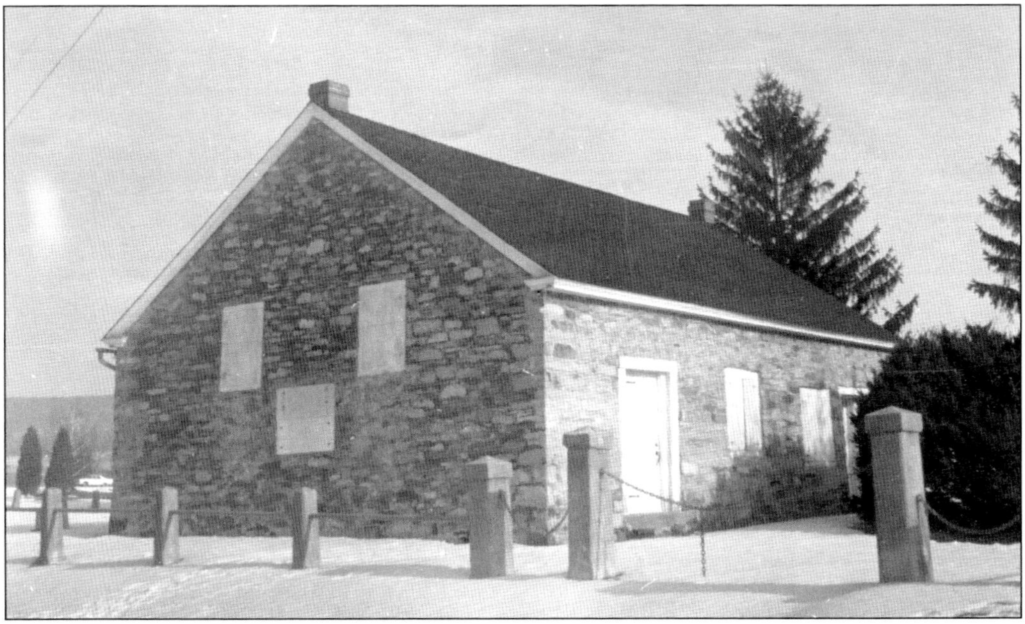

**OLD STONE CHURCH, BRIAR CREEK.** This structure, erected in 1808, was the first church building of the Methodist Episcopal denomination in the forks of the Susquehanna River. It was a rallying point for Methodists from Milton, Lewisburg, Northumberland, the Wyoming Valley, and surrounding countryside. The congregation is gone, but annual services are still held, and the building has been the site of historical pilgrimages.

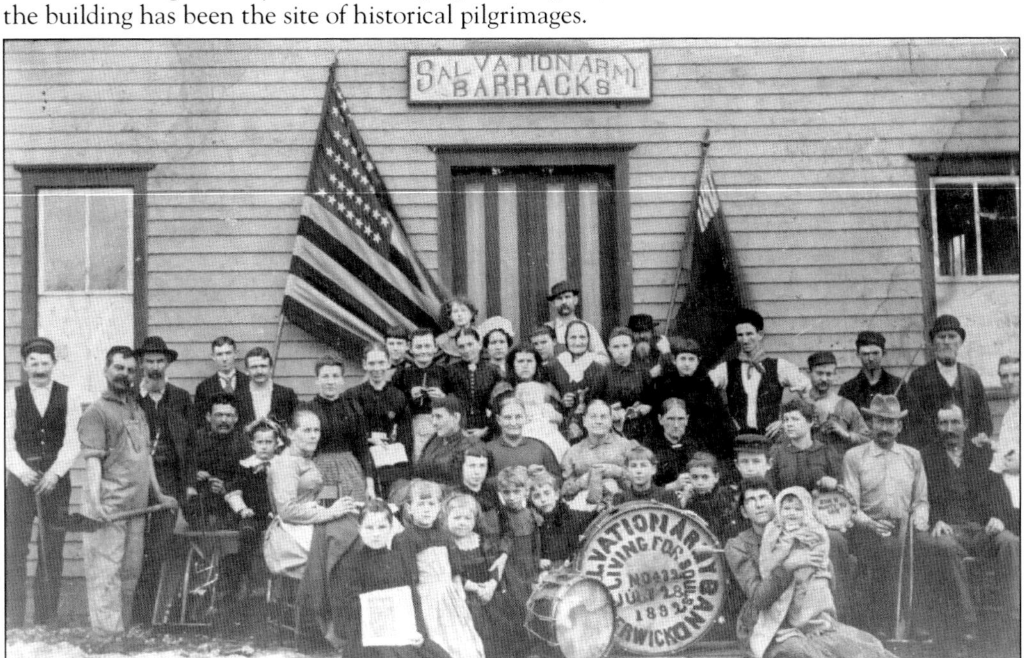


**SALVATION ARMY BARRACKS IN BERWICK, 1892.** At the time this photograph was taken in 1892, the barracks was located on the southeast corner of Market and Cemetery Streets in Berwick. The membership of the Salvation Army in Berwick was quite large. Captain Fuss was the commander at the time.

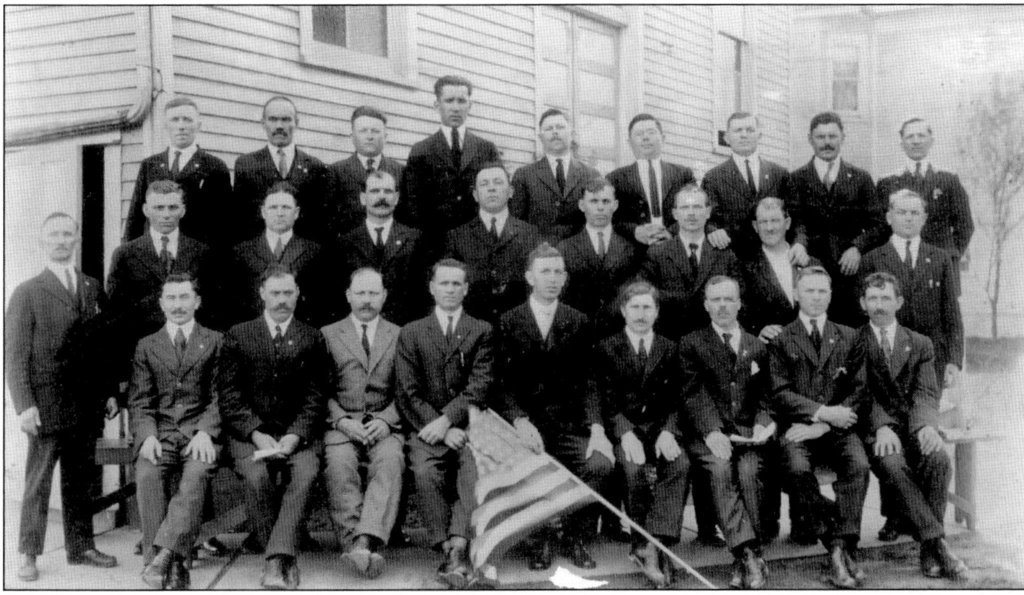

**CITIZENSHIP CLASS, 1921.** This group of Russian immigrants is pictured in front of Holy Annunciation Russian Orthodox Church in Berwick. Last names only are given for those pictured here. From left to right are (first row) Yevich Jr., Laytar, Basala, Pirnik, DeLong, Yevich Sr., Hamalyak, Jurbala, and Berbich; (second row) Mihaly, Rusinko, Kutchka, Stenko, Patrick, Yedinak, Oram, Karas, and Wladika; (third row) Radvak, Kutzarik, Kost, Harrison, Kundrat, Matzko, Korba, Krepich, and Lacomey. (Courtesy of Beverly Parker.)

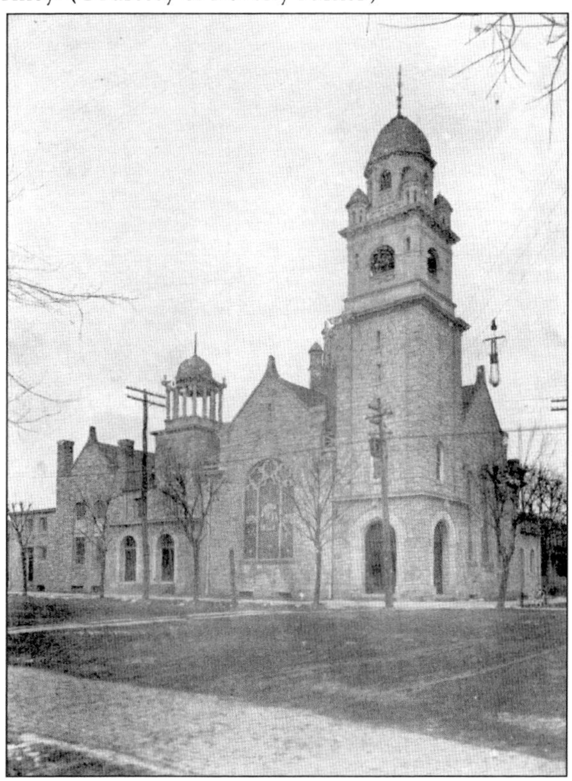

**FIRST UNITED METHODIST CHURCH.** This Berwick church traces its roots to 1792 when it was visited by circuit rider Rev. William Colbert. It became an organized church in 1805. Located at the corner of Market and Second Streets, the church is known for its stained-glass windows and unique tower. It also is the point at which the annual Run for the Diamonds begins every Thanksgiving.

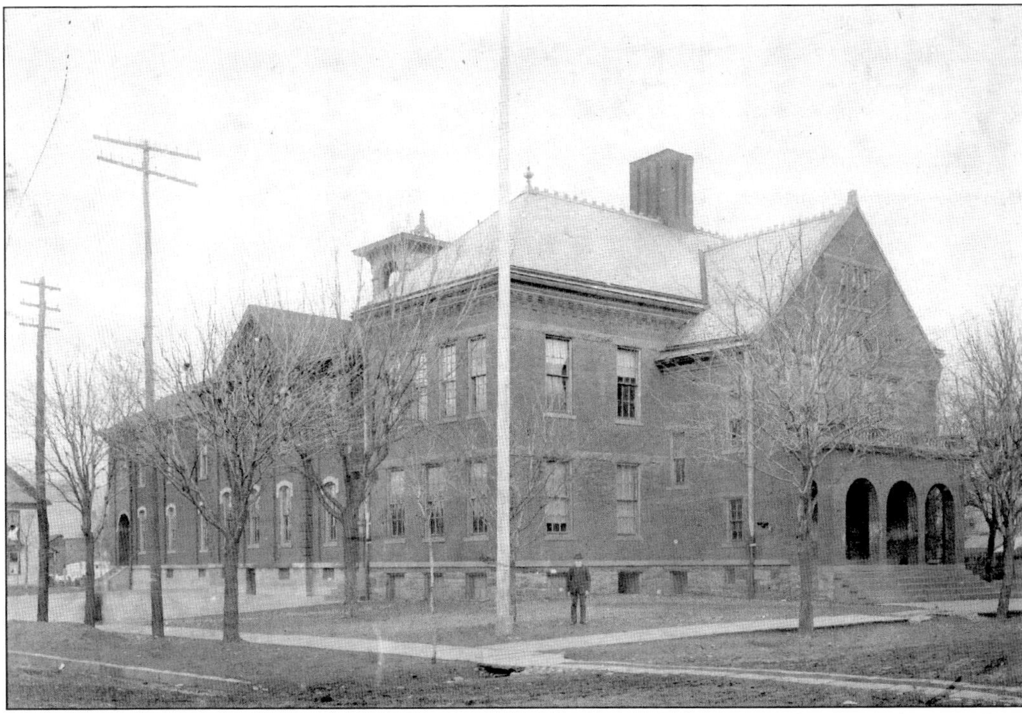

**MARKET STREET SCHOOL, BERWICK.** This building opened in 1870 and was used as a school for over a century, until 1974. Additions were made in 1875 and 1893. The building was later used to house offices of the school district. It has since been torn down to make way for the new public library.

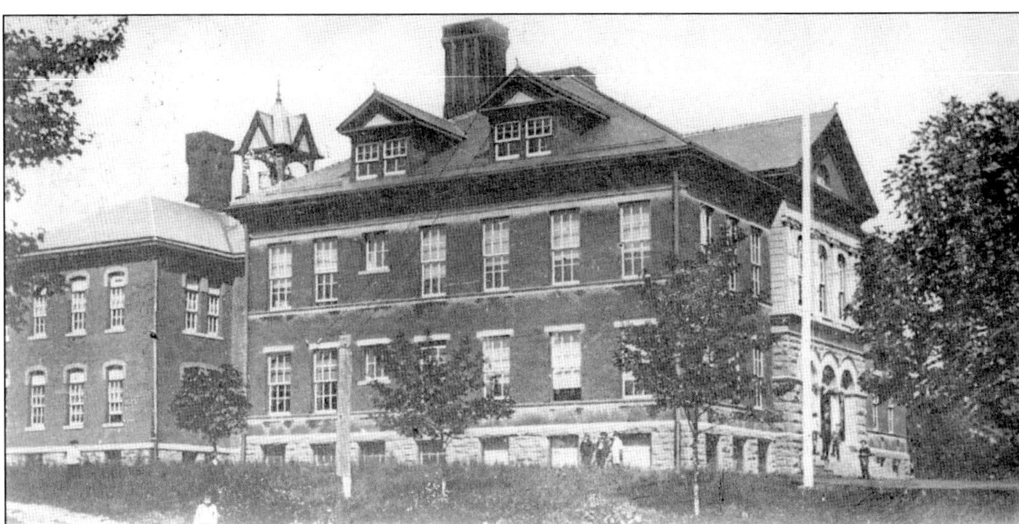

**BERWICK HIGH SCHOOL, C. 1906.** The main portion of the building was erected in 1876 on West Third Street. Additions were made in 1901 and again in 1920, when Berwick and West Berwick were consolidated. The building served as a high school until 1959 and a junior high until 1975. The YMCA was housed in the additions in recent years, and the original building was razed to provide parking for it.

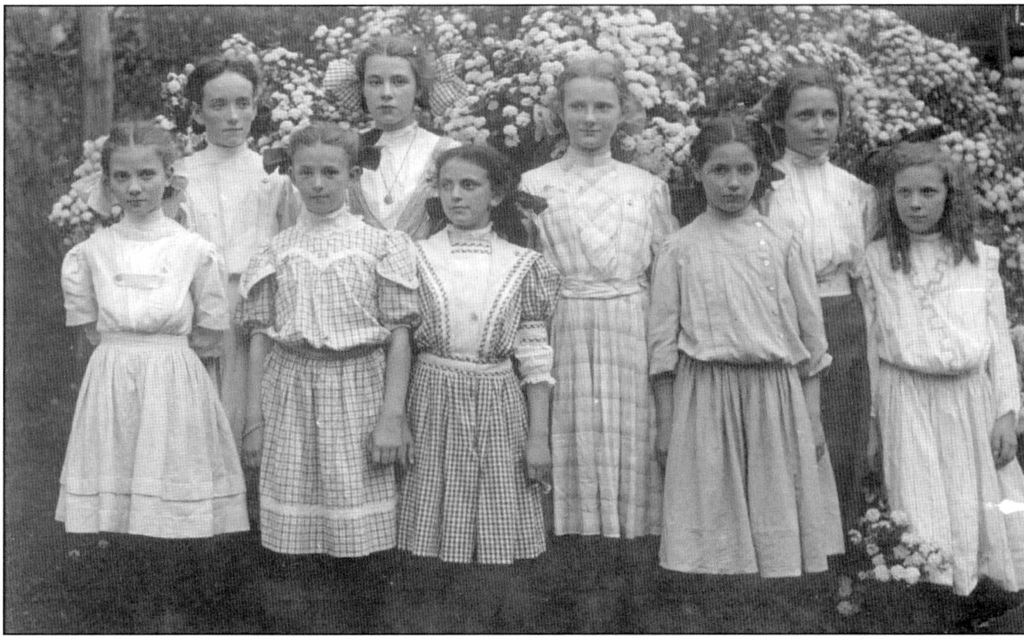

**RED CROSS CLUB IN BERWICK, 1908.** American Red Cross clubs were formed and still exist throughout the country in schools and colleges. Students who belong are involved in offering Red Cross–related services to their schools and communities. Some of those services include disaster relief, health and safety awareness, coordinating and helping with blood drives, and other community service projects.

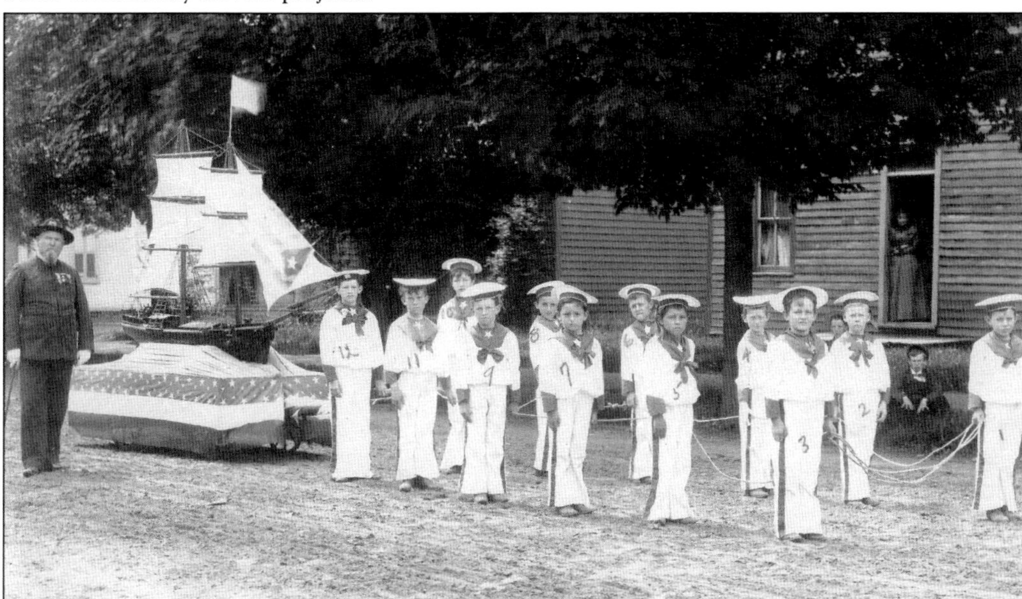

**BOYS' DRILL TEAM.** The boys are in formation for a Berwick parade in 1897. The team was coached by Col. A. D. Seely, a Civil War veteran and Berwick's drillmaster. The boys from left to right are Haber Distlehurst, Ernest Finch, Fred Fowler, George Linville, Herb Levy, Frank Laubach, Chester Hughes, Elmer Young, Casper Frantz, Paul Fowler, Ray Stackhouse, and Theodore Heller.

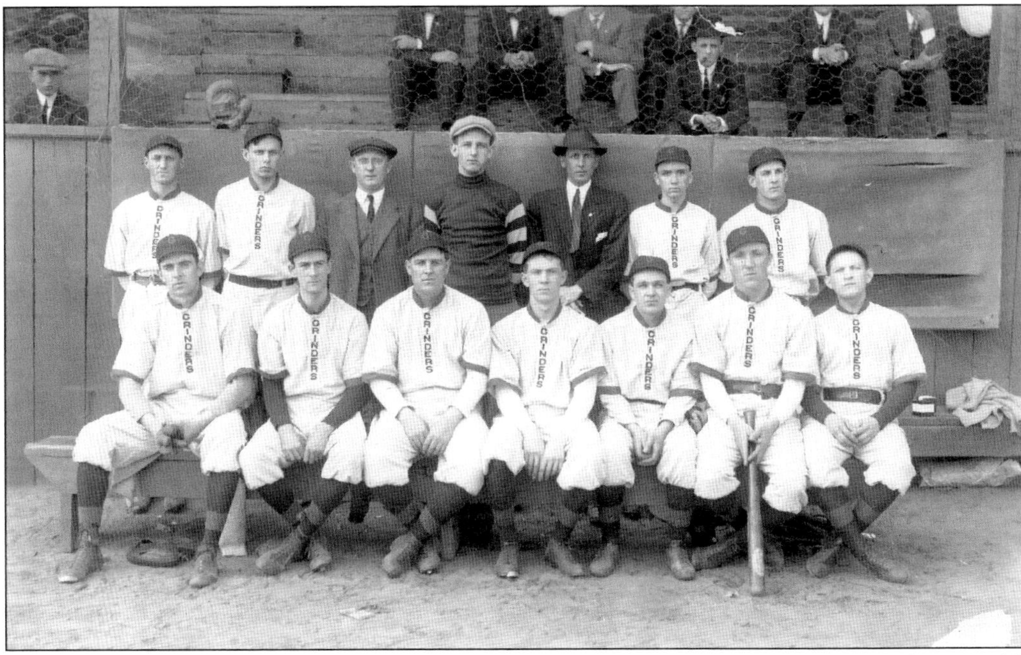

**GRINDERS' CLUB.** Organized in 1911, the club was originally a debating society that quickly expanded to include social and athletic activities. The club forbade intoxicants and gambling on its premises. In 1912, the club won the pennant in the Pennsylvania League of baseball clubs. It won first prize in 1913 in a New York parade for its presentation of *Uncle Tom's Cabin*.

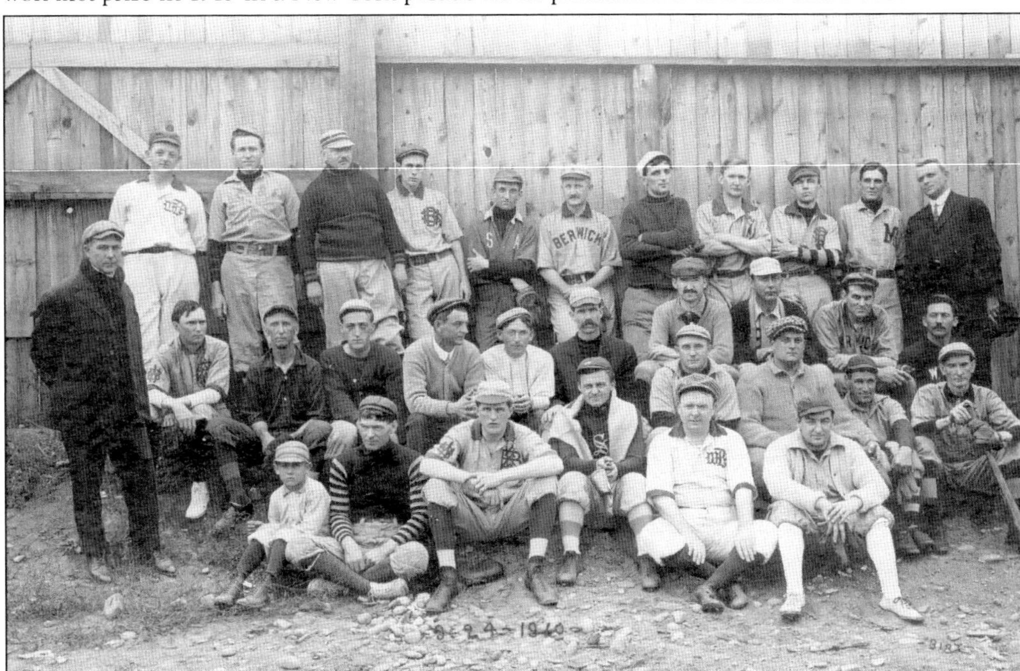

**BERWICK BASEBALL TEAM.** This photograph is dated September 24, 1910. The identities are not known. Every town and village had a baseball team—it was and continues to be one of America's favorite pastimes.

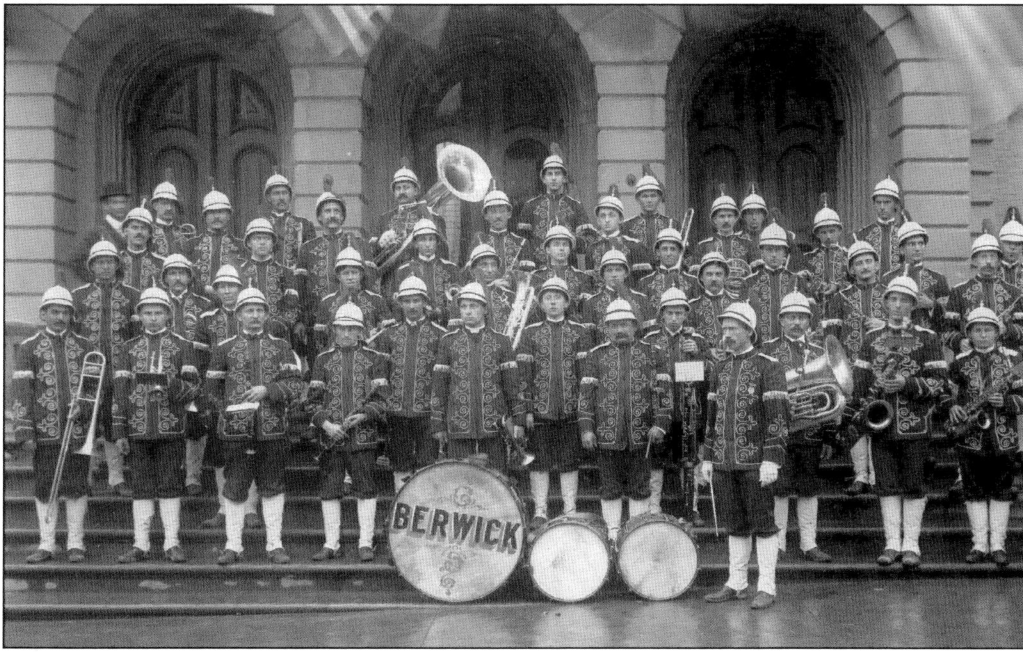


**Berwick Band, 1890.** Organized in 1868, the band made its first public appearance on Decoration Day on May 30, 1870. It marched to the top of the hill and began to play, but just as the first note was blown, a ceremonial cannon nearby roared in a tremendous explosion that shook the earth, stopped the band music, and split the lips of most of the players.

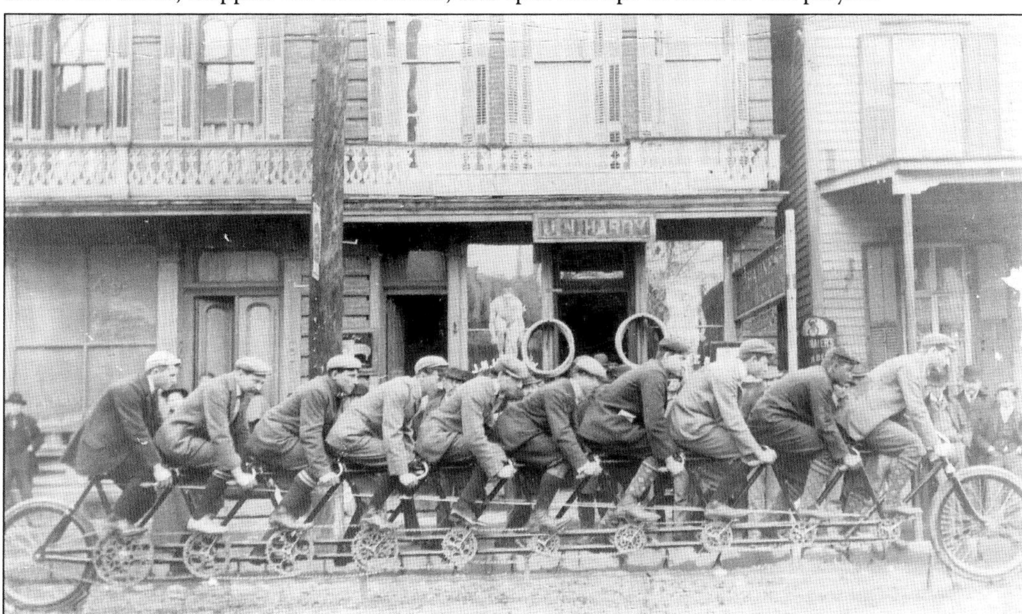

**The Oriten in Berwick, 1898.** Charles Metz built the 10-seat Oriten in 1896 for the Orient Bicycle Company in Waltham, Massachusetts. The bicycle weighed 305 pounds, was 23 feet long, and had no brakes or gears. Shown here from left to right are John Harry, Charles Harry, George Harry, James Harry, William McMichael, Ralph Laubach, Edward Averill, Bruce Kepner, Edwin Schenk, and Charles Brittain.

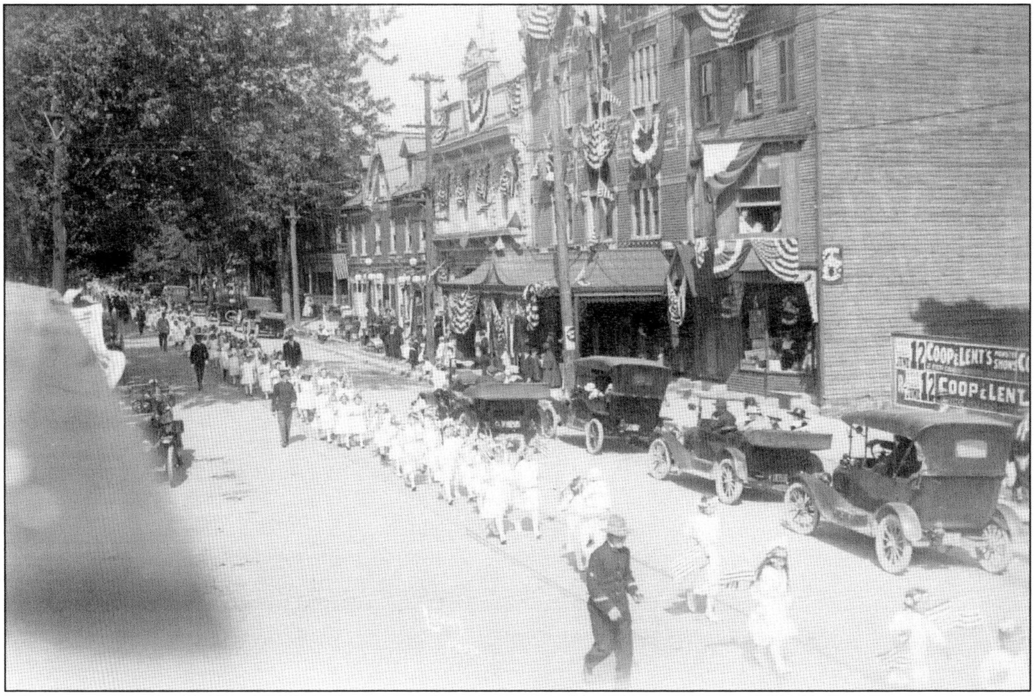

**PATRIOTIC CELEBRATION, 1917.** Although the occasion is not known, the spirit of patriotism is clear, as evidenced by the buntings and the children parading with flags. Besides a number of vintage cars, there are trolley tracks, the Palace Theatre, and a sign reading "Singer Sewing Machines."

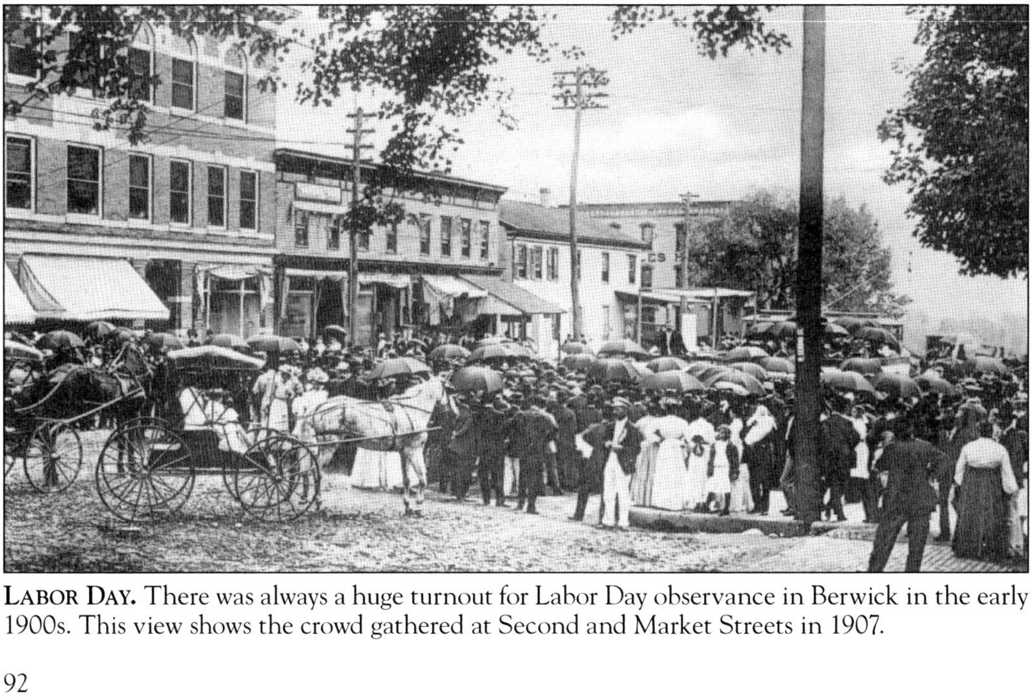

**LABOR DAY.** There was always a huge turnout for Labor Day observance in Berwick in the early 1900s. This view shows the crowd gathered at Second and Market Streets in 1907.

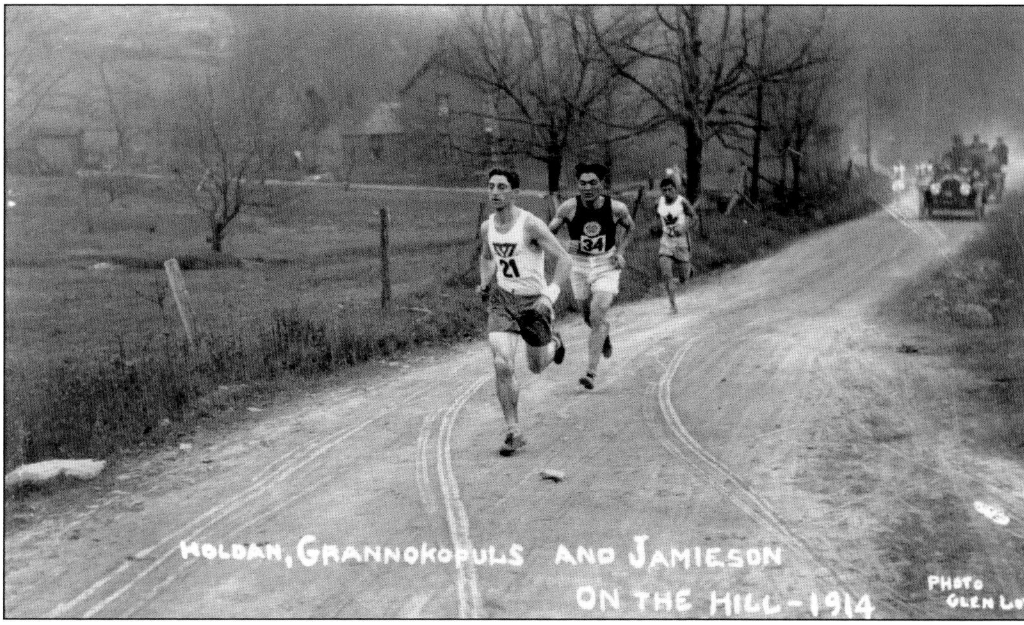


**Run for the Diamonds, 1914.** On this fair, mild, and calm day in 1914, George Holden of New York City leads the field cresting the one-and-a-half-mile hill. Holden won the race before a crowd estimated at 15,000 to 20,000 spectators. The winning margin was less than 10 seconds, and the winning time was 50 minutes, 29 seconds. Other runners pictured are Nick Grannokopulis and Arthur Jamieson. (Courtesy of Margaret Livsey.)

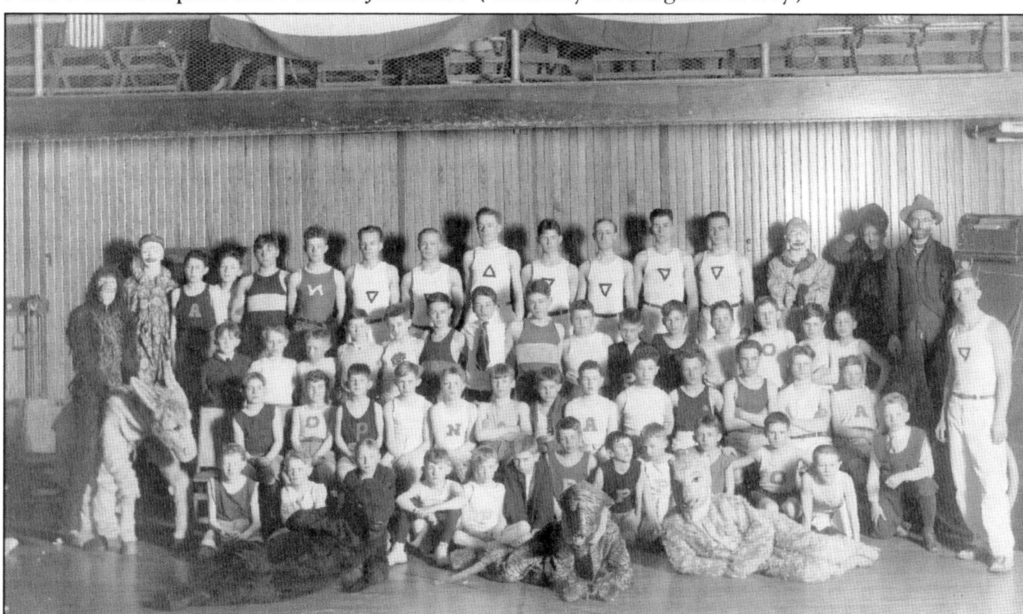

**YMCA Circus, 1914.** Initially called the Industrial Young Men's Christian Association of Greater Berwick, the old Berwick YMCA building at Second and Market Streets was erected in 1884 for $30,000 and contained a 5,000-volume library, considered one of the best in the area. By 1914, the building included a gymnasium, swimming pool, and bowling alley. This photograph shows children posing for a circus day picture in the gymnasium in 1914.

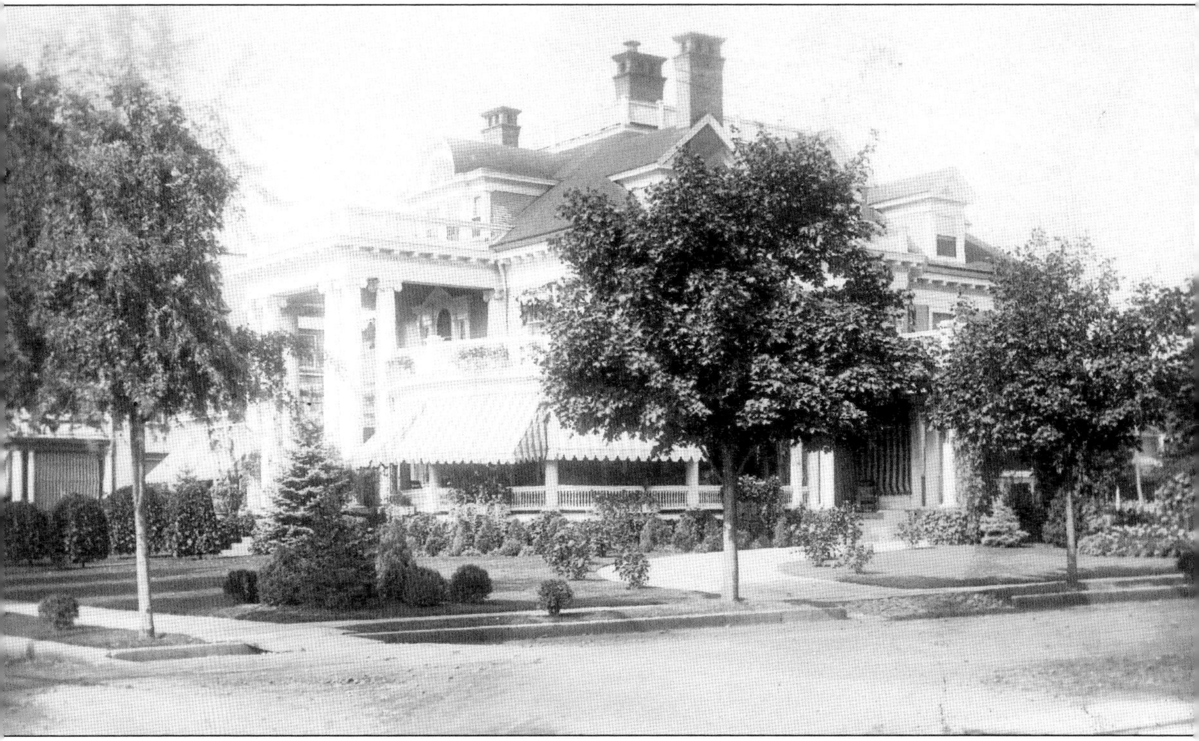

**CRISPIN MANSION.** This embellished Georgian-style house was built in 1903 by Frederick Eaton, president of American Car and Foundry, and his wife, Elizabeth Furman, during an era of prosperity due to the expansion of the industrial firm. The house was given to their daughter Mae Lovely Eaton upon her marriage to Clarence Crispin in 1904. The mansion stands today mostly unchanged along East Berwick's riverfront promenade.

# *Five*

# River Communities

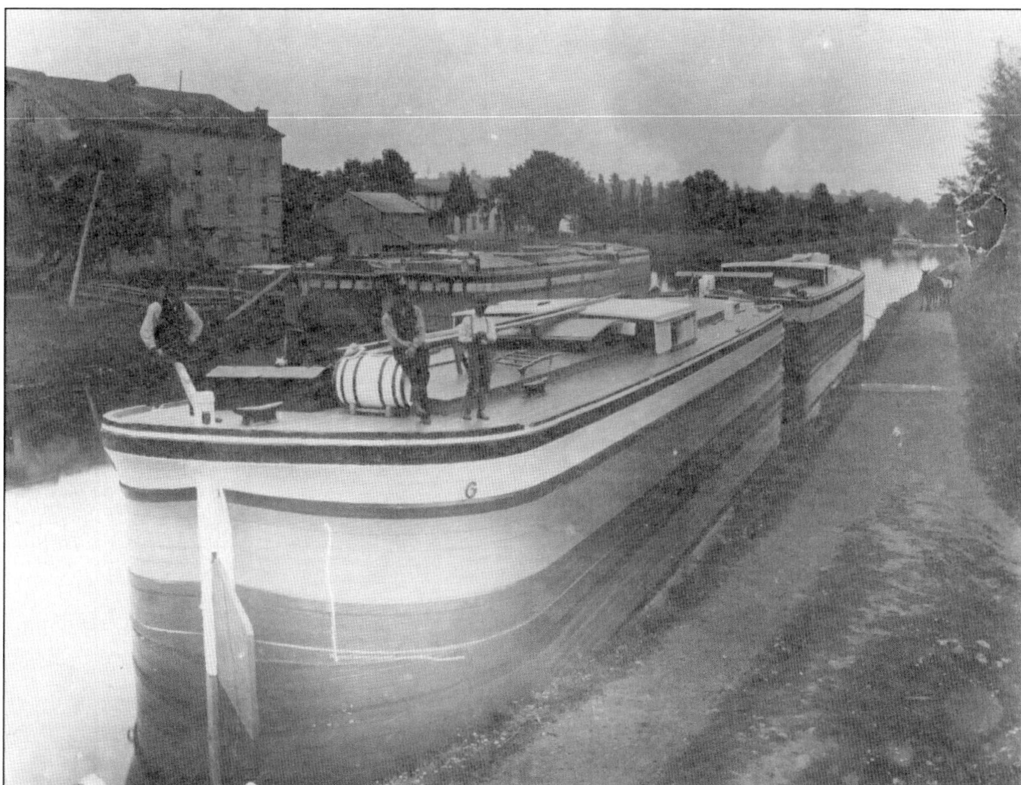

**Canal Boat, Espy.** The canal boats shown here were 65 feet long and carried 15 tons of merchandise. The boats were pulled at about four miles per hour by horses or mules walking on the towpath, seen at the right. Many attempts were made to make the boats faster by mechanical means before the invention of steam, but none seemed to work.

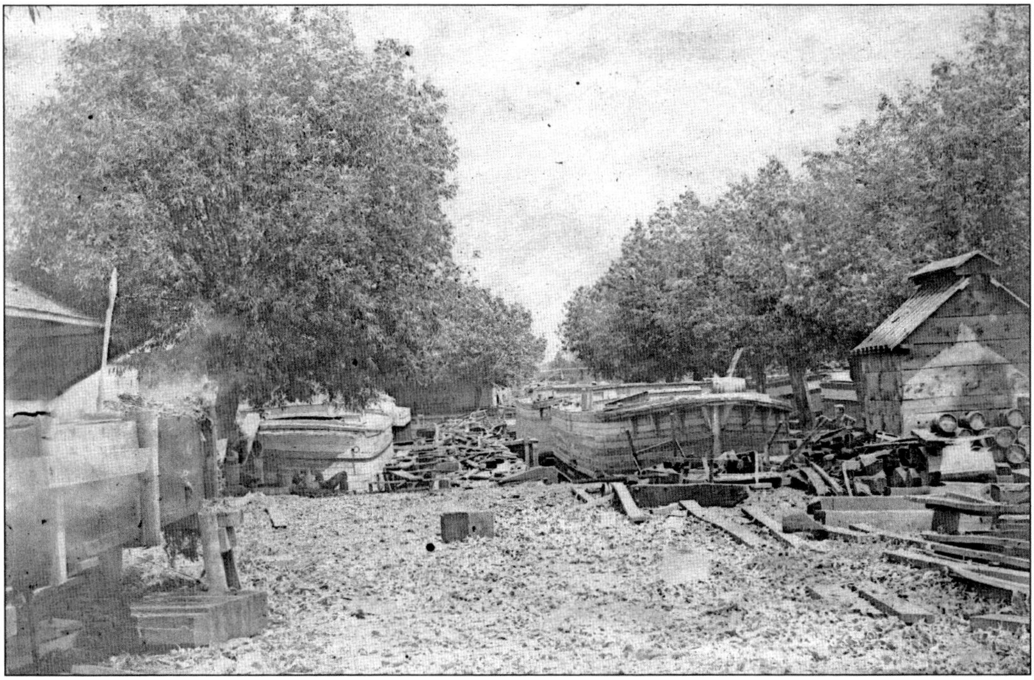

**ESPY BOATYARD.** The first canal boat was built by George and Thomas Webb in 1834 in Espy. The canal boat business sprang up quickly with the following companies: Barton and Edgar; Kressler and Vansickle; Fowler, Tronsue, and McKamey; and the Pennsylvania Canal Company. The Pennsylvania Canal Company bought the others and prospered until 1901, when the boatyard was destroyed.

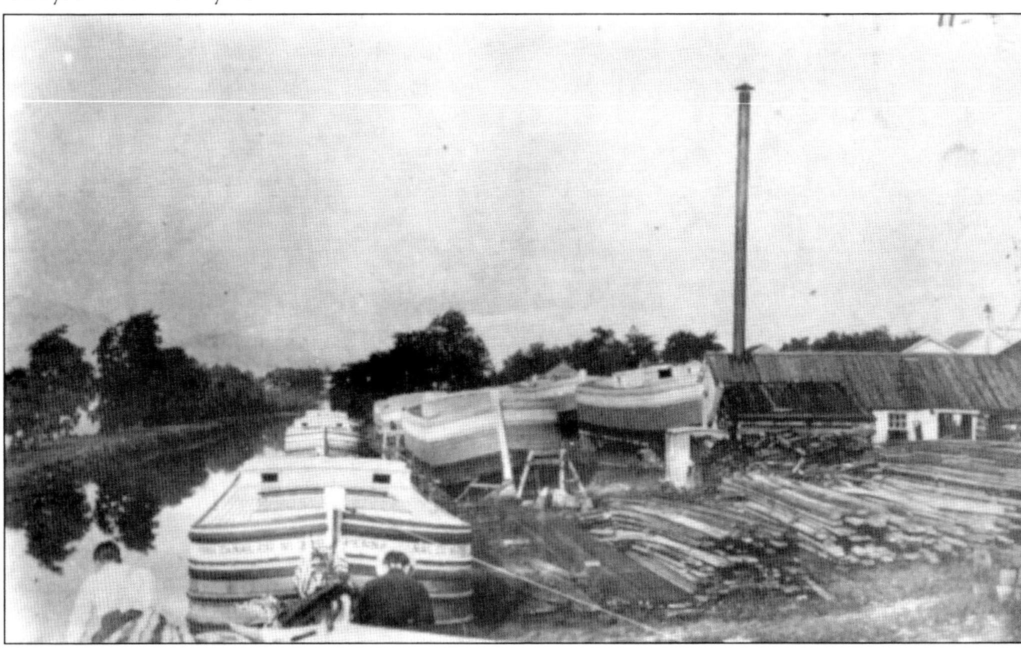

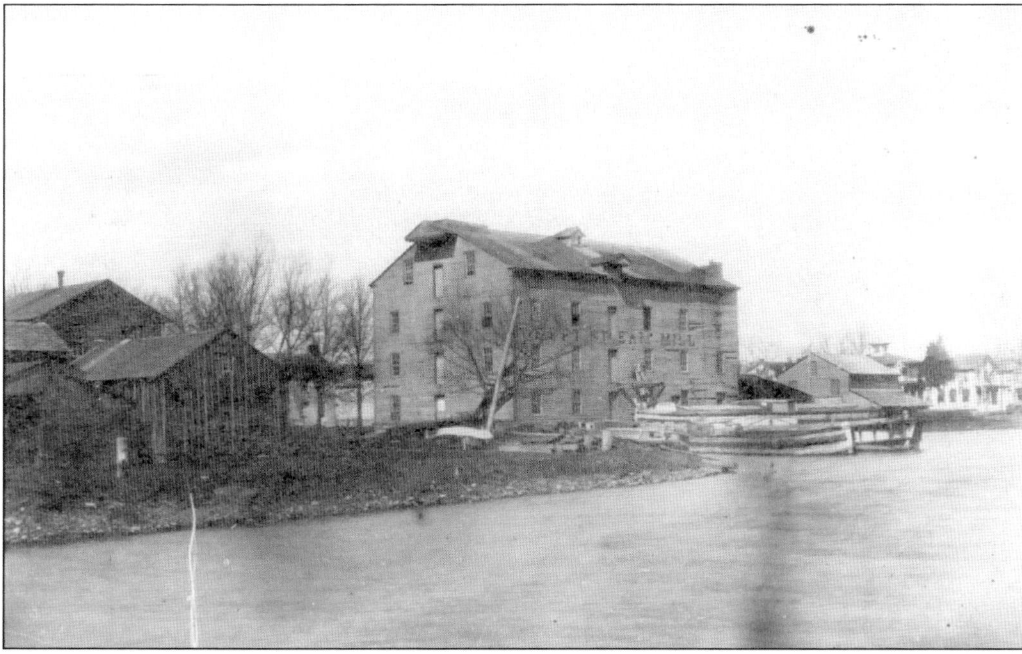

**ESPY STEAM MILL.** The Espy Steam Mill was part of the Espy boatyard. It was located beside the Espy basin, a wide point in the canal. Steam was used to bend the lumber that was used in making the canal boats. The boatyards turned out 50 new boats every year and repaired 200. The steam mill was probably destroyed along with the boatyards in 1901.

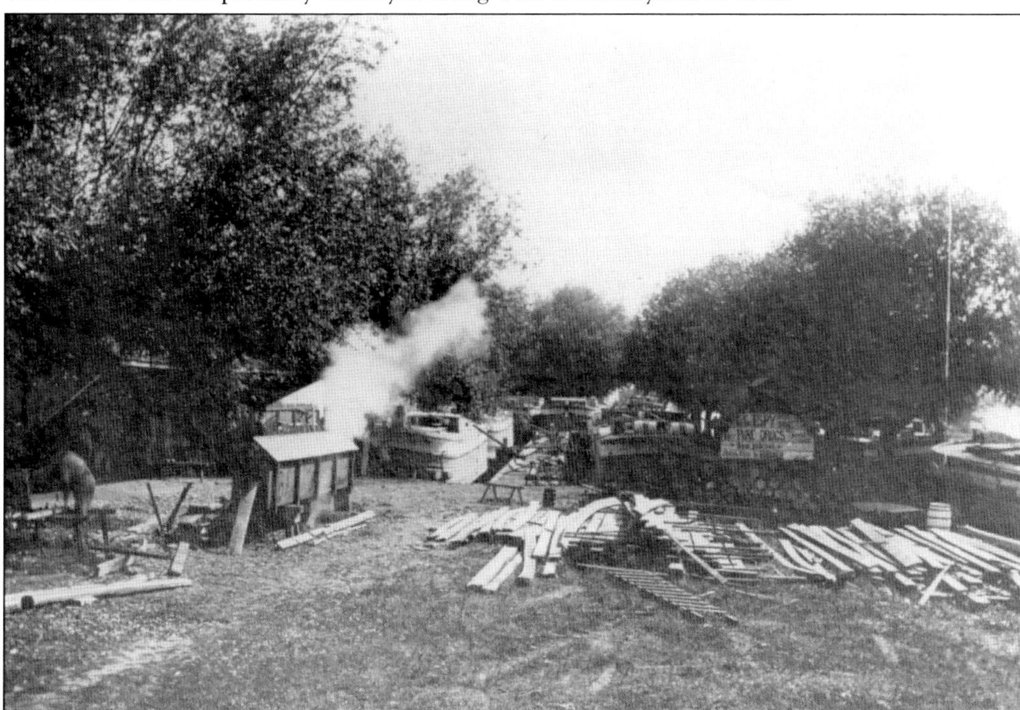

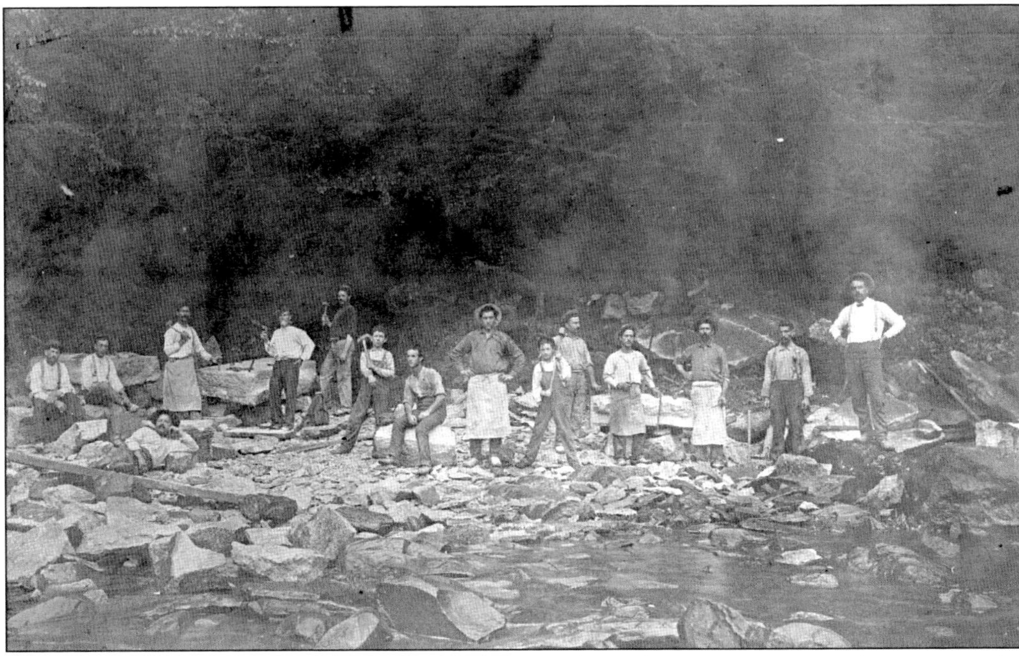

**MIFFLINVILLE BRIDGE CONSTRUCTION WORKERS.** Shown here are workers at the construction site of the Mifflinville Bridge in 1907. The work was well under way with three spans completed when the flood of 1904 destroyed the bridge. The work was resumed and was progressing when, in December 1907, a second flood caused the entire span to collapse. Forty men went down with the bridge; all but seven were rescued. The bridge was finally completed and opened for travel in 1908. (Courtesy of Mifflinville Village Committee.)

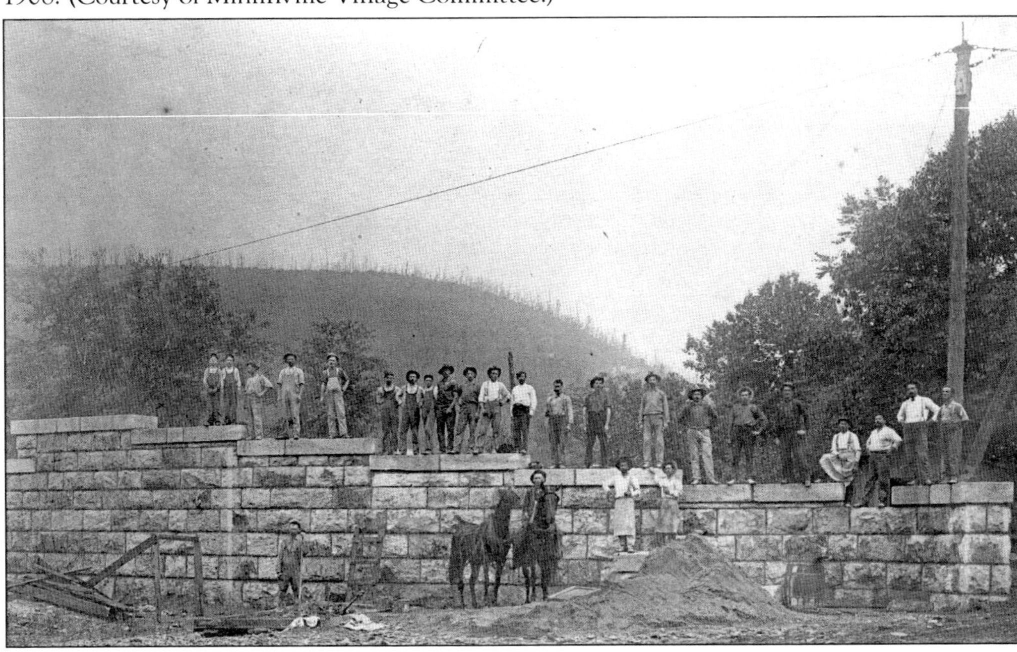

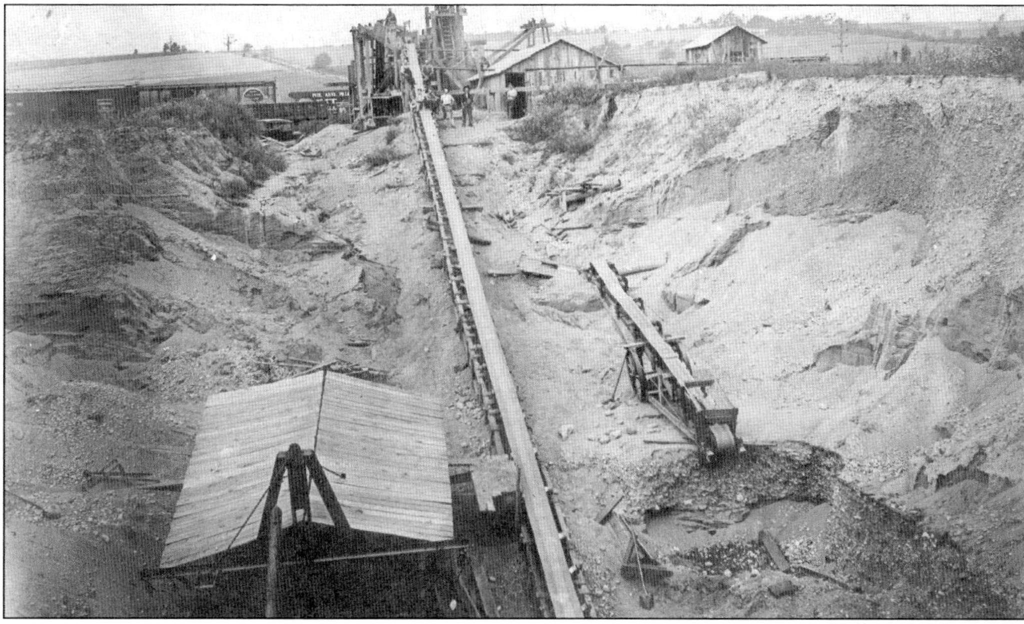

**The Sand Pit at Lime Ridge.** The sand pit was most likely part of the limestone quarries developed by Abram Miller in the early 1800s. Isaac Low, Miller's son-in-law, soon joined him in business. Sand was used in the production of lime, limestone, and cement products. Limestone was used in iron making in Danville and Bloomsburg. Lime was used for mortar in the construction of the first brick buildings in Wilkes-Barre.

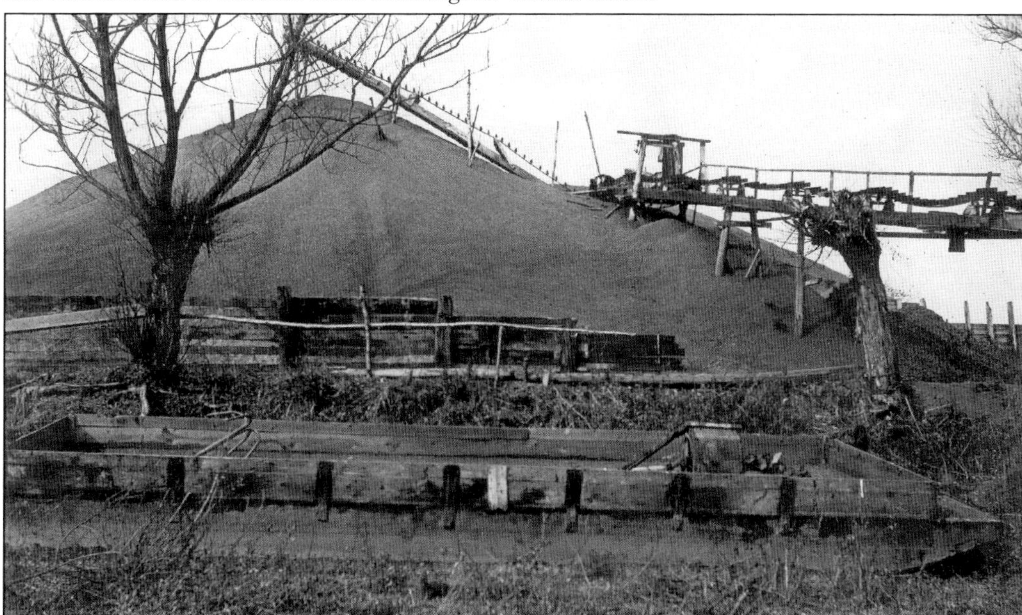

**River Coal, c. 1920.** A large pile of river coal rests alongside the Susquehanna River between Bloomsburg and Espy. The riverbed held vast quantities of coal fragments deposited there by floods and runoff coming from the tributaries throughout the anthracite mining areas. In the latter part of the 19th century, dredging the river to extract the free coal became an industry. It continued into the mid-20th century.

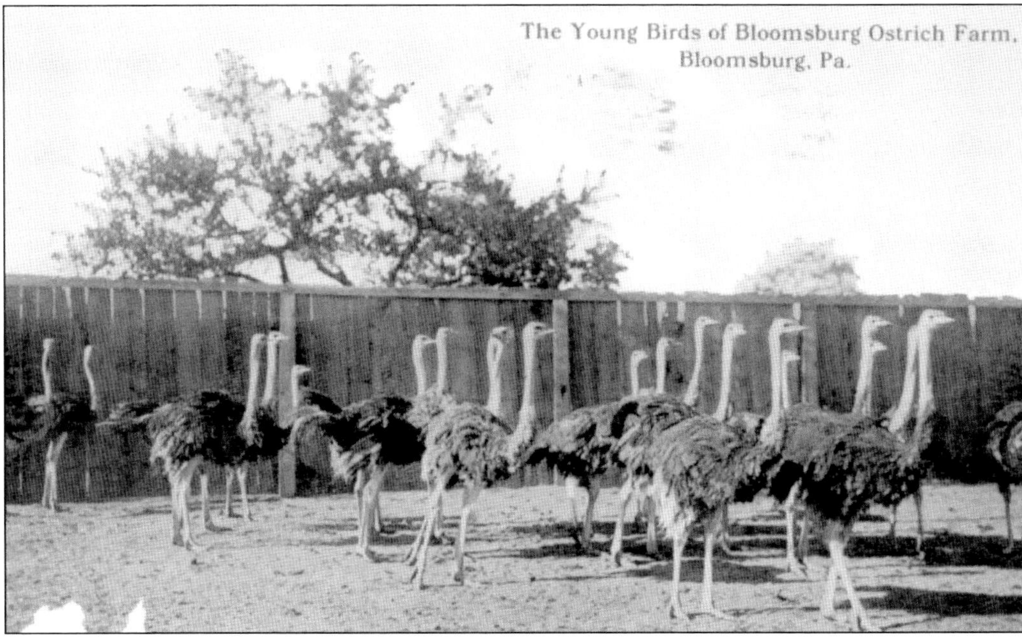


**BLOOMSBURG OSTRICH FARM AND FEATHER COMPANY.** In 1910, the Bloomsburg Ostrich Farm and Feather Company, also known as the African Farm and Feather Company, was the first and only ostrich farm in a northern latitude. It was located at present-day Edgar Avenue and Old Berwick Road in Espy. President and founder W. H. Hile procured the first of his stock in Africa. He developed the farm into a showplace and a tourist destination. There was great demand for the plumes for use in ladies' hats and as home decorations. The operation was short-lived, as the demand died out when fashions changed.

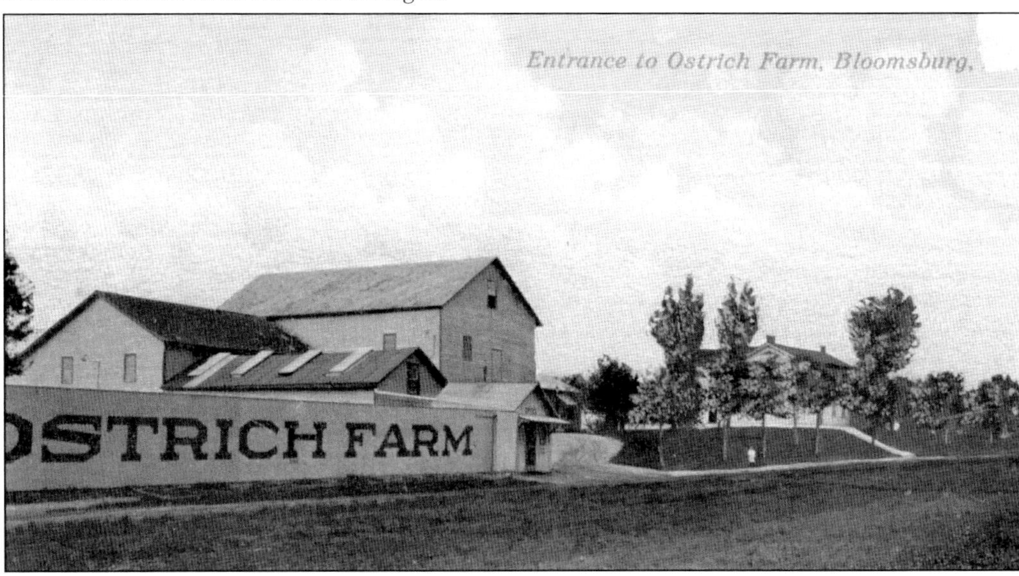

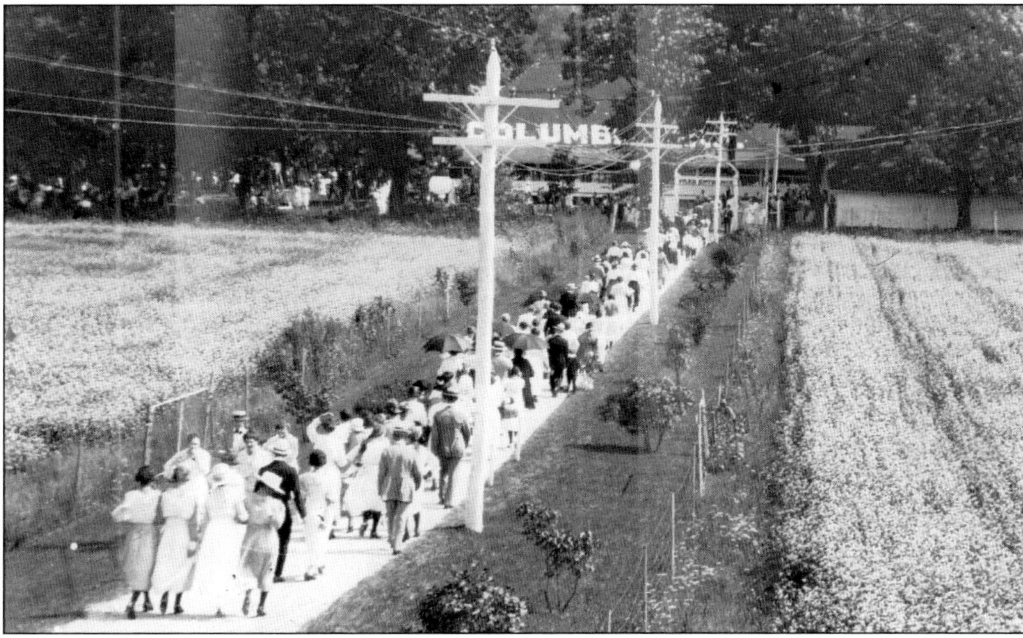

**Columbia Park.** Columbia Park, located just east of Lime Ridge, was an amusement resort operated by the trolley company. It was originally known as Shawnee Park, named for the tribe of Native Americans who formerly made their home there. The trolley company renamed it Columbia Park and outfitted it with amusement devices, swings, pavilions, a swimming pool, and summer cottages available to rent. For nearly 20 years, it was the most popular spot along the trolley line, as county residents came for eating, dancing, games, and athletic events. Admission was free. The above photograph shows the pathway to the entrance around 1910. The photograph below shows the pavilion. (Above, courtesy of Bloomsburg University Archives.)

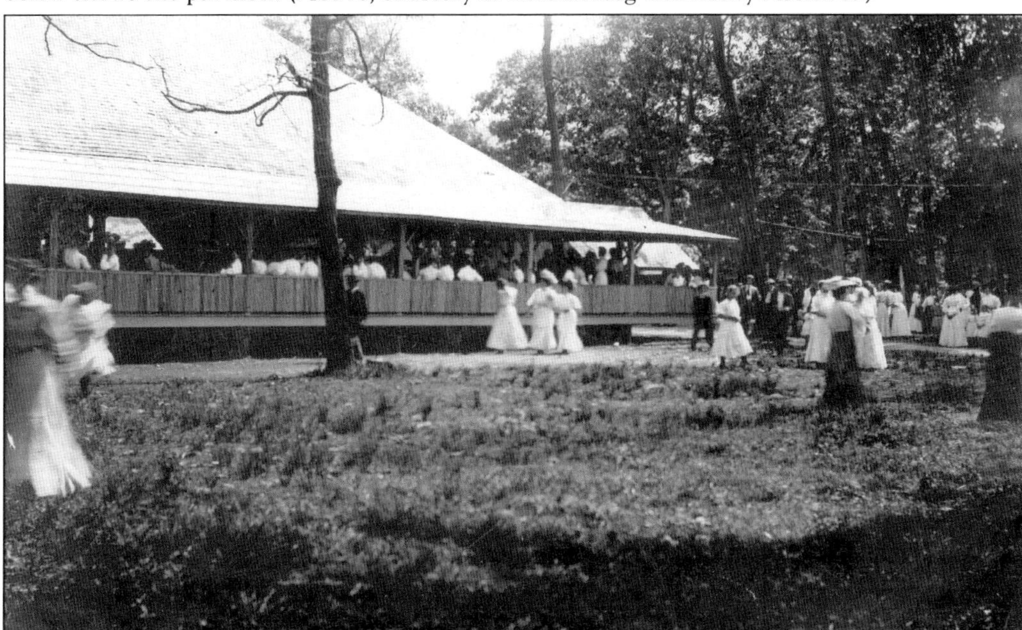

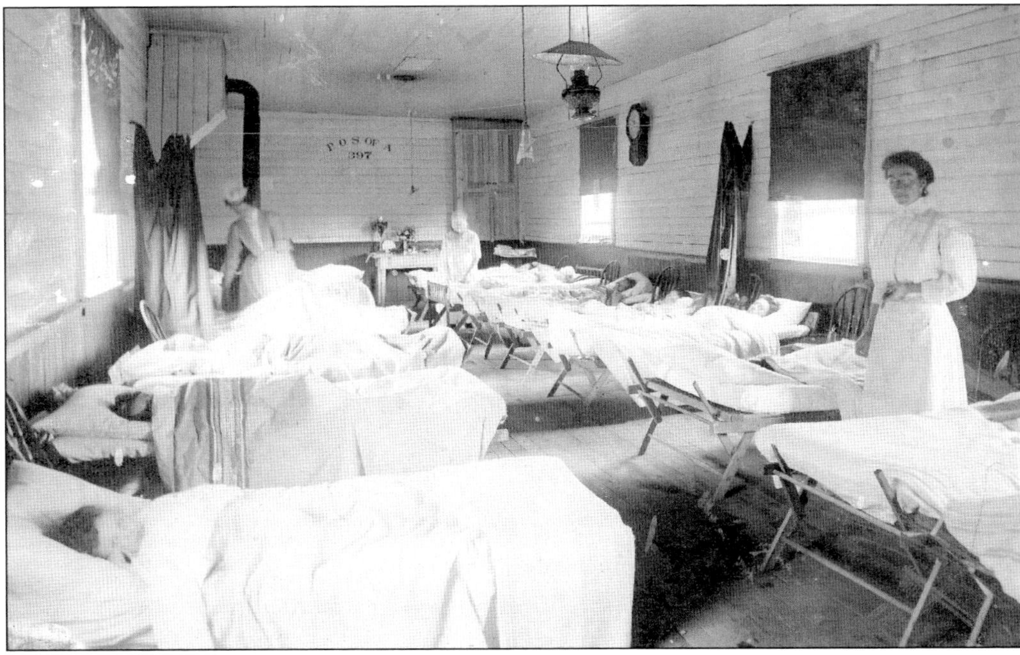


**LIME RIDGE PATRIOTIC ORDER SONS OF AMERICA.** Camp 397, Patriotic Order Sons of America, served as a temporary hospital in the August 1910 typhoid epidemic. Detective work revealed the epidemic was caused by impure milk. Many of the victims ate ice cream made from that milk. Twenty-one cases were treated.

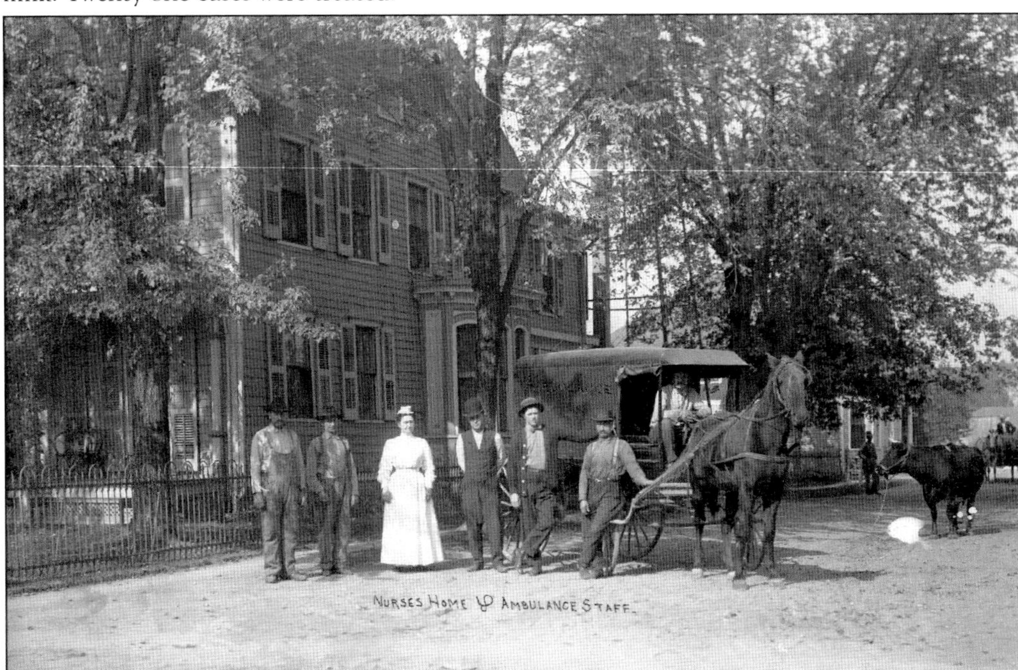


**LIME RIDGE NURSES' HOME.** The nurses' home and ambulance staff at Lime Ridge were located at the intersection of Lowe's Road and Old Berwick Road. This photograph was probably taken in 1910 during the typhoid epidemic.

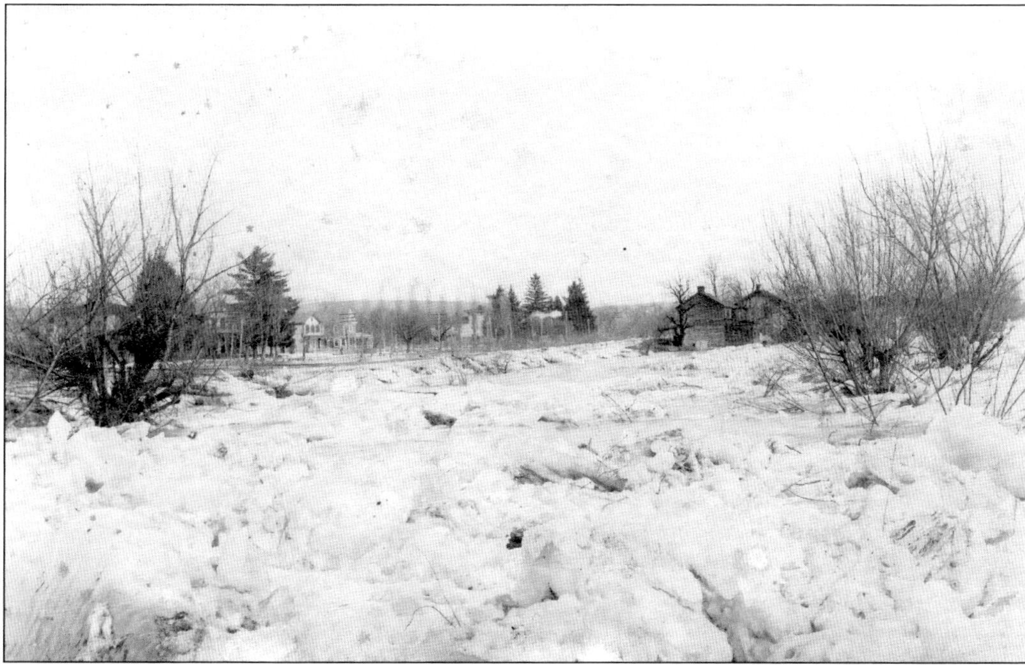

**FLOOD, MARCH 1904.** This is a view of the Susquehanna River at Espy showing ice and water from the March 1904 flood. Old Berwick Road is visible in the background.

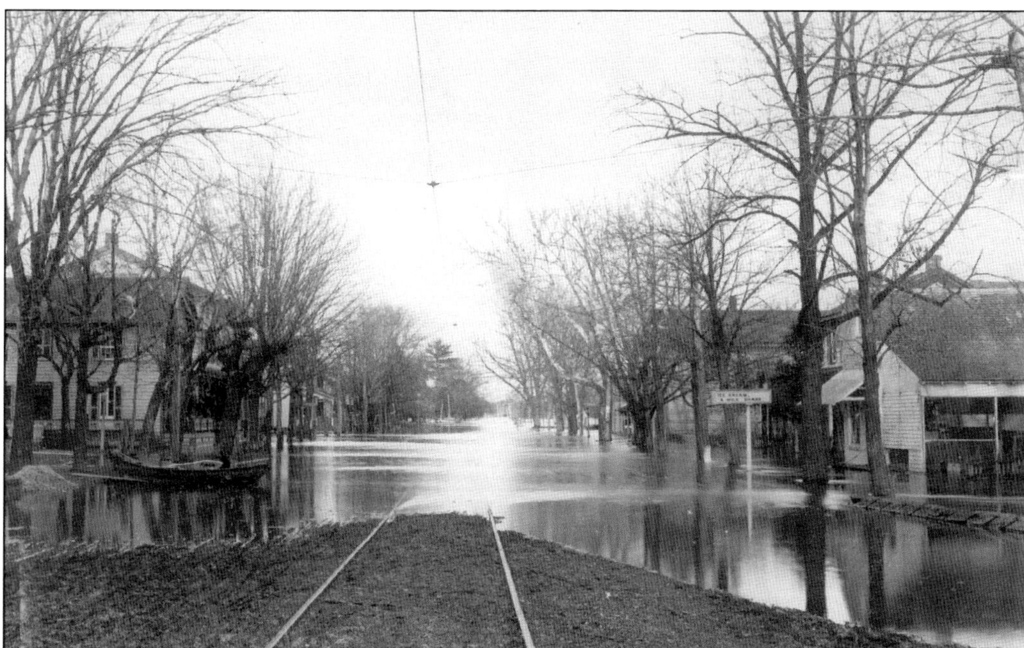

**FLOOD SCENE, 1904.** Old Berwick Road and the trolley tracks running through Espy are under water thanks to the 1904 spring flood. The rowboat seen in the foreground at left was the only dependable means of transportation in this situation, and even after the water receded, the unpaved road was a sea of mud. The sign in front of the store at right reads, "Ice Cream & Milk Shake."

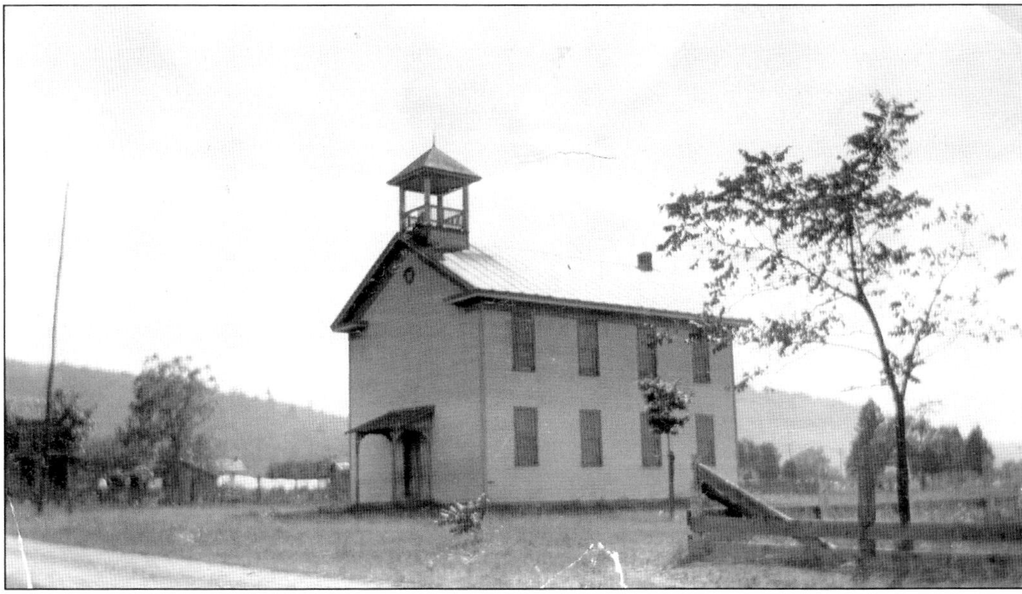

**Almedia School House.** Almedia was once known as Afton. It was home to one school, Almedia School House. First through fourth grades were taught on the first floor. Grades five through eight were on the second floor.

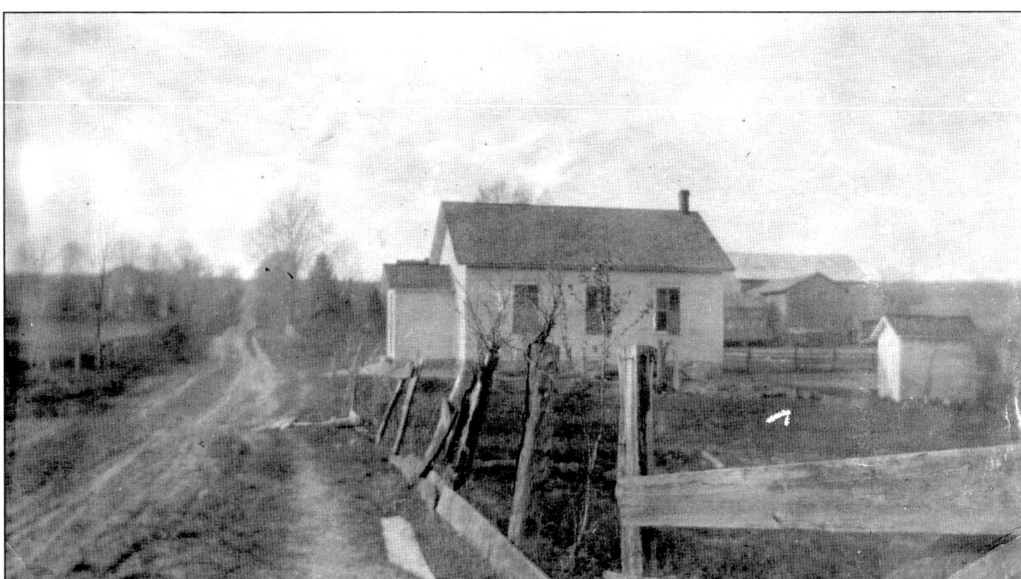

**The Miller School.** The Miller School was located near the limestone quarry in Lime Ridge north on Keefer's Lane. The school was in use during the late 1800s and early 1900s, and it has since been torn down. The earliest schools in Centre Township were taught in private homes, as was common in early days.

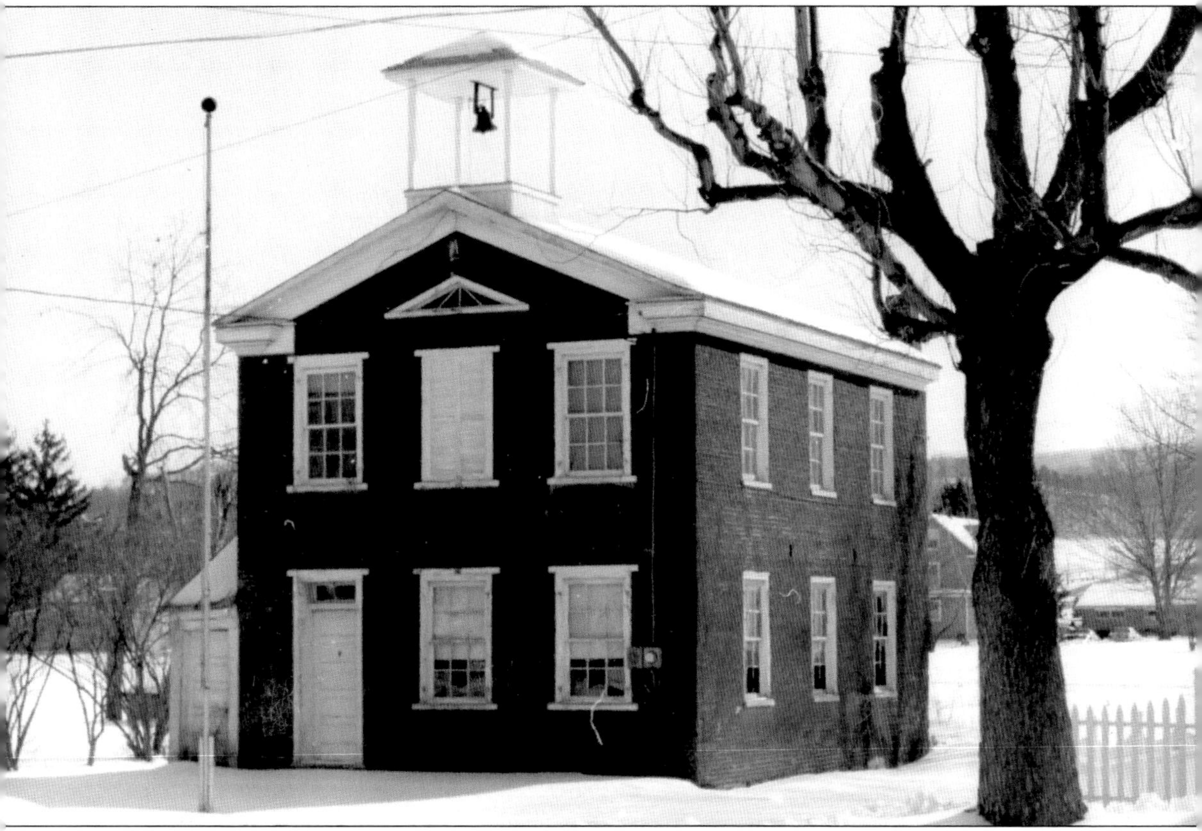

**MIFFLINVILLE GERMAN SCHOOL.** On Third Street in Mifflinville, the German college, built around 1850, was intended to serve the children of German-speaking residents. These citizens who came from Berks and Lehigh Counties wanted to retain their culture through the language and were reluctant to have their children learn English. Eventually it became a public school and also served as a meeting hall for the Patriotic Order Sons of America.

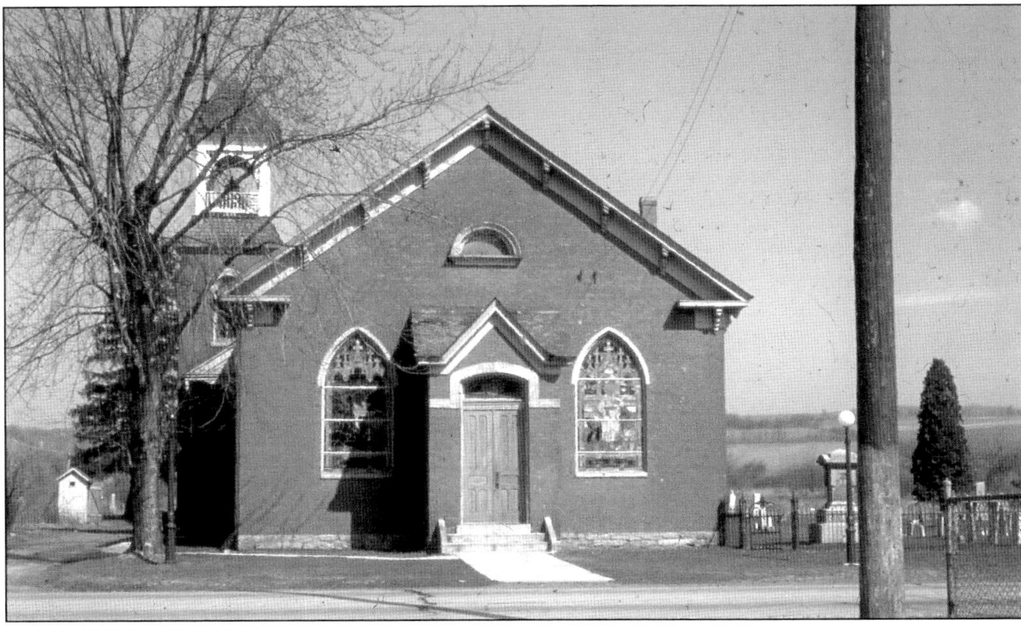

**LIME RIDGE UNITED METHODIST CHURCH.** The congregation of the Lime Ridge United Methodist Church was formed in 1832 and met in private homes. In 1834, land was donated for a church. Everyone contributed materials, money, and labor for eight years, and the church was dedicated in 1842. A tornado damaged the belfry in the late 1800s. Today it is still a functioning church.

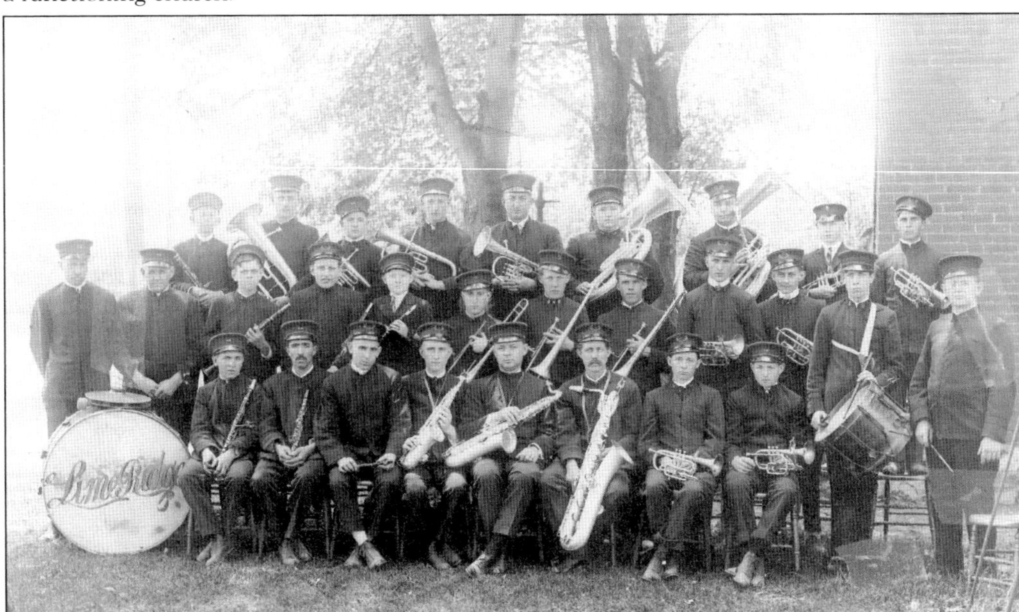


**LIME RIDGE BAND.** At the start of the 1900s, it was estimated that there were at least 15,000 small-town bands. The members were amateur musicians recruited from the ranks of the townsmen. The Lime Ridge Band had 29 members of varying ages and with an assortment of instruments. This small community, established in the mid-1840s and originally known as Centreville, was halfway between Bloomsburg and Berwick.

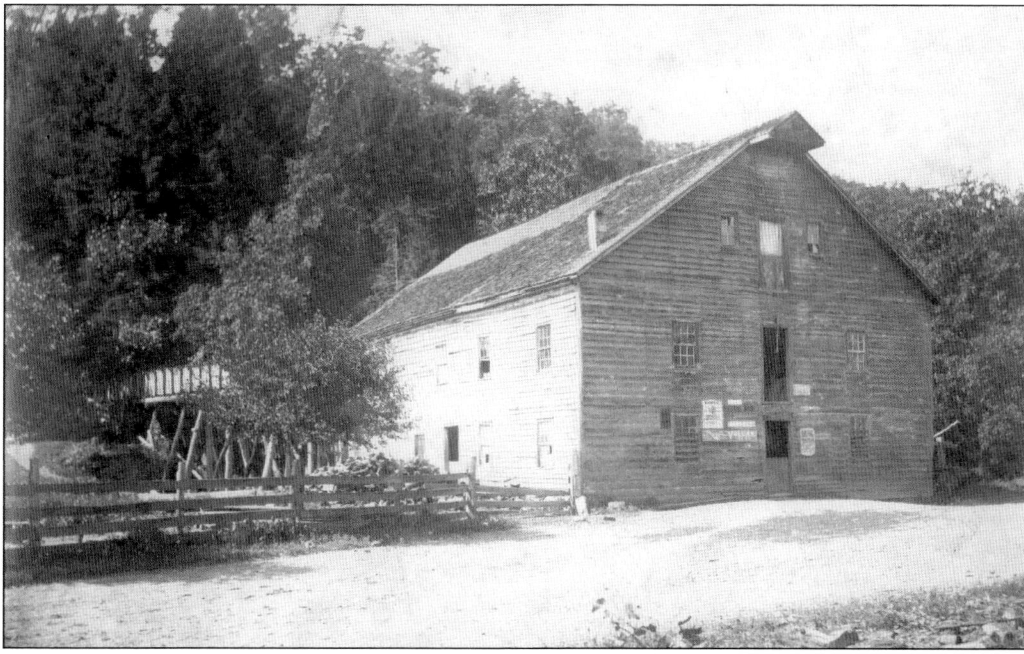

**BROWN'S MILL.** Brown's Mill, near Mifflinville, was built by John Brown soon after the Wyoming massacre of 1778. It had the capacity to grind 100 bushels of buckwheat per day. It was the second-oldest gristmill in the county. (Courtesy of Mifflinville Village Committee.)

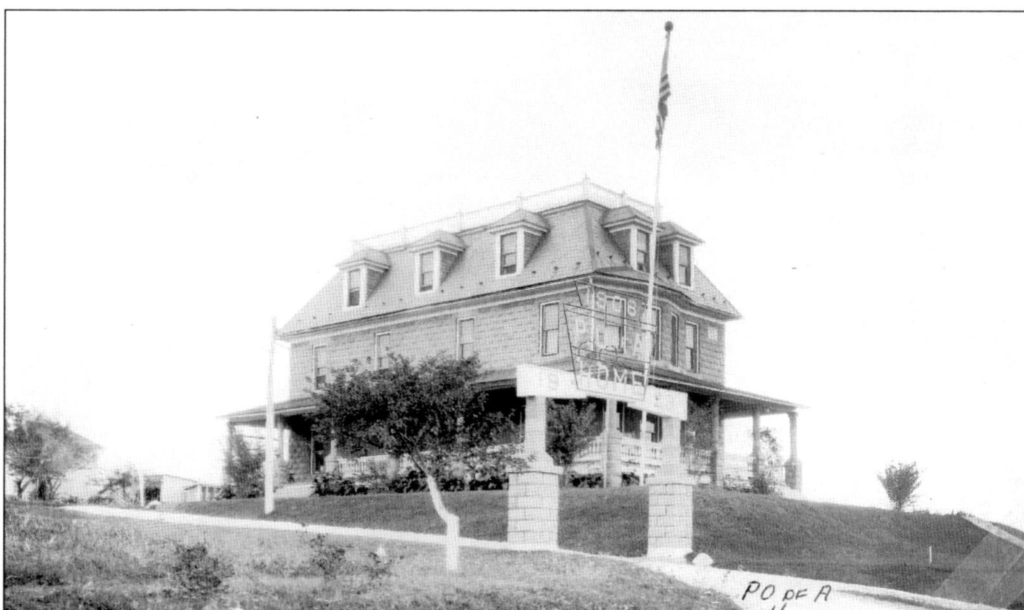


**PATRIOTIC ORDER OF AMERICA ORPHANAGE AT MIFFLINVILLE.** The Patriotic Order of America was an auxiliary branch of the Patriotic Order Sons of America, a fraternal organization that promoted attention to national issues and encouraged patriotism. The auxiliary became the driving force behind the establishment of the orphanage at Mifflinville. The home was for children of members of the organization.

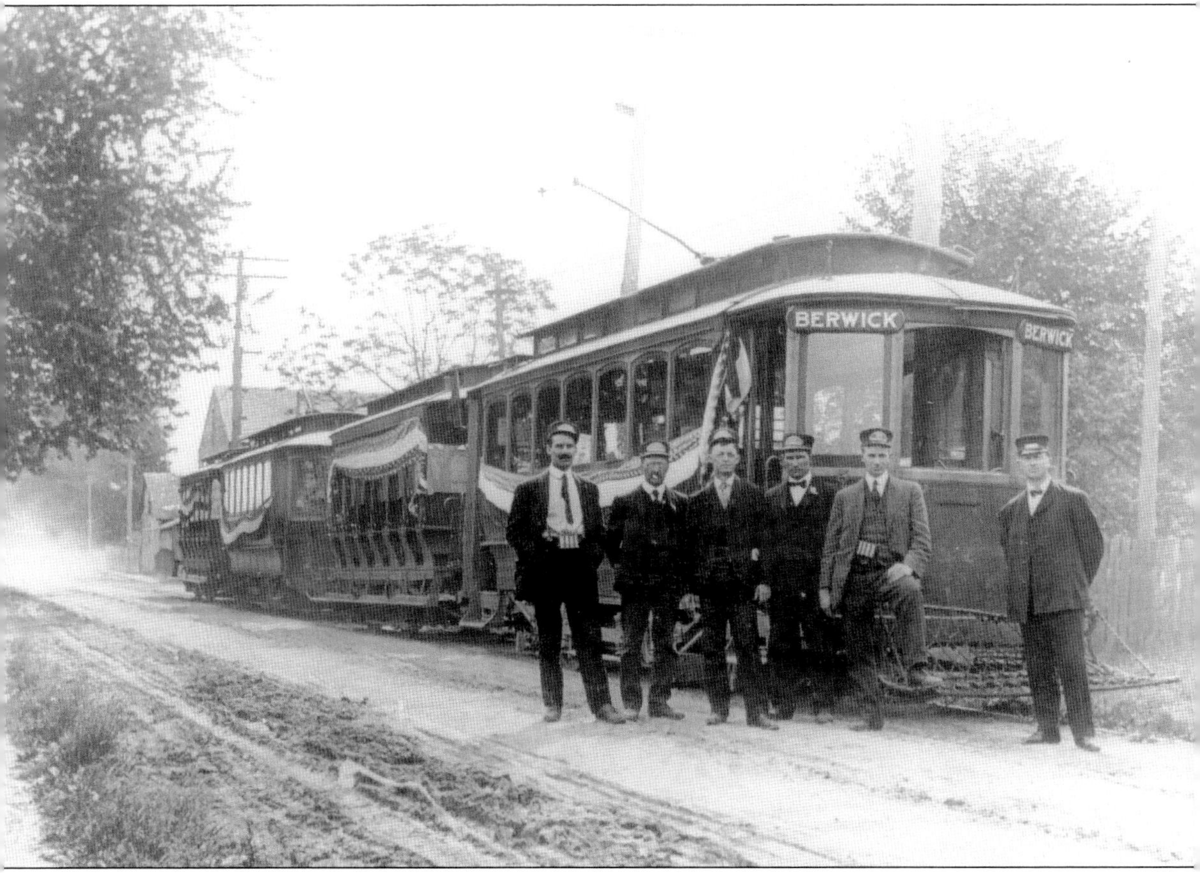


**TROLLEY CARS AND CREWS.** Two closed cars, two open cars, and their crews pose along the route from Berwick to Bloomsburg around 1910. After completing the trolley line in Bloomsburg, the next priority was to reach Berwick, which occurred on September 28, 1901. This was always the most profitable route for the company because it was the most heavily populated, traveling through Espy, Almedia, and Lime Ridge. Riders from these communities went to the larger towns to both work and shop. (Courtesy of Bloomsburg University Archives.)

# *Six*

# CATAWISSA AND THE SOUTHERN COUNTY

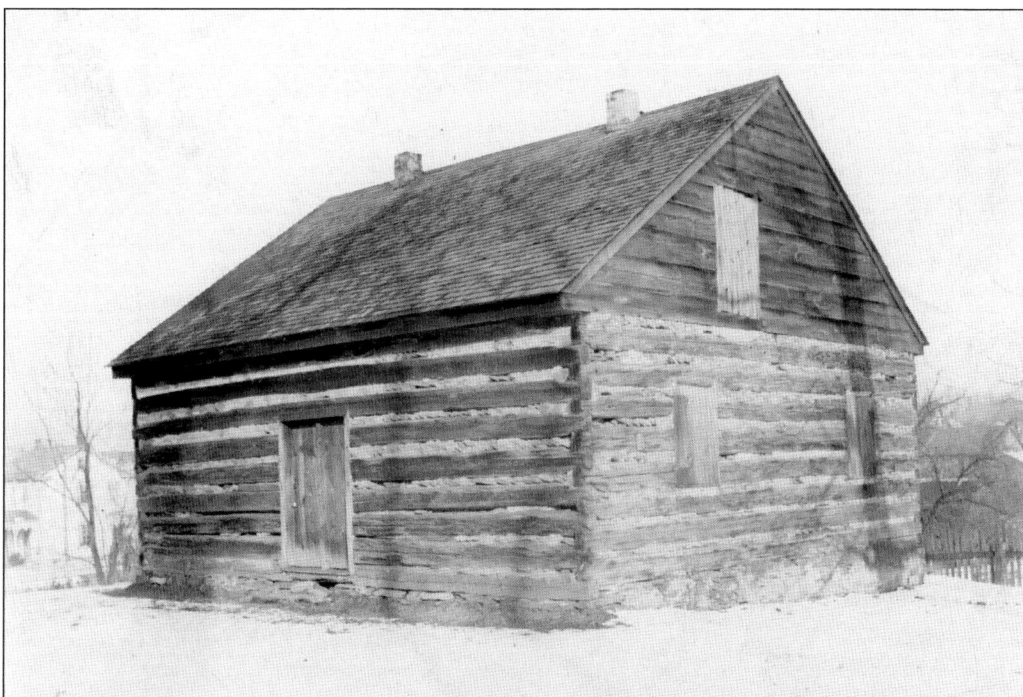

**CATAWISSA FRIENDS MEETINGHOUSE.** The land for the Catawissa Friends Meetinghouse was included in a purchase from the Native Americans by the Colonial government of Pennsylvania in 1768. One early member of the Religious Society of Friends was Moses Roberts of Berks County, who settled in Catawissa with his family about 1775. The last meeting at this site, now identified by a Pennsylvania Historical Marker, was held on August 26, 1921.

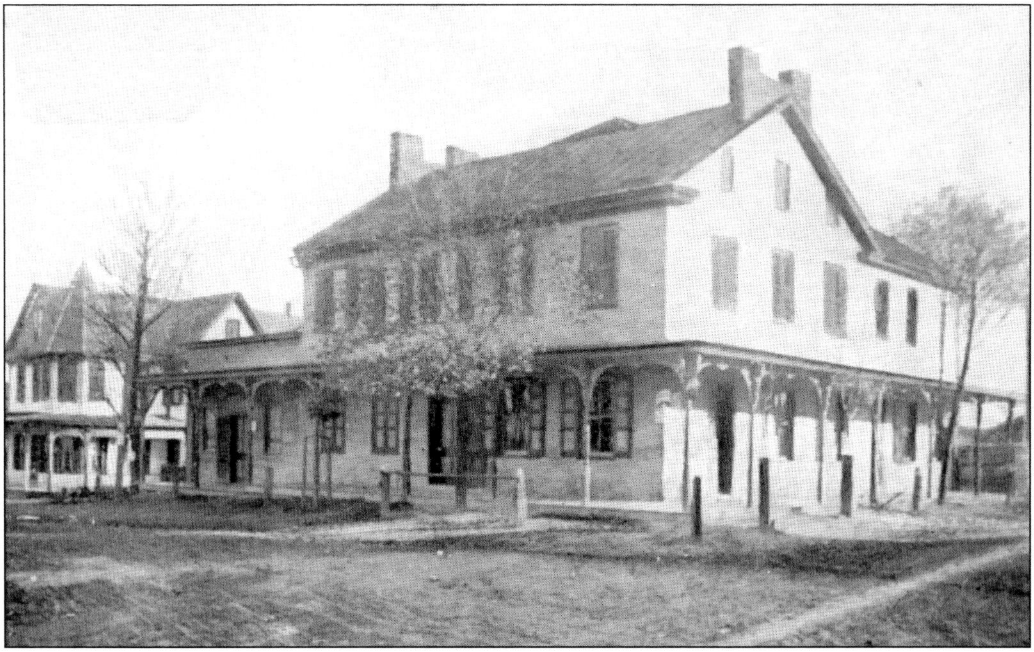

**NUMIDIA HOTEL, C. 1901.** The Numidia Hotel was located in Numidia at the intersection of Route 42 and Ringtown Mountain Drive. At the time of this photograph in 1901, Samuel Dyer was the proprietor, and the hotel also had an exchange stable. In 2008, the building was known as JD's Inn.

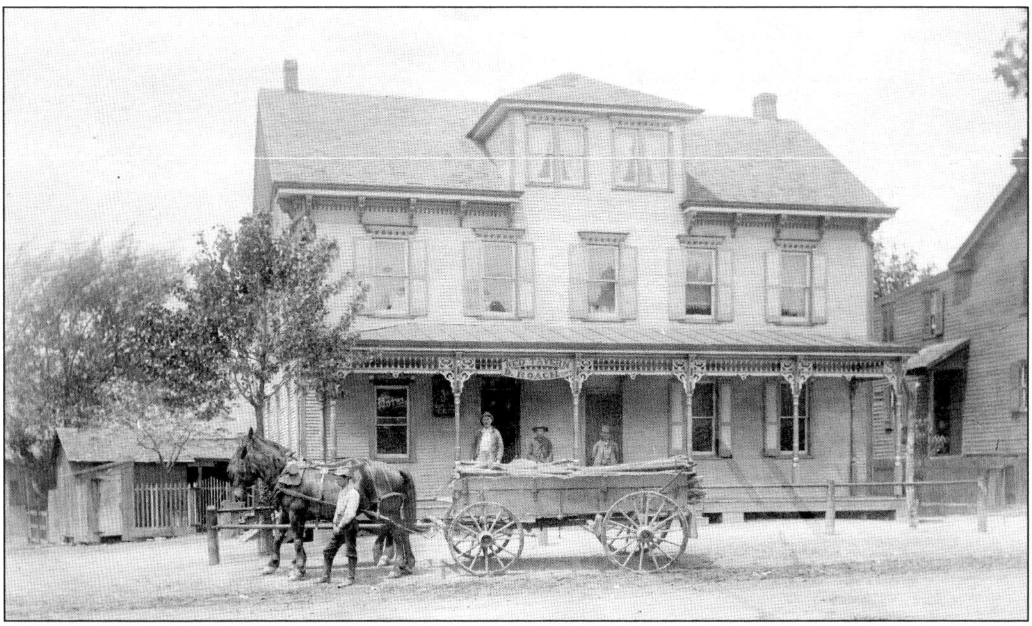

**THE RED TAVERN.** John Rhodenberger built the original Red Tavern around 1800 in what was then Catawissa Township. The area later became known as Montana and then as Aristes. The tavern became a meeting place for travelers during stagecoach days. The story goes that the owner hung a red lantern on the front porch to help guide travelers, giving it the name the Red Tavern. The photograph shows the second Red Tavern, built by U. F. Fetterman in 1890.

**CATAWISSA OPERA HOUSE.** The Catawissa Opera House, built in 1869 as a Masonic hall, never operated as an independent opera house. It housed storerooms, meeting rooms, and a social hall. A number of businesses have operated in this building. Numerous plays and skits were held in the social hall over the years. The words "opera house" were first painted on the building front in July 1891, reflecting the popular trend at the time for this venue of entertainment.

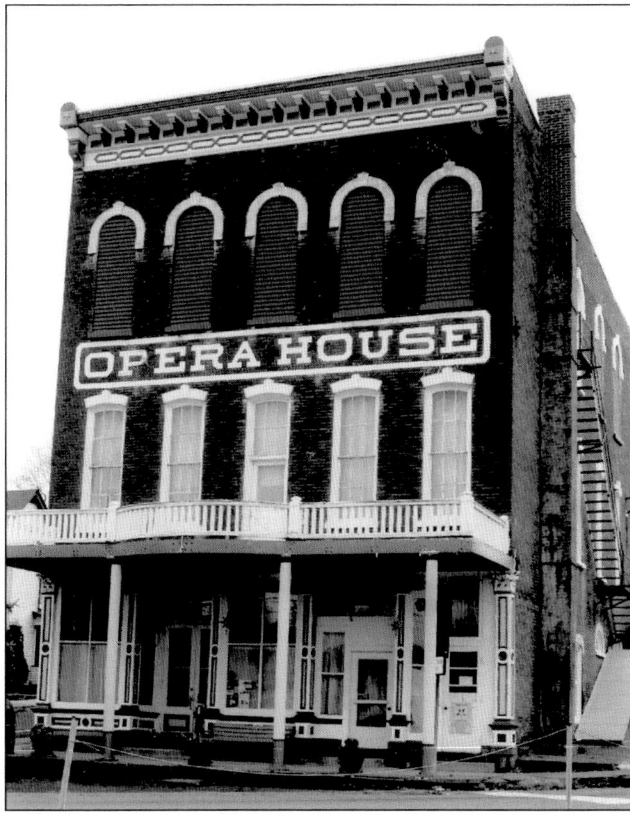


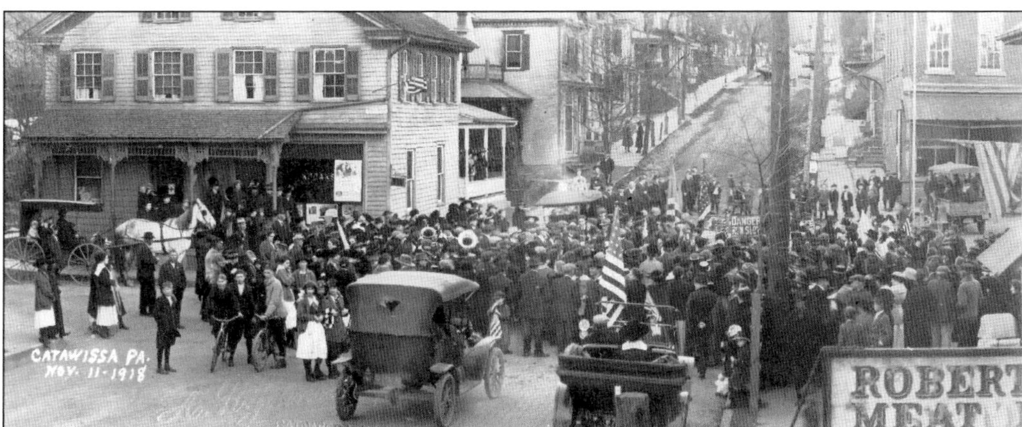


**WORLD WAR I ARMISTICE CELEBRATION.** The signing of an armistice on November 11, 1918, by Germany and Allied forces brought an end to World War I. Elaborate ceremonies took place to celebrate the occasion of Armistice Day, now called Veteran's Day. This scene took place at the intersection of Main, Fourth, and Mill Streets in Catawissa. Note the opera house in the upper right corner.

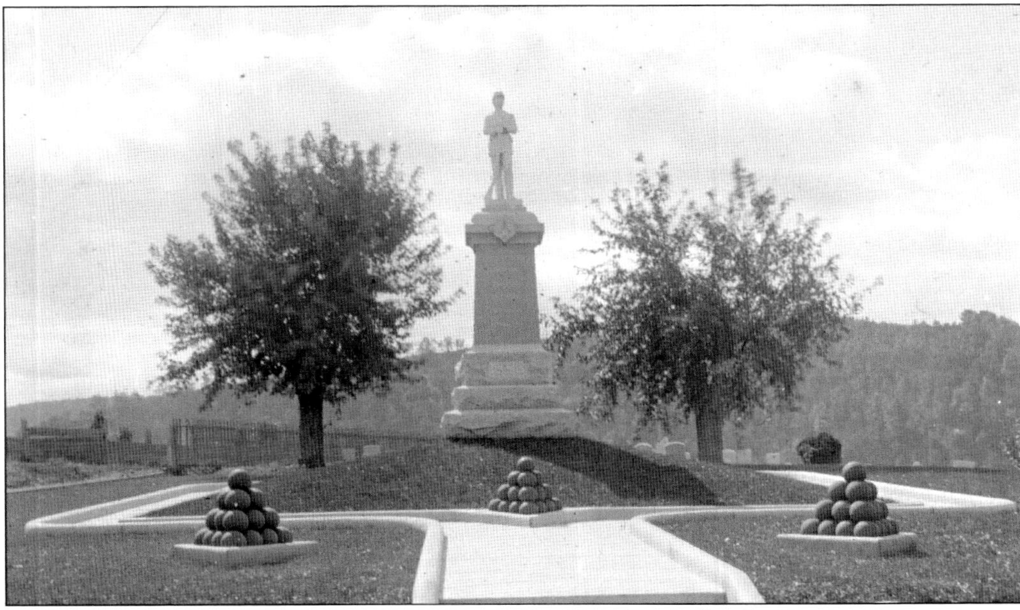

**CATAWISSA SOLDIER'S MONUMENT.** Catawissa was the first Columbia County community to honor with a monument the memory of the brave men who gave up their lives in service to their country. Frederick B. Smith, proprietor of the Catawissa Marble and Granite Works, erected the monument on land donated by Christian Brobst in Union Cemetery. The monument was dedicated on October 7, 1899.

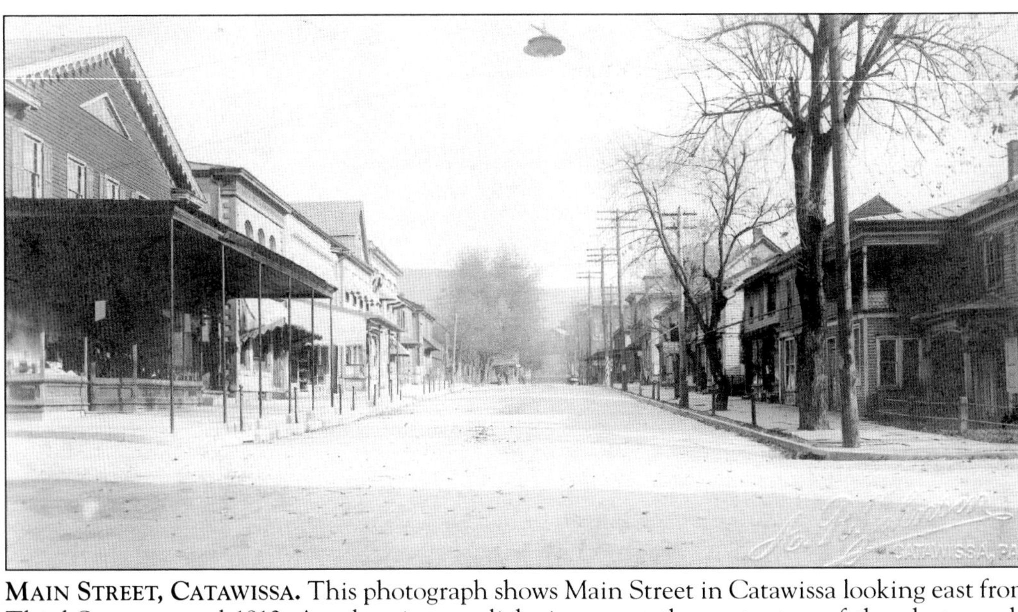


**MAIN STREET, CATAWISSA.** This photograph shows Main Street in Catawissa looking east from Third Street around 1910. An electric streetlight is seen at the center top of the photograph. The opera house can be seen at the end of Main Street before going up the hill to the Catawissa Borough School in the background.

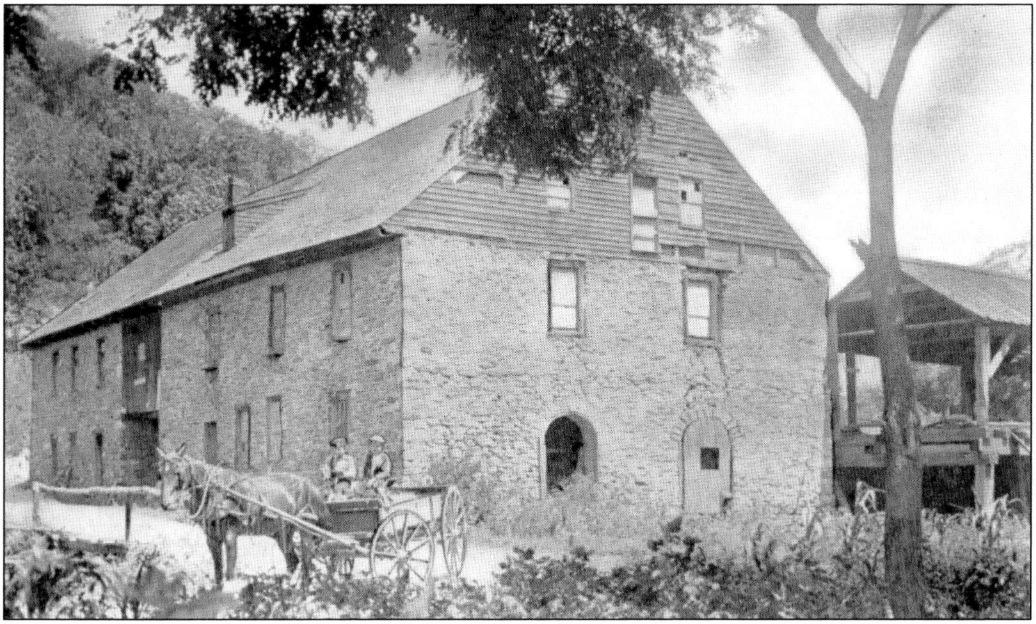

**THE OLD STONE MILL, CATAWISSA.** Known as the Christian Brobst Mill, the old stone mill in Catawissa was built in 1799 and expanded in 1802. The mill produced flour, plaster, and lumber. It was located along Catawissa Creek on the north side of Hollingshead Bridge. The mill changed hands many times over the years. Last owned by J. H. Geary, it was destroyed by fire in 1910.

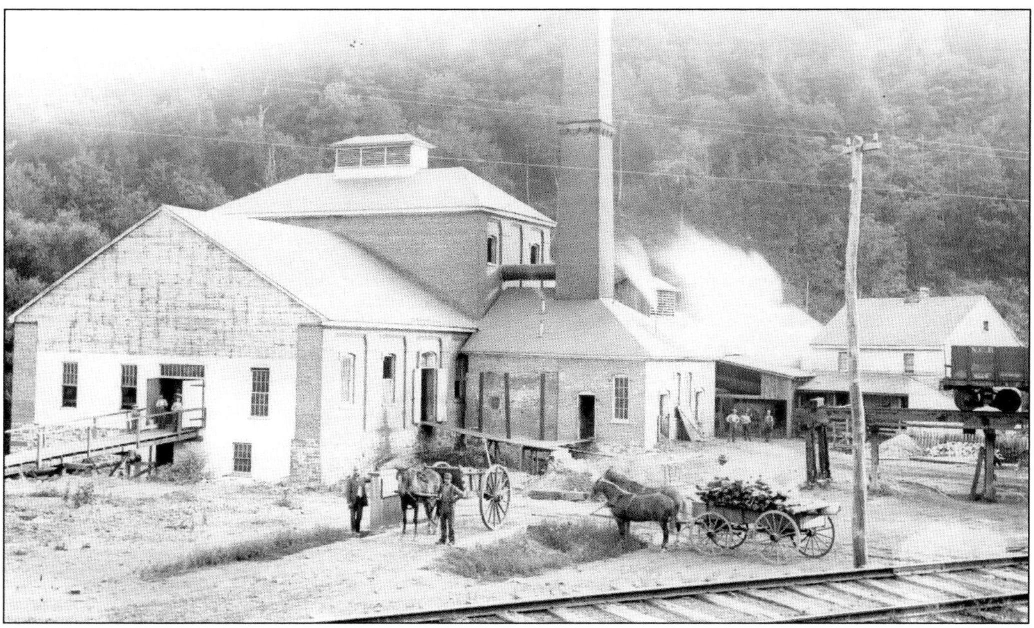

**CENTRAL FORGING COMPANY, C. 1918.** Located on the north side of Catawissa Creek and chartered in 1918, Central Forging Company manufactured forged steel unions. Originally the site of the paper mill, it functioned as such from 1811 until 1901, surviving a fire in 1883. In 1913, it was sold to new owners and was used for the manufacture of toys until becoming Central Forging Company. Later it became the Catawissa Valve and Fittings Company.

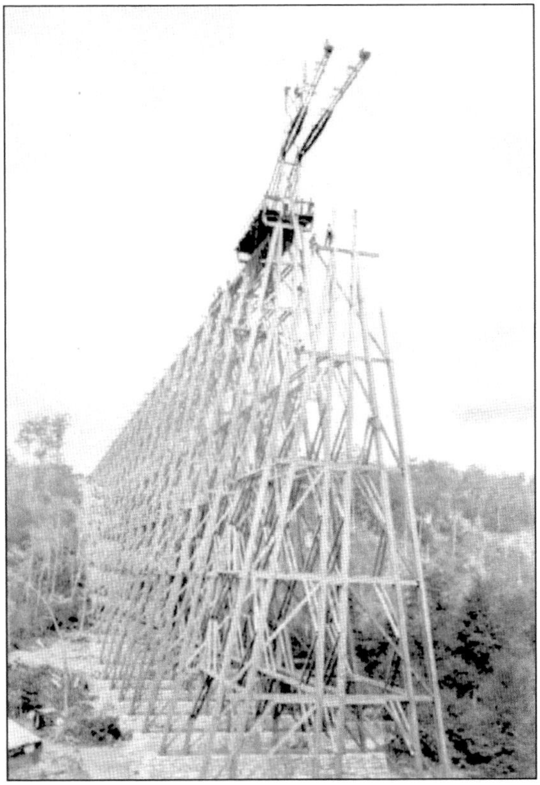

**Catawissa Railroad Trestle Bridge, Mainville.** The Catawissa, Williamsport, and Erie Railroad was the first railroad in Columbia County. The first train arrived in Catawissa on July 16, 1854. When the initial railroad went bankrupt in 1860, it was sold and became the Catawissa Railroad. In 1872, it was acquired by the Philadelphia and Reading Railroad. At one time, Catawissa was considered an important railroad center.

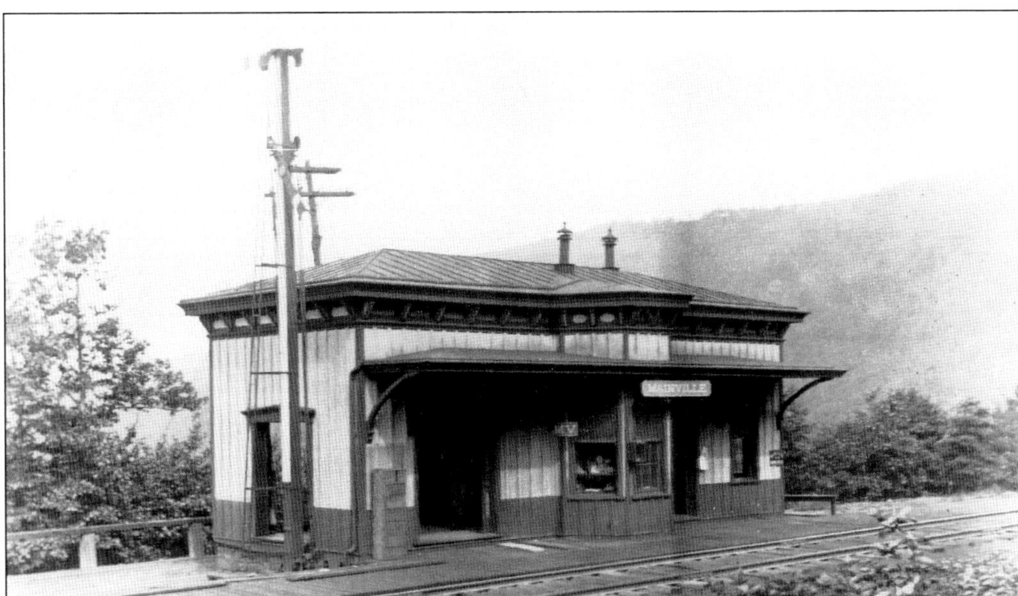


**Mainville Railroad Station.** The station was located across Catawissa Creek from the village of Mainville on the tracks of the Danville, Hazleton, and Wilkes-Barre Railroad. Nearby and parallel was the track of the Catawissa branch of the Philadelphia and Reading Railroad. The cross-creek community of a half-dozen houses was known as Mainville Station. (Courtesy of Mainville Historical Group.)

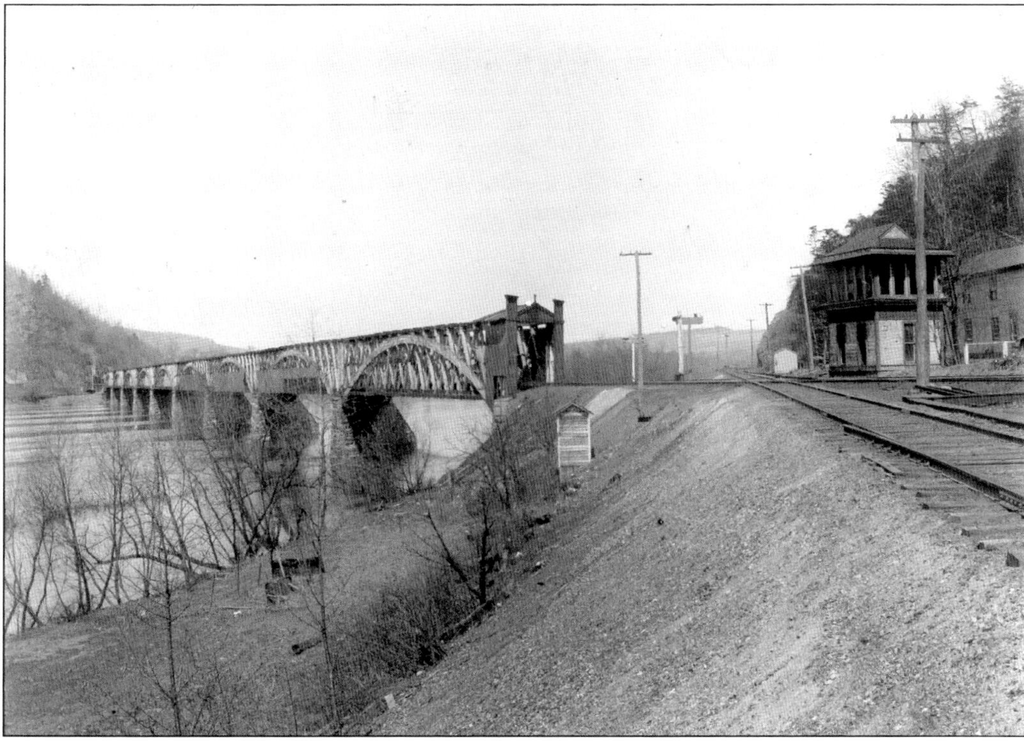

**CATAWISSA RAILROAD BRIDGE.** The old Catawissa Railroad bridge and the switch tower can be seen in this photograph.

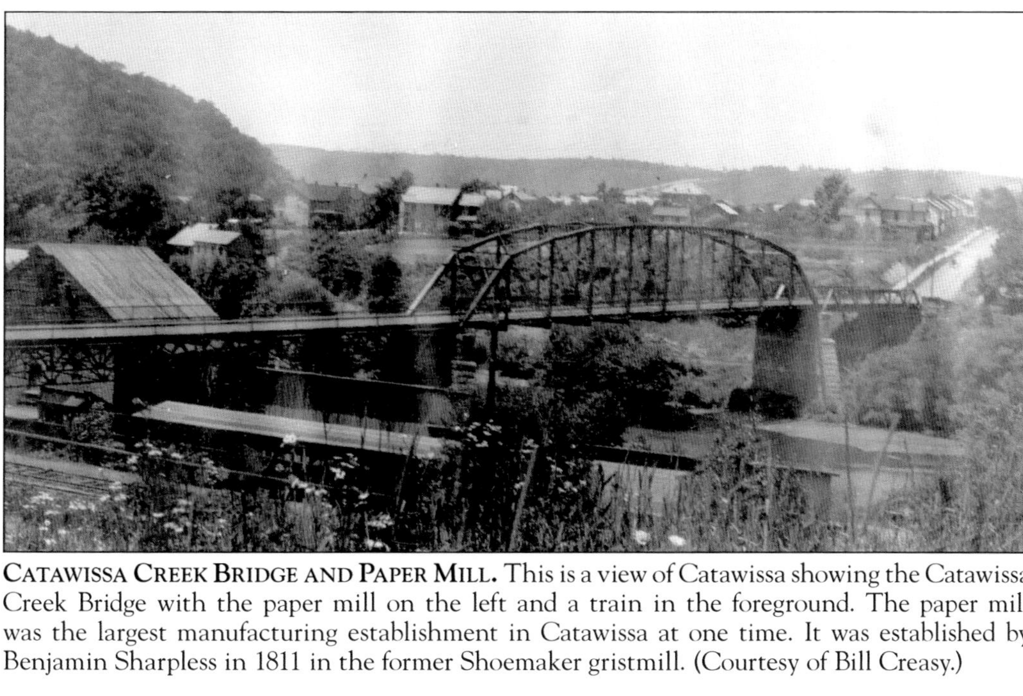

**CATAWISSA CREEK BRIDGE AND PAPER MILL.** This is a view of Catawissa showing the Catawissa Creek Bridge with the paper mill on the left and a train in the foreground. The paper mill was the largest manufacturing establishment in Catawissa at one time. It was established by Benjamin Sharpless in 1811 in the former Shoemaker gristmill. (Courtesy of Bill Creasy.)

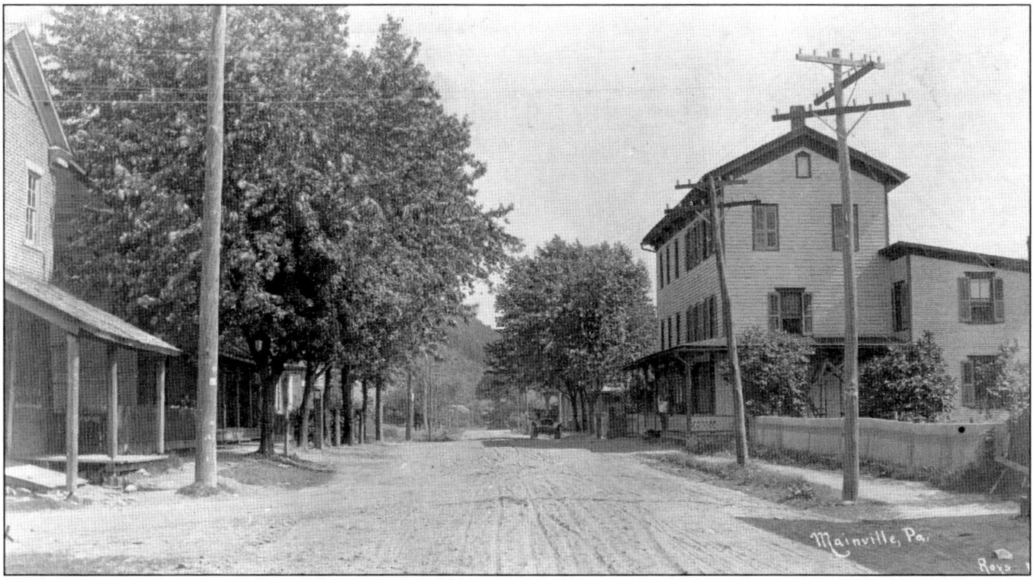


**MAINVILLE DRIVE, MAINVILLE.** The view is looking south toward Nescopeck Mountain. On the left is the Patriotic Order Sons of America building; on the right is the Main Hotel. In the left foreground is the road to Mifflinville. (Courtesy of Mainville Historical Group.)

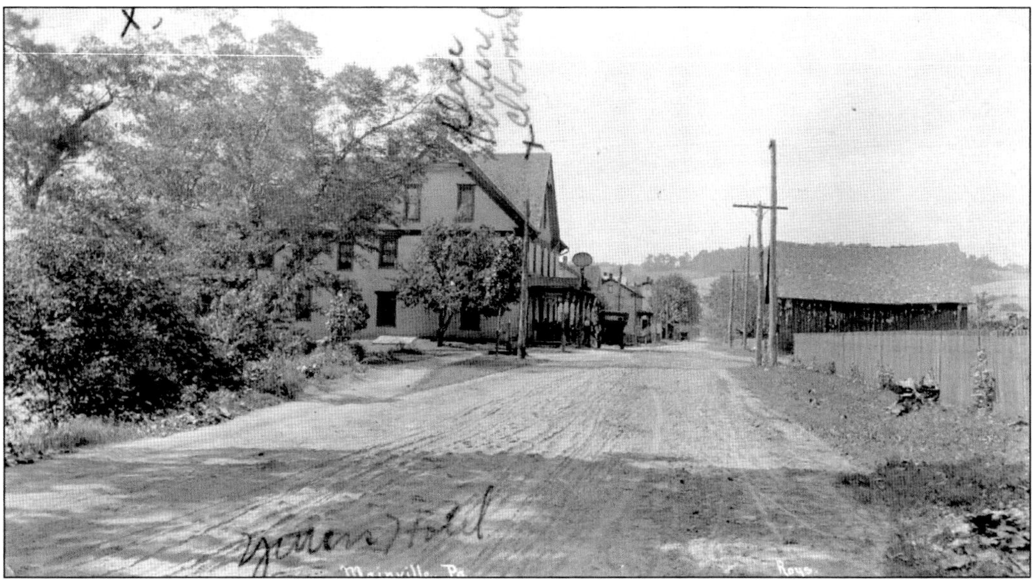

**DOWNTOWN MAINVILLE.** This view shows Main Street in Mainville looking north before 1910. At left is the Yetter boardinghouse, which backed the Catawissa Creek at the center of the village. Just beyond it is the Main Hotel. (Courtesy of Mainville Historical Group.)

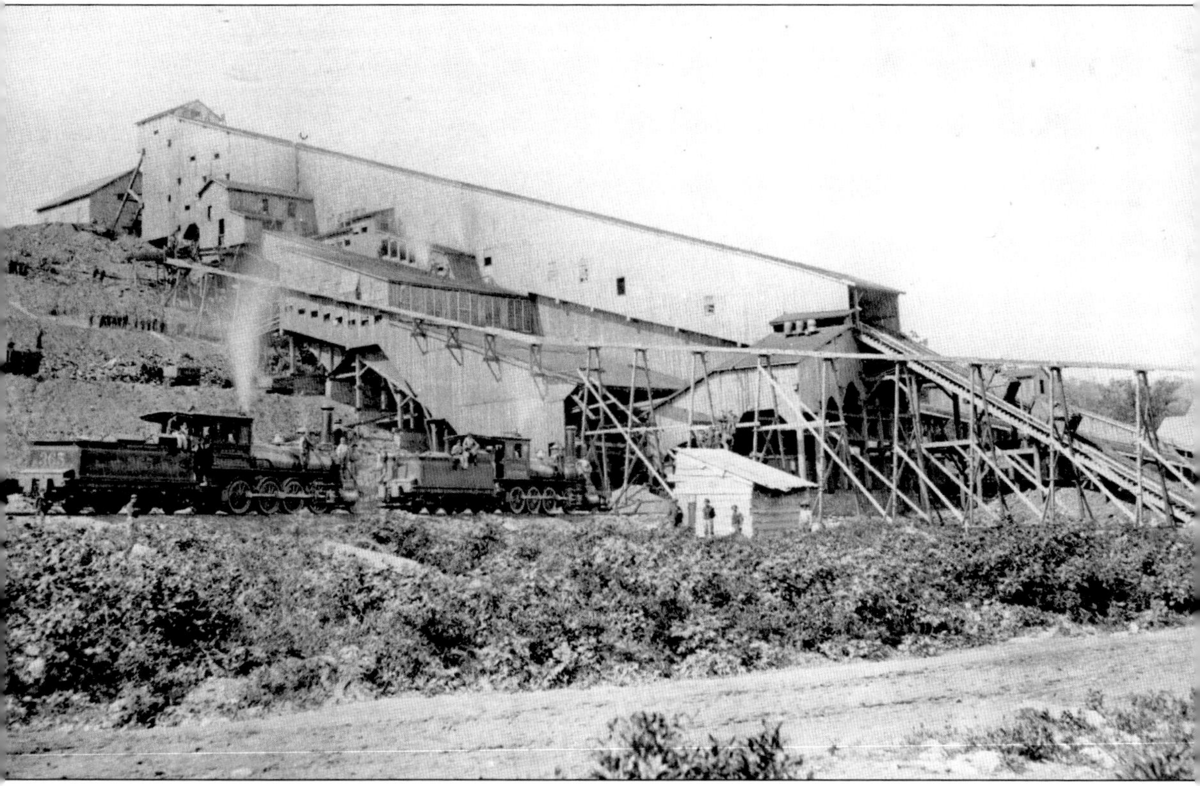

**THE LOGAN COLLIERY.** The Logan Colliery at Centralia was operated by Lewis A. Riley and Company in the west end of the town. The two Lehigh Valley Railroad consolidation-type locomotives in front are the *Hazel Dell* and *Logan*. The photograph was taken in 1881. (Courtesy of Thomas J. Dempsey.)

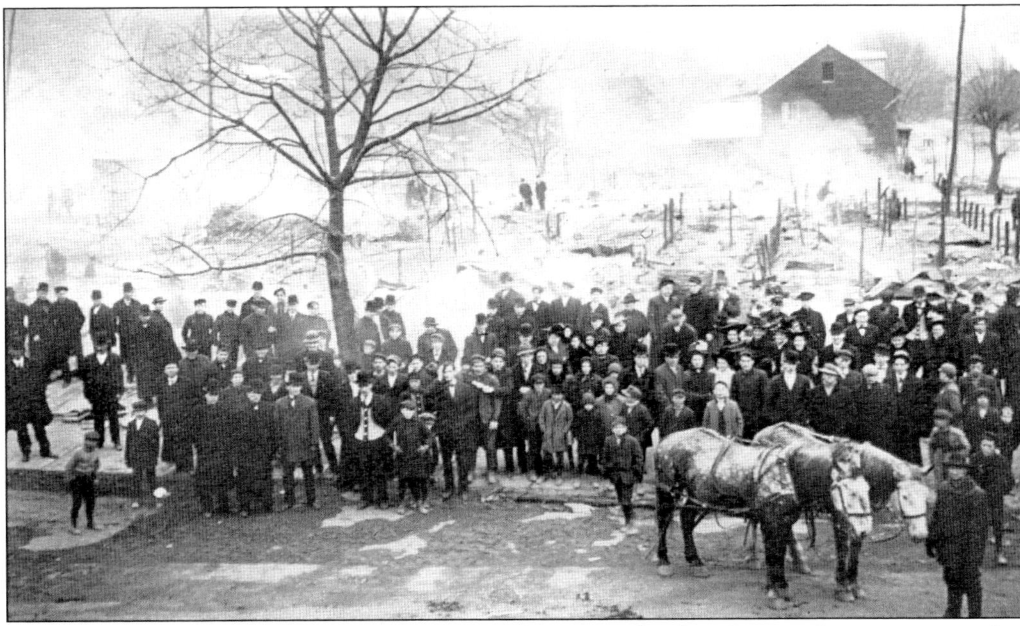

**Centralia Fire, 1908.** One of the biggest fires in Columbia County history occurred in Centralia on December 4, 1908. The fire started in the Palace Theatre at 519 Locust Avenue. It spread north and south of the theater and rounded the corner onto East Center Street to the south and East Railroad Street to the north. It eventually burned itself out. The fire was allegedly arson, but no one was ever brought to justice. (Courtesy of Thomas J. Dempsey.)

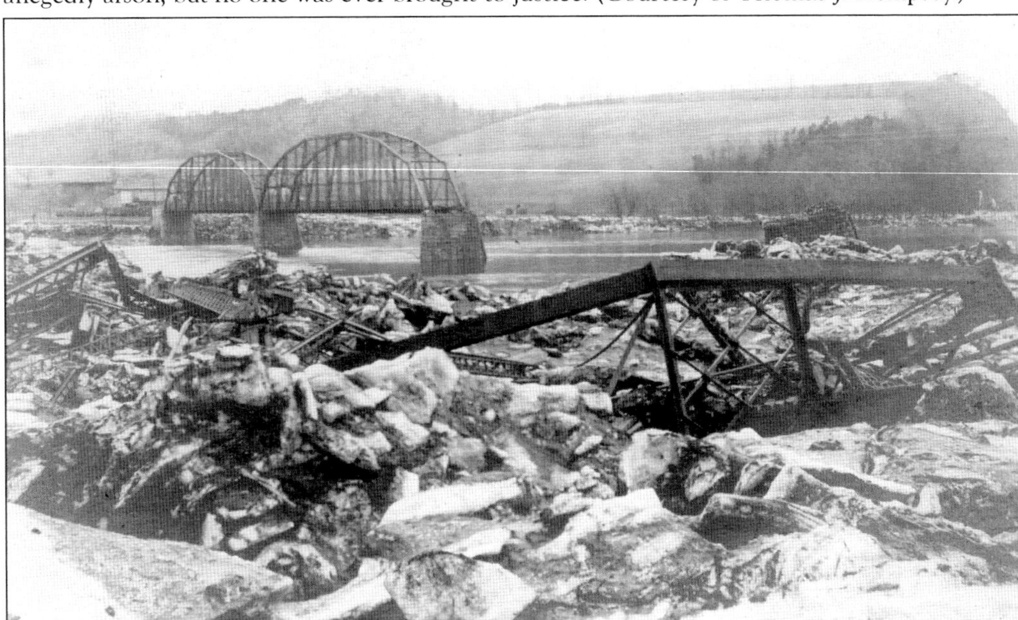

**Flood at Catawissa, 1904.** The photograph shows wreckage from the Catawissa Bridge that was torn loose and crushed by the ice gorge following the flood of March 1904. Ice blocked the train rails, stalling trains until the tracks could be cleared. The wreckage ended up on the shoreline near Catawissa and took months to remove.

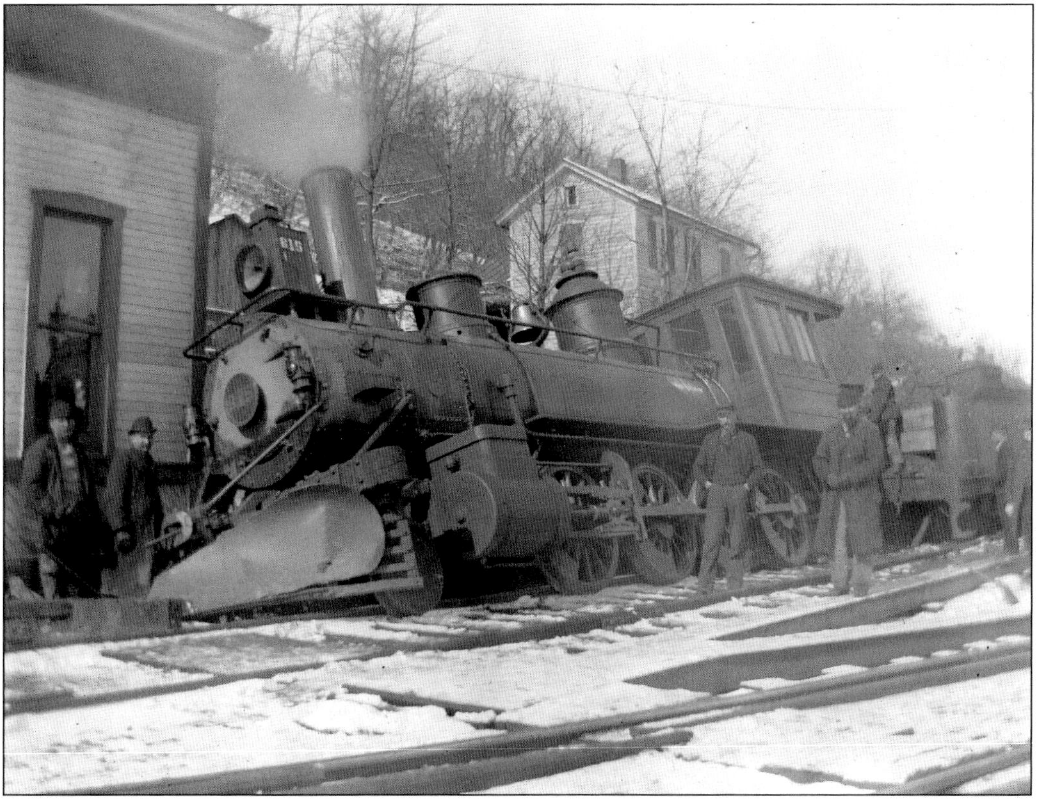

**Derailed Train at Catawissa.** Work crews tend to a derailed steam engine at the switch house near the Catawissa Bridge.

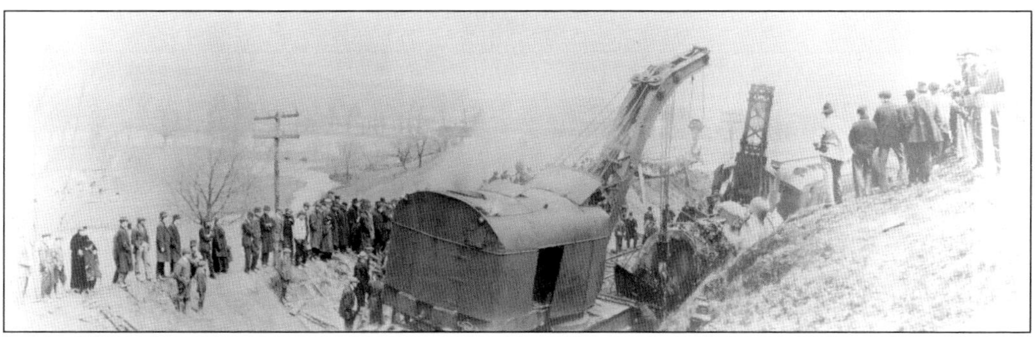

**Train Wreck Near Rupert.** Work crews tend to the twisted wreckage of engine 986 on the Catawissa division of the Philadelphia and Reading Railroad near the Rupert station. The photograph was taken on April 3, 1916. (Courtesy of Rex Oman.)

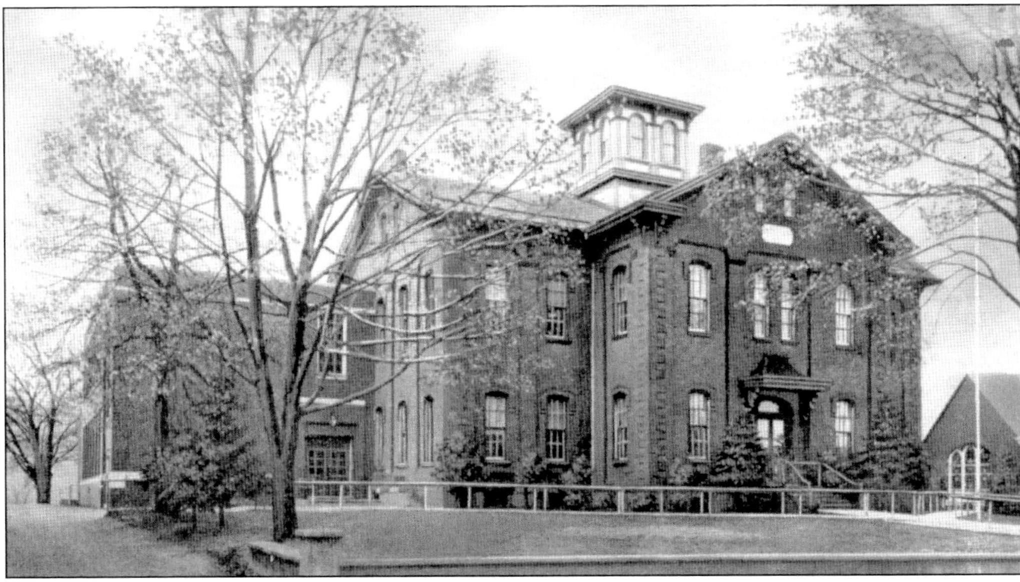

**Catawissa Public School.** The Catawissa Public School opened in 1882 and housed both elementary and high school classes. Located at the intersection of East Main and Church Streets, it was the first public high school in Columbia County. It ceased operation as a high school in 1962 when Catawissa became part of the Southern Columbia School District. The elementary school closed in 1976. Today apartment houses stand where the school was.

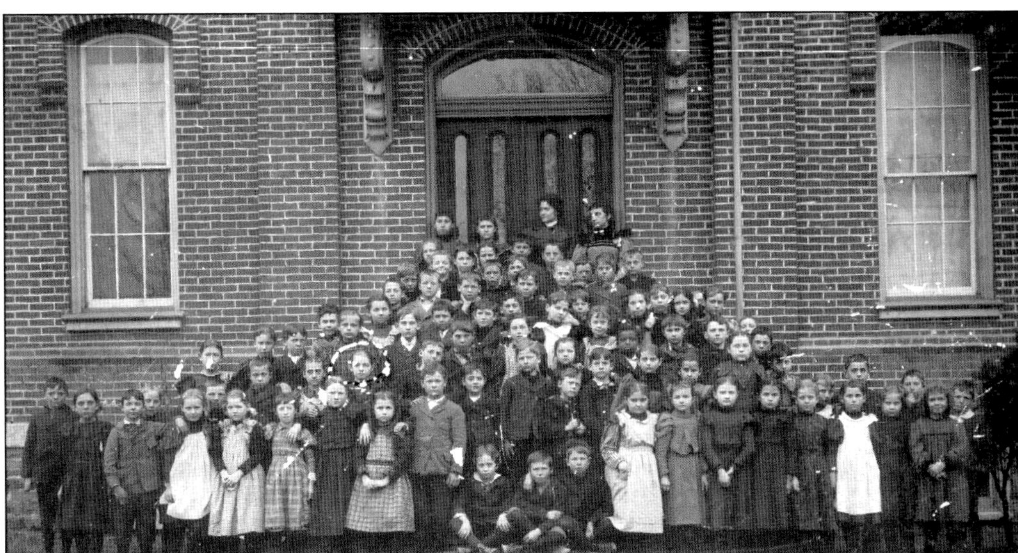

**Elementary Students at Catawissa Public School, 1898.** Enrollment at Catawissa Public School had approached 500 students by 1897. An addition was made to the existing building, which had been erected in 1882.

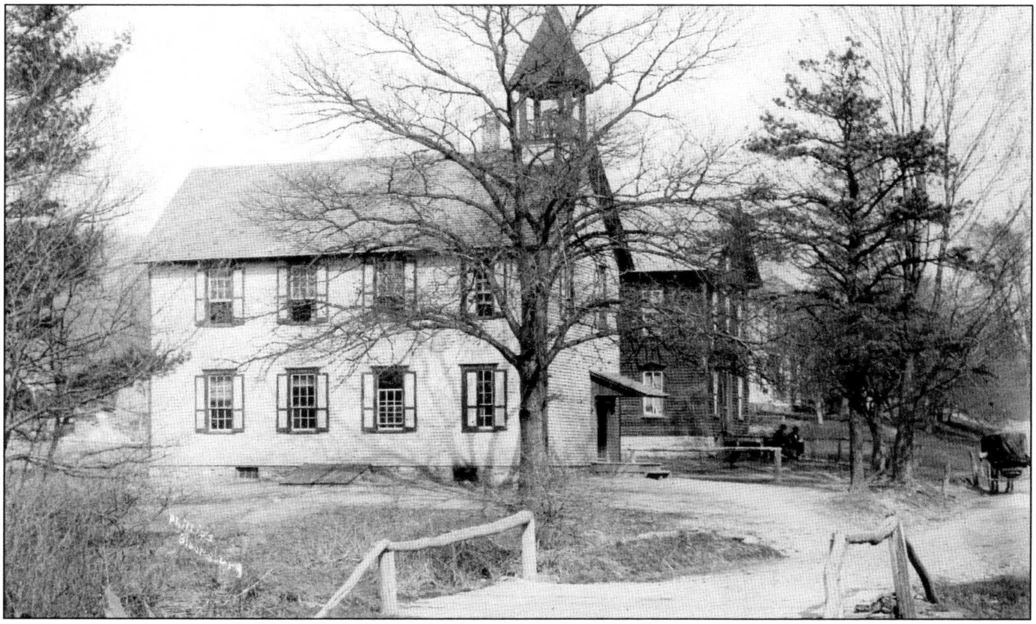

**Locust Township Public School, 1908.** Locust Township Public School was in a small village called Newlin about one mile east of Numidia. The elementary grades were on the ground level, and the high school was on the second floor. In the early 1900s, many rural townships began building high schools as part of their educational system. In the 1950s, many small, rural schools were consolidated into larger districts.

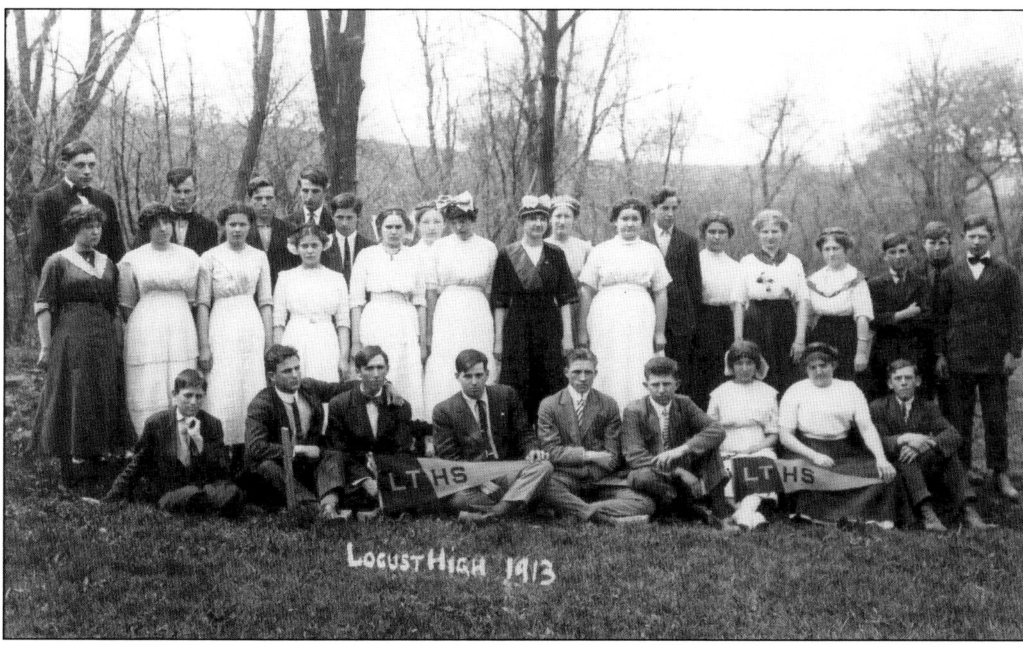


**Locust Township High School, Class of 1913.** At the dawn of the 20th century, only 11 percent of the U.S. population graduated from high school. In many cases, children of high school age had to go to work to help support the family.

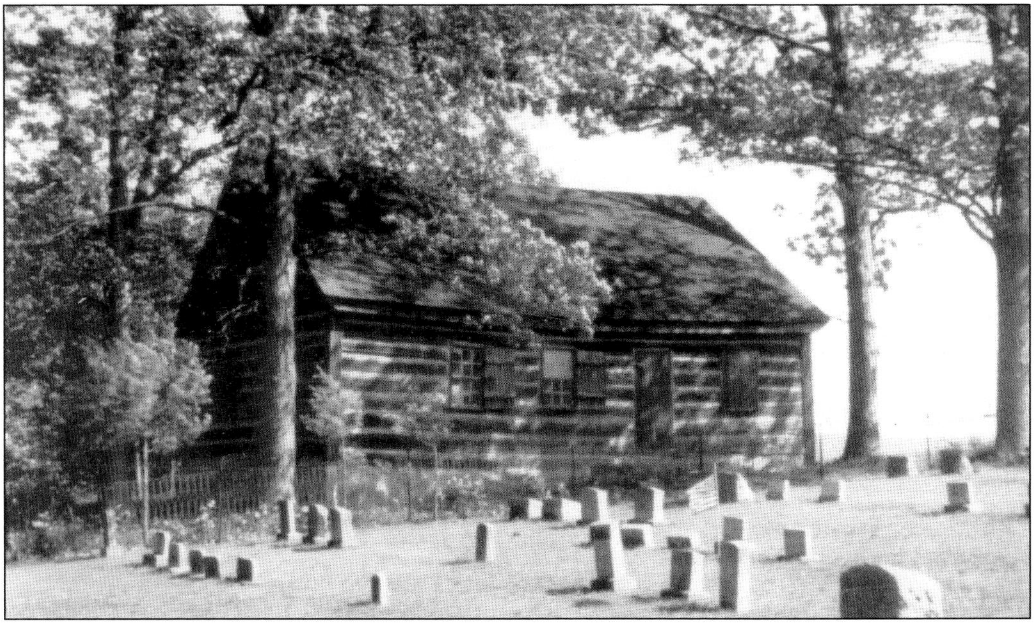

**ROARING CREEK FRIENDS MEETINGHOUSE.** Built in 1795 or 1796 and located in Locust Township, the Roaring Creek Friends Meetinghouse is a log construction with the two-cell design. The men and women met separately. This was more typical of the early English Quaker pattern and less typical of the American Friends meetinghouse design. This meetinghouse is no longer in use.

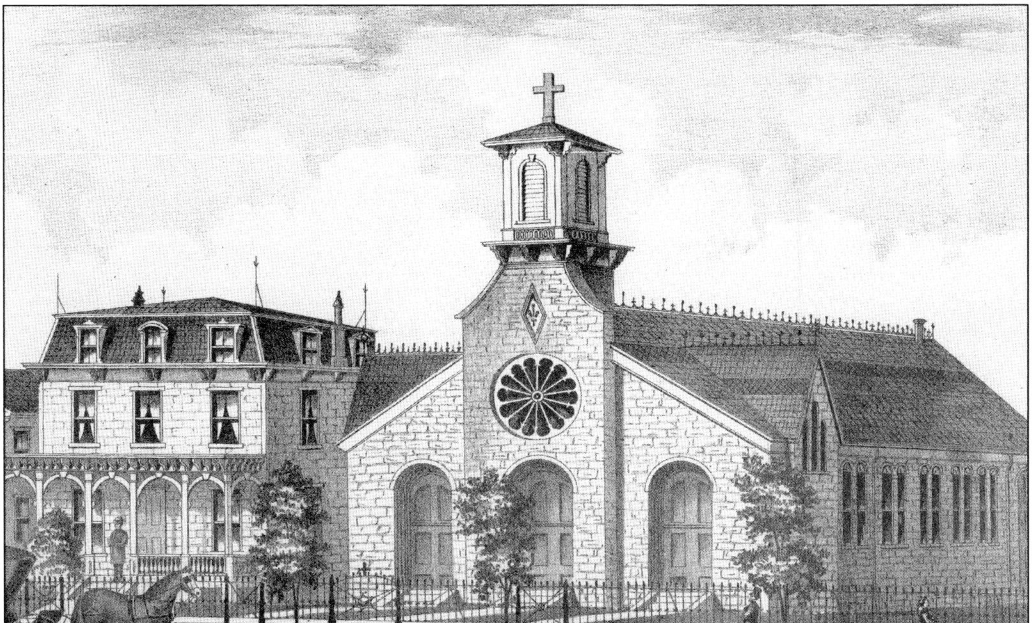

**ST. IGNATIUS CATHOLIC CHURCH, CENTRALIA.** The cornerstone of St. Ignatius Catholic Church in Centralia was laid on July 18, 1869, by Bishop J. F. Shanahan on property donated by the Locust Mountain Coal and Iron Company. The church was demolished in 1997 due to the underground mine fire that was the demise of Centralia.

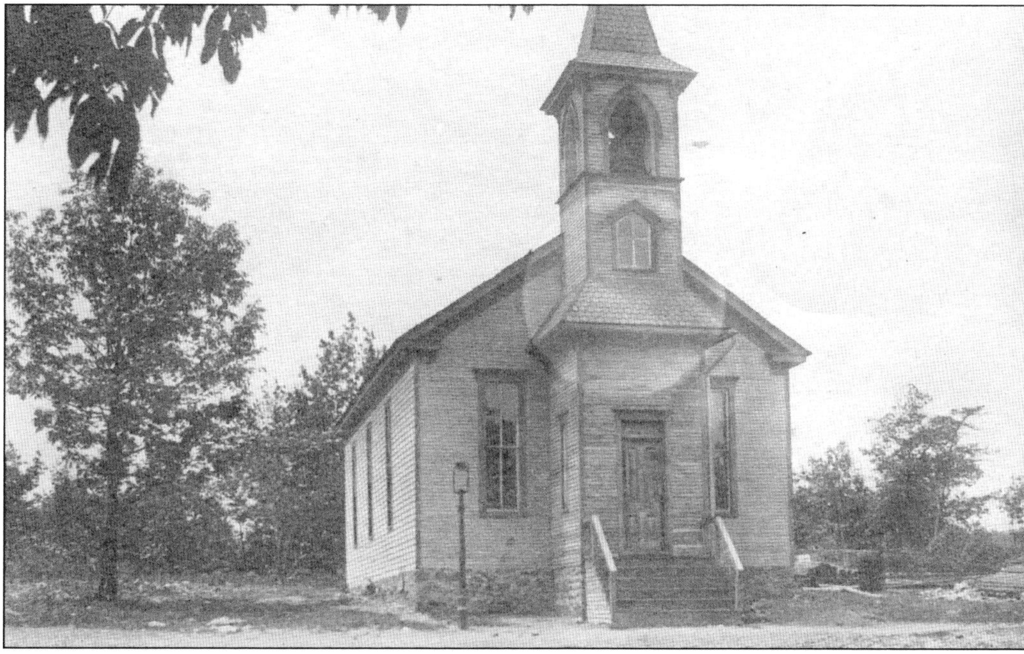

**THE WHITE SCHOOLHOUSE AND CHURCH.** One of the institutions that played a prominent role in days gone by was the village church. The White schoolhouse and church, pictured here in 1870 in Aristes, served both as a schoolhouse and worship house for a time. It was not uncommon for early churches to serve as schoolhouses.

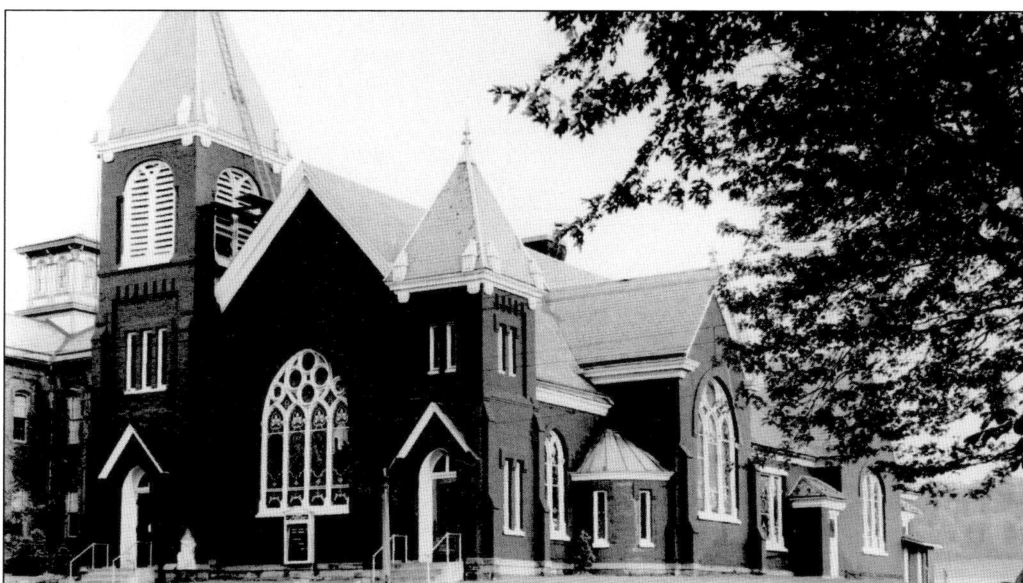

**ST. JOHN'S LUTHERAN CHURCH, CATAWISSA.** In 1804, the cornerstone was laid on land donated by Christian Brobst. Initially St. John's served both Lutheran and German Reformed congregations. In 1845, a faction desiring to have services in English started St. Matthew's Lutheran Church. St. John's erected a new edifice in 1890. Services were conducted in German until 1892. In 1983, both churches merged again and became Christ United Evangelical Lutheran Church.

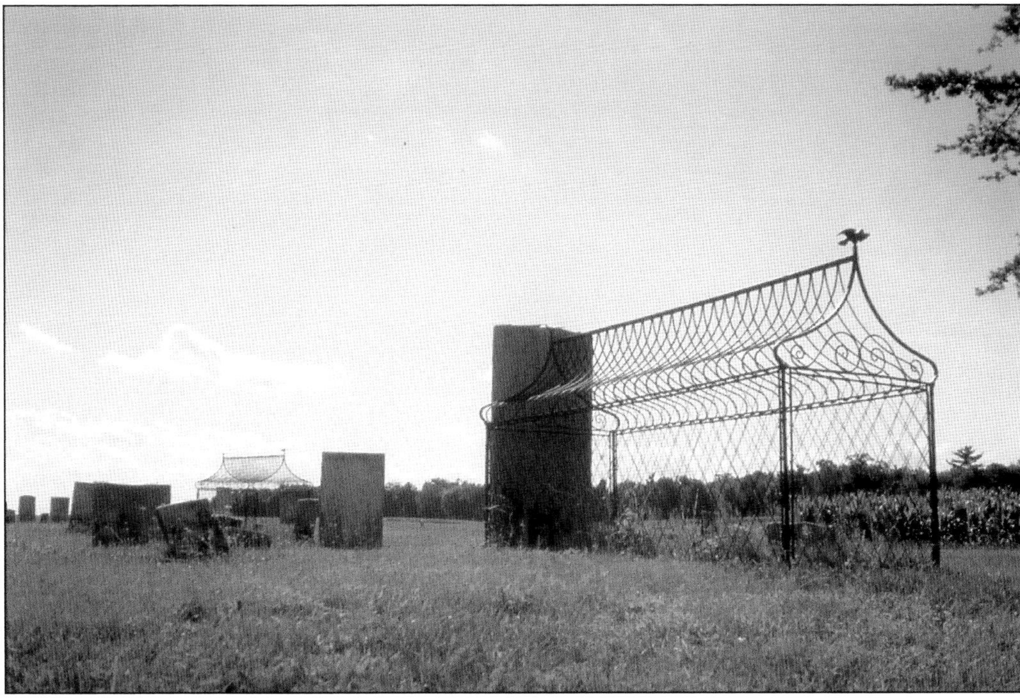

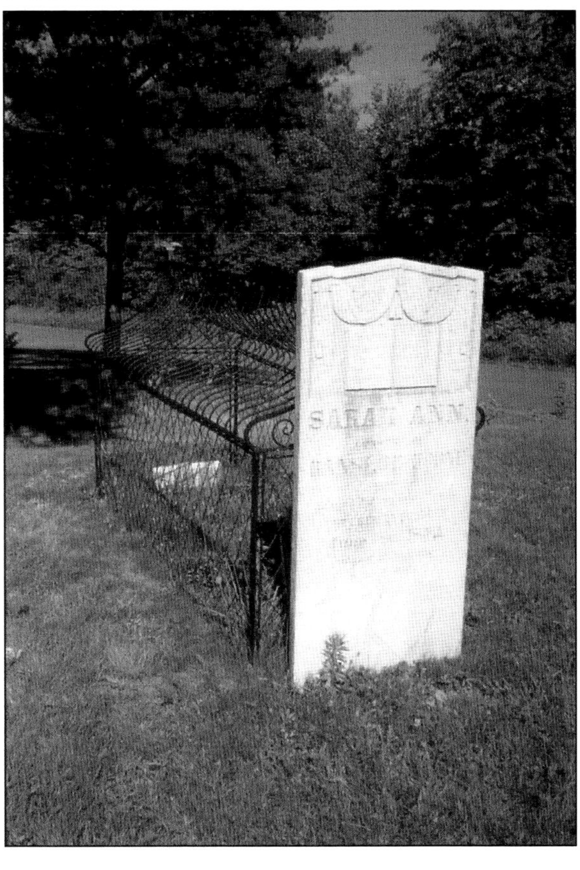

**THE HOODED GRAVES.** The Hooded Graves are located in Franklin Township in the old Mount Zion graveyard across from the former Clayton School. Local historian Ann Diseroad believes the most plausible reason for the hoods is that they served as "mortsafes," or "structures intended to prevent theft of a body by anatomy instructors, doctors, or medical students." Bodysnatching was not an uncommon practice in the mid-1800s. (Courtesy of Ann Diseroad.)

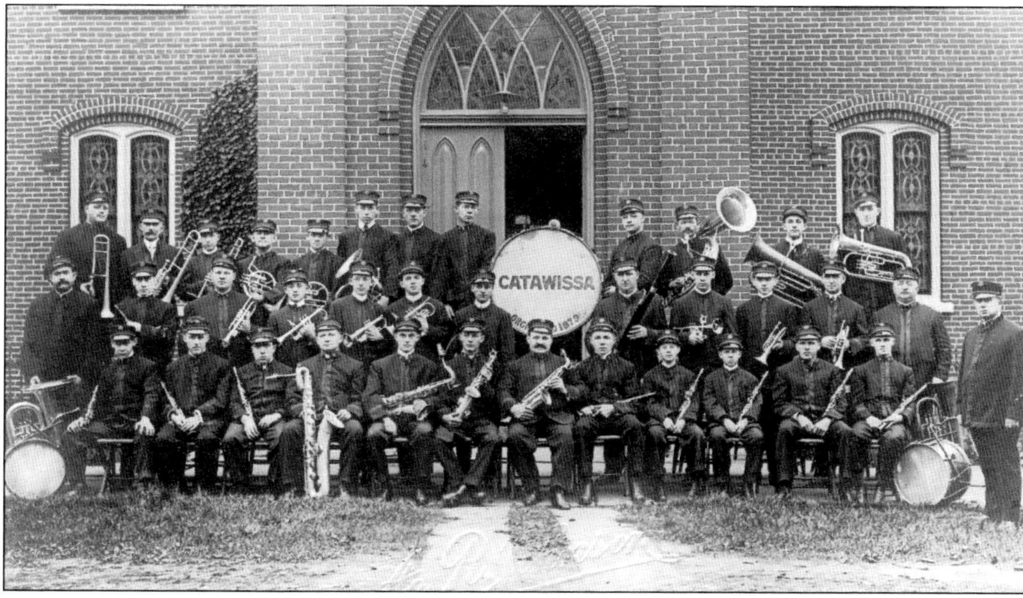


**CATAWISSA MILITARY BAND.** The Catawissa Military Band has been providing music for over 130 years. It began as the Mechanics' Band, made up largely of workers in the Catawissa Railroad Company shops. It merged with the Catawissa Brass Band in 1872. Partly because many of its members volunteered for active duty during the Spanish-American War, it became known as the Catawissa Military Band.

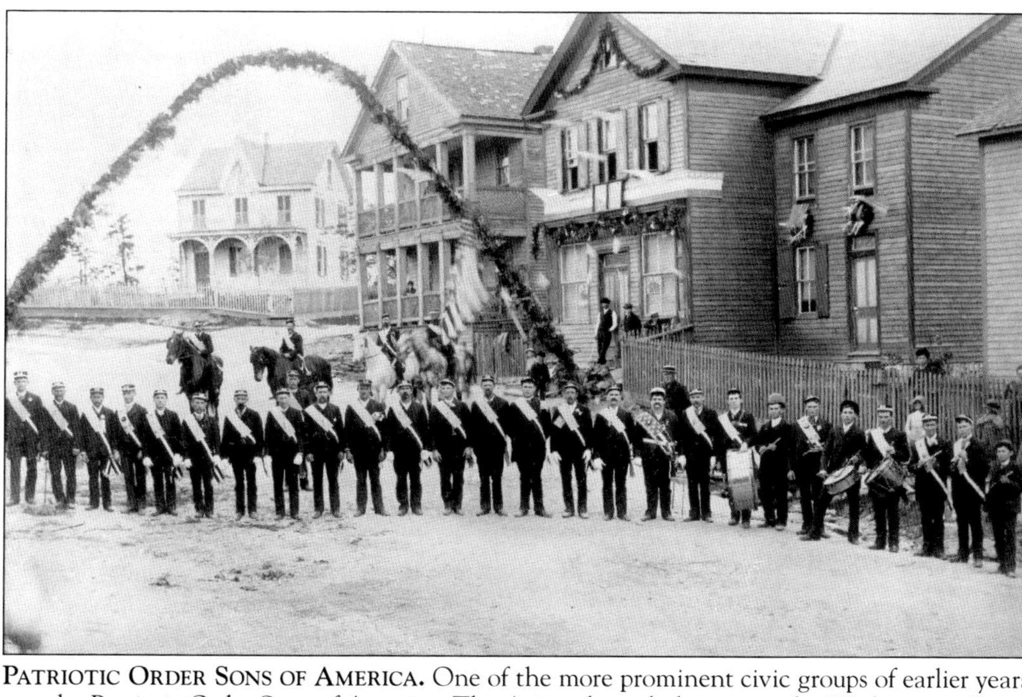

**PATRIOTIC ORDER SONS OF AMERICA.** One of the more prominent civic groups of earlier years was the Patriotic Order Sons of America. The Aristes branch, known as the Washington Camp No. 38, is shown lined up for a Memorial Day parade on May 30, 1890. Aristes, formerly known as Montana, was observing its 100th anniversary that year.

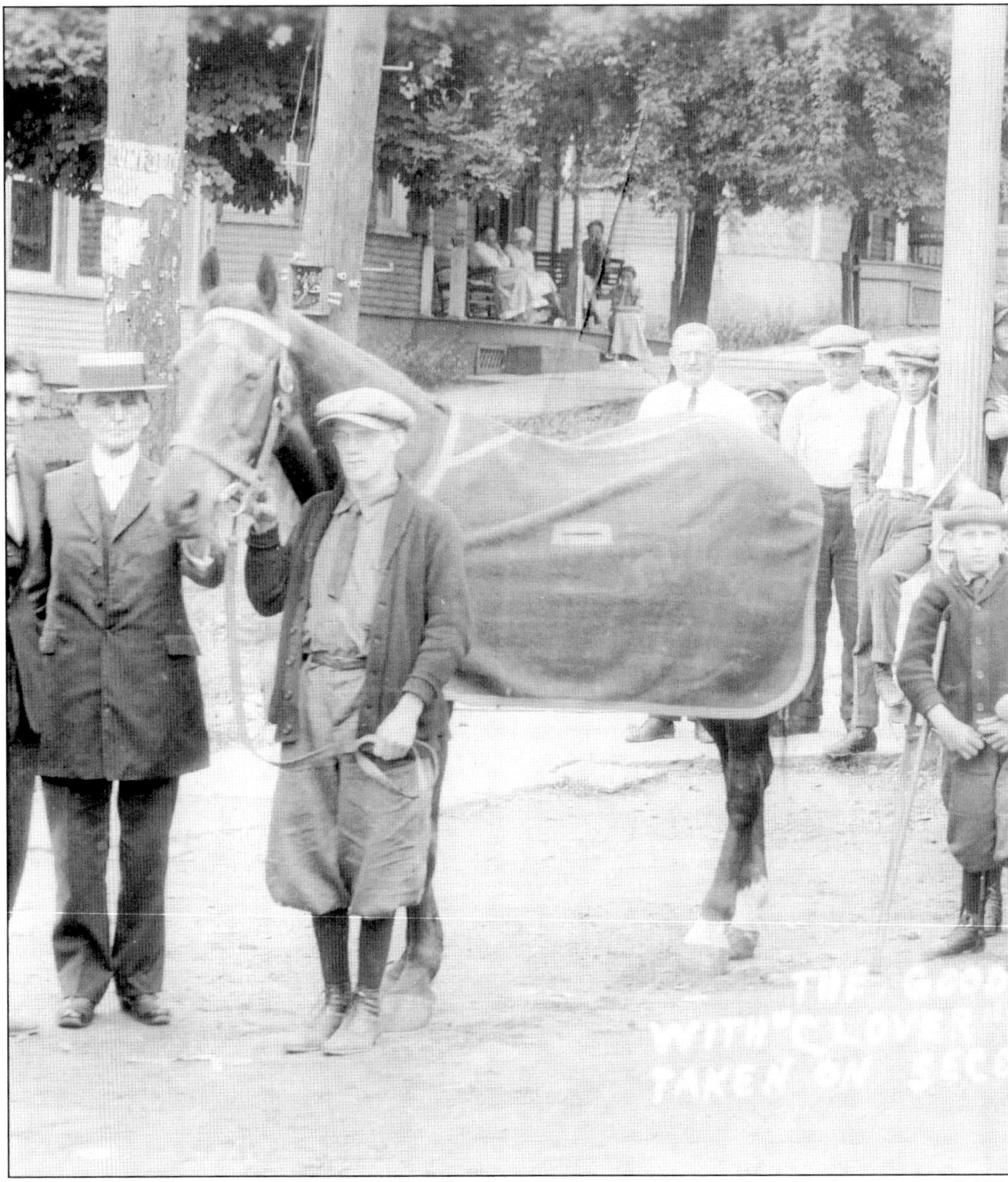


**CLOVER THE HORSE.** Clover was reportedly the world's oldest horse when he died in April 1924 at 53 years of age. He was owned by Rev. Uriah Myers, who drove him on his rounds while visiting members of his congregation for more than 35 years. Myers served St. Matthew's Lutheran Church in Catawissa from 1883 to 1921.

# About the Society

For nearly a century, the Columbia County Historical and Genealogical Society has been preserving and interpreting the story of the region's people, industries, and institutions. Originating as a county historical society in 1914, the society grew by merger with the Central Susquehanna Valley Genealogical Society in 1999. With over 600 members, the society sponsors a library, museum, research service, Web site, and various public programs on historical themes. The museum's collection of local artifacts and treasures includes canal boat horns, Wirt fountain pens (the first successful fountain pen), local Hyssong pottery, thousands of Native American artifacts, and numerous stereopticon slides. In the society's research facilities, a knowledgeable all-volunteer staff helps answer family history queries by visitors and correspondents from all across the country. The society's Web site, www.colcohist-gensoc.org, provides indexed access to over 20 databases, including 200,000 names of local people, 8,000 photographs, naturalization papers, and much more.

Consistent with our mission to preserve history on a local level, this book was printed in South Carolina on American-made paper and manufactured entirely in the United States. Products carrying the accredited Forest Stewardship Council (FSC) label are printed on 100 percent FSC-certified paper.

MADE IN THE USA